W9-DHM-132

RELIGION AND THE RISE OF SCEPTICISM

The Catholic
Theological Union
LIBRARY
Chicago, Ill.

WITHDRAWN

DEC 3 1 1969

WITHDRAWN

BOOKS BY FRANKLIN L. BAUMER

THE EARLY TUDOR THEORY OF KINGSHIP

MAIN CURRENTS OF WESTERN THOUGHT

RELIGION AND THE RISE OF SCEPTICISM

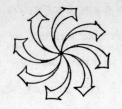

BL
2747
.8
.B35

Religion and the Rise of Scepticism

BY FRANKLIN L. BAUMER

HARCOURT, BRACE & WORLD, INC. • NEW YORK

The Catholic
Theological Union
LIBRARY
Chicago, Ill.

A HARBINGER BOOK

© 1960 BY FRANKLIN L. BAUMER. ALL RIGHTS RESERVED. NO PART OF THIS PUBLI-CATION MAY BE REPRODUCED OR TRANSMITTED IN ANY FORM OR BY ANY MEANS, ELECTRONIC OR MECHANICAL, INCLUDING PHOTOCOPY, RECORDING, OR ANY INFOR-MATION STORAGE AND RETRIEVAL SYSTEM, WITHOUT PERMISSION IN WRITING FROM THE PUBLISHER. LIBRARY OF CONGRESS CATALOG CARD NUMBER: 60-10918. PRINTED IN THE UNITED STATES OF AMERICA.

TO MY MOTHER

ACKNOWLEDGMENTS

I owe a debt of gratitude to both the Guggenheim Foundation and the Fund for the Advancement of Education for enabling me to take time off in past years from my regular academic work. It was while I held fellowships from them that I first began to read and think about the history of scepticism. However, the specific idea for this book grew out of a series of lectures which I had the privilege of delivering, for two successive years, at a summer conference sponsored jointly by the Council for Religion in Independent Schools and the Department of the Master of Arts in Teaching at Yale University. The interest shown and the questions raised by the teachers who heard these lectures on "Religion and the Sceptical Tradition" encouraged me to pursue the idea further and to expand the lectures into a book. In 1955, Connecticut College's invitation to deliver the Henry Wells Lawrence Memorial Lecture gave me the opportunity to try my ideas out on a college audience. Needless to say, the book also profited immeasurably from the good talk and stimulation of intimates, associates, and graduate students. Of these I should like to single out for special mention my wife and Charles and Adelaide Walker, who, in running conversations over several years, have not only encouraged me, but also helped to clarify and sharpen my ideas. Throughout, the Yale University Library has been a home to me, and its staff has given me unfailing and kindly assistance.

FRANKLIN L. BAUMER

Pierson College, Yale University
December 1, 1959

CONTENTS

RELIGION AND THE RISE OF SCEPTICISM

The Sceptical Tradition

1.

Goethe once said that "the deepest, the only theme of human history, compared to which all others are of subordinate importance, is the conflict of scepticism with faith." [1] One does not have to subscribe completely to this statement in order to appreciate that it raises an extremely important problem, a problem, moreover, which has increasingly agitated thoughtful people from Goethe's time to our own. That problem is the relationship between religion and civilization. Are the epochs "that are ruled by faith" the great epochs of history, and are the sceptical epochs "essentially sterile," as Goethe thought? (It should be noted that Goethe himself used the words "faith" and "scepticism" in a quite broad sense.) Is religion one of the essential components of a creative and imaginative civilization? This question, however, begs another question which Goethe did not raise. Why are some epochs more sceptical than others? Why, for instance, is the twentieth century one of the great sceptical epochs of history? Why does religion (the word needs to be defined, of course) come with such special difficulty to twentieth-century man?

[1] Goethe, *Wisdom and Experience*, trans. and ed. Hermann J. Weigand (New York: Pantheon Books, 1949), p. 72.

To answer this second question in any depth requires more than a philosophical and psychological analysis of the twentieth-century mind. It requires digging back into the past, at least as far as the sixteenth and seventeenth centuries and at certain points even farther, and showing how past experience has helped to shape present experience. Present-day religious scepticism, in other words, would not be what it is, would certainly not be as pervasive as it is, had it not been for the development of a powerful sceptical tradition over four centuries and more. The tracing of this tradition in the West—in broad outline only, for it would require volumes to write a full-dress history—is my theme. Since the shaping of this tradition was largely the work of intellectuals I shall deal largely with their ideas rather than with the spread of scepticism to nonintellectual groups. The latter, though of immense importance, is a whole story in itself. Moreover, with some few exceptions the intellectuals in question are western Europeans, for, as I see it, it was they rather than Americans who were largely responsible for the main lines of development. Clearly, however, this European story has relevance for America and Americans. Indeed, the American story can scarcely be understood without reference to it. American intellectuals are conversant with and have appropriated all the sceptical arguments of their European cousins. Moreover, despite surface appearances, they are scarcely less impregnated with the sceptical "world view" at the present time. There is considerably more scepticism among the intellectual leaders of this country than we usually think or care to admit.

At any rate, so far as Europe is concerned, the wide spread of scepticism among the intelligentsia and non-intelligentsia alike—what one church historian has called the contemporary "secularization of the West"—would seem to be beyond reasonable doubt. Christians themselves and Christian sympathizers freely admit it. A Church of England commission report of 1945 on the "Conversion of England," for example, showed full realization of a "whole-sale drift from organized religion" and "the present irrelevance of the Church in the life and thought of the community." Almost as if echoing this statement, an English layman, a noted student of the history of religious thought, observed in 1952 "the secular drift from God" which, he said, had "proceeded to unheard-of lengths"; "we are under no illusions now about the extent of the drift from Christianity." [2] An American Christian, reporting on Christian Europe in 1953, sent back this dismaying news: forty million baptized Roman Catholics in France, but only six million who were active members of the Church; only two million out of twenty-seven million Anglicans attending communion at Easter; and much the same situation elsewhere. Sixty per cent of a group of 680 young Norwegians, when polled, said they were not much interested in the Christian religion. "The greatest religious *discovery* of the twentieth century," he wrote, "is that Europe, the cradle of Christian culture, is its own *major* mission field." [3] About the same time a prominent German theologian warned of the rise of secularism in the postwar generation which, he said, was separated from any kind of church by a far wider gulf than were the "atheists" and "anticlericals" of former times. "We are living in a time," he said, "when

[2] Basil Willey, *Christianity Past and Present* (Cambridge, England, 1952), p. 7.

[3] Stewart W. Herman, *Report from Christian Europe* (New York: Friendship Press, 1953), p. 12; see also pp. 48-9. These figures square pretty well with those reported by James H. Nichols in his *History of Christianity, 1650-1950. Secularization of the West* (New York: Ronald Press, 1956), chap. 34, and with the conclusions of two English sociologists, B. Seebohm Rowntree and G. R. Lavers, concerning England and Wales and the Scandinavian countries.

in all civilized countries the tide of secularism is slowly but continually rising and the proportion of people still attached to any kind of church even in the Anglo-Saxon countries is steadily diminishing." [4] These are only a few examples of what amounts to a universal alarm sounded by Christians since the last great war. The question in their minds is obviously not whether the "secularization of the West" is fact or fiction, but rather what can be done to combat the fact. Of course, they also report new vitality in the churches—such things as physical recovery since the war, interesting new types of association and evangelism, and new theologies. But those who face facts have no illusions about the seriousness of the problem confronting them.

Several independent investigations by sociologists corroborate these observations, at least for England and Wales. The results of a survey made by B. Seebohm Rowntree and G. R. Lavers shortly after the war were, briefly, as follows. Relying chiefly on a system of "indirect interviewing" of about one thousand persons, "carefully selected as being typical of the whole," they concluded, first of all, that church attendance had fallen off alarmingly, both relatively and absolutely. In the city of York, for example, three censuses in 1948 showed that only 13 per cent of the adult population attended Christian churches, as compared with 35.5 per cent in 1901 and 17.7 per cent in 1935. Other conclusions were that anticlericalism was widespread in the towns; that in the lives of "a large majority of people of all classes of the community" the Church was no longer relevant; that "very likely a majority of the whole population" had rejected Christian doctrine, including the belief in a personal life after death; that many of these same people

[4] Karl Heim, *Christian Faith and Natural Science* (New York: Harper and Brothers, 1953), p. 24.

were actually agnostics; and that many teachers found it difficult or impossible to teach religion in the schools as enjoined by the Education Act of 1944. Significantly, however, they also discovered in many quarters a "spiritual hunger," "a wish that there was something in which to believe," as well as considerable instinctive conviction that Christian ethics were best. But, they concluded, "it is inconceivable to us" that the churches "will ever again be a dominant force in the religious life of the nation, although the corporate worship that they make possible will remain a source of strength and inspiration for a great many individuals." [5]

Some of the recorded answers concerning matters of belief are worth quoting because of their unmistakable historical lineage. "The nobs," said a working-class housewife, "try to make working folk believe [religion is true], so that they won't kick up a fuss" (religion is the opiate of the people). Asked what he thought about a life after death, a middle-aged male teacher in a secondary school replied, "I don't know, and I don't see how anybody can know" (agnosticism). An "upper middle-class man" declared he was indifferent to religion because he had "travelled too much and seen too many different religions to believe that there is such a thing as a true religion" (a conclusion not infrequently drawn from the modern study of comparative religion). "I believe Christianity cannot be sustained as a theological system," said a serious-minded man of the professional class, "and doubt whether its ethics . . . can survive the decay of belief in their supernatural sanction." The headmistress of a girls' secondary school wrote off the New Testament as "a text book for a very elementary stage of human understanding." "When you have simple people—

[5] B. Seebohm Rowntree and G. R. Lavers, *English Life and Leisure* (London, 1951), p. 373.

children or nearly illiterate grown-ups—you have to teach them in simple terms, by stories and so on. . . . What is needed now is what I would call an advanced text book, a sort of Newer Testament, fit for the twentieth-century level of thought" (two statements reminiscent of the nine-teenth-century "warfare between science and theology" and suggesting that Christianity has become outmoded as a system of thought).[6] Almost the only major modern criticism missing from the list is the psychological or Freudian.

The figures adduced by Geoffrey Gorer are very similar to those of Rowntree and Lavers: nearly one-quarter of the English people do not believe that they belong to any religion whatever, and the figure is even higher for the men; less than one-sixth of the population are regular in church attendance; 42 per cent "very seldom" or "never" say private prayers. As to the dogmatic content of religion, three-fifths of those interviewed state definitely that they do not believe in hell or the devil, and over one-half of the remainder say they are uncertain. More than one-half say that they do not believe in a life after death, or else do not know what to believe. Only 6 per cent of the whole population—according to this survey—profess full belief in the Christian dogma on this point. Mr. Gorer concludes:

with its [the belief in hell] virtual disappearance, it could be argued that the major supernatural sanctions of Christianity have also disappeared, for implicitly, if there is no belief in hell the concept of Judgment also becomes meaningless; and then all that is left of Christianity is a system of ethics with closer resemblance to such a system as Confucianism than to any of the major historical religions.[7]

[6] *Ibid.*, pp. 354-57.
[7] Geoffrey Gorer, *Exploring English Character* (London, 1955), p. 253.

In the face of these facts and their general admission even by champions of the churches, the editorial statement in the February, 1950, issue of the *Partisan Review* makes curious reading indeed. Introducing a symposium on "Religion and the Intellectuals," the editors threw out this bombshell:

One of the most significant tendencies of our time, specially in this decade, has been the new turn toward religion among intellectuals and the growing disfavor with which secular attitudes and perspectives are now regarded in not a few circles that lay claim to the leadership of culture. There is no doubt that the number of intellectuals professing religious sympathies, beliefs, or doctrines is greater now than it was 10 or 20 years ago, and that this number is continually increasing or becoming more articulate.

Ironically, however, this bombshell proved to be a dud. For the majority of the "intellectuals," European as well as American, who were invited to contribute to the symposium exhibited no such "new turn toward religion," in fact quite the reverse. Several, to be sure, admitted that there might be something to it, especially among intellectuals in the literary world, although the tendency was to interpret it less as a genuine religious renaissance than as a sort of "nostalgic longing." But as for themselves—this obviously does not apply to persons like W. H. Auden and Paul Tillich, who were among the contributors—they would have none of it and associated it with all the things they liked least in contemporary culture: irrationalism, traditionalism, and loss of intellectual nerve. The fact is, the editors of the *Partisan Review* notwithstanding, that secularism, or religious scepticism as we shall normally call it in this book, has made greater inroads among the intelligentsia than in any other class. The English philosopher C. E. M.

Joad was certainly right when he wrote two years later—paradoxically, in a book explaining why he personally had been recently converted to a religious view of the universe —that religious doubt "was never so widely spread or so deeply ingrained [as it is today]." "In the circles in which I have moved," he said, "consisting mainly of left wing and left centre politicians, journalists, writers, artists and dons, it is a comparatively rare thing to find an educated man who is also a Christian." [8] The evidence in Rowntree and Lavers' survey, which includes the depositions of many "intellectuals," bears out this statement, and the evidence for it will mount as we proceed farther in this book.

2.

The editors of the *Partisan Review* were, however, right in one respect. They overshot the mark when they proclaimed a new age of religious "conversion and return"; but they were correct in sensing that at mid-century, European (and American) intellectuals were not so complacent nor so jubilant about their religious scepticism as once they had been in the days of "triumphant naturalism." They stated only a simple truth when they said that "at present many thinkers sound an insistent note of warning that Western civilization cannot hope to survive without the re-animation of religious values." Clearly, something new has entered the picture. The scepticism is still there, still powerful, still persuasive. But into the picture has now crept a new note of worry and warning whose source is undoubtedly the world crisis in which many intellectuals now feel themselves to be living, and which would appear, at least to some of them, to be not unrelated to the general decline of reli-

[8] Cyril E. M. Joad, *The Recovery of Belief, A Restatement of Christian Philosophy* (London, 1952), p. 21.

gious conviction. Proof of this new note is to be found in
the spate of recent books, articles, and discussions on such
subjects as "religion and culture," "Christianity and civilization," "decadence," "the disinherited mind," "the age of
longing," etc. These effusions are the outer expression of
an inner and intensely serious debate—a debate which, to
be sure, began decades ago but which is now vocal and
urgent as never before. In other words, scepticism has now
become a problem where once it seemed a release and a
relief.

Precisely what is the problem and to whom is it a problem? Suffice it to say at this point—a detailed answer is
deferred to Chapters IV and V where it can be seen more
clearly to unroll in a historical sequence—that it involves
both sceptics and believers and that it has both subjective
and objective aspects.

The subjective aspect, which concerns more particularly
the sceptics, centers in the psychological state of individuals. The title of a collection of essays published over
twenty-five years ago by the psychologist Carl Jung exactly epitomizes this mental state: *Modern Man in Search
of a Soul*. Jung detected in "modern man," specifically in
the hundreds of educated persons, mostly Protestant, who
came to him for counsel, a vast "spiritual need" which
could not be explained simply in terms of Freudian categories. In his view this need was bound up with an acute
sense of the meaninglessness of life which arose from a
combination of two causes, one of long standing and the
other of very recent origin, viz., the decline of religious
life and conviction, and at the same time the collapse of
faith in the rationalist millenium, the latter of which was
occasioned by the shock of the Great War and its after-
math. Thus, on Jung's analysis, modern man's scepticism
has become a burden to him, accentuating rather than

removing his tensions. Rowntree and Lavers, it will be recalled, similarly observed a "spiritual hunger" among people who professed scepticism of church doctrine, as also do
many novelists and poets who have made it their business to
describe the mental state of "modern man." Even the contributors to the *Partisan Review* symposium recognize this
tension, as can be inferred from their frequent allusions to
the spiritual "starvation," the "nostalgic longing" of
"countless intellectuals."

Many intellectuals, sceptics as well as Christians, see this
inner conflict reacting outward on civilization. This is the
objective side of the problem, the point so to speak at which
the problem enters history and affects not merely individuals but quite possibly the collective ideals and behavior of
whole societies.

Civilization, as is well known, has become a problem to
Europeans since the publication of Oswald Spengler's *Decline of the West* in 1918. It has been widely felt and even
simply assumed—on the impressive evidence of two major
wars, the flight of whole nations to collectivistic systems,
man's inhumanity to man as exhibited in concentration
camps and other forms of barbarism—that the West has
entered a "time of troubles" and that it may even conceivably "go under," as Spengler predicted, unless the crisis is
properly diagnosed and a cure provided.[9] Significantly, religion figures prominently in this great contemporary debate
over the civilization problem. An older point of view, first
well developed during the eighteenth-century Enlightenment, dismissed religion—at least the religion of creeds and
priests—as irrelevant or even inimical to the progress of

[9] For a discussion of this problem as many European intellectuals see
it, see Franklin L. Baumer, "Twentieth-Century Version of the Apocalypse," *Cahiers d'Histoire Mondiale* (*Journal of World History*), Vol. I,
No. 3 (January, 1954), pp. 623-40.

civilization. Edward Gibbon, for instance, saw a cause-and-effect relationship between the rise of Christianity and the decline and fall of the Roman Empire, and some of the French *philosophes* were convinced that religion (as they understood the term) obstructed the progress of knowledge, social justice, and international peace, and even contaminated morals. In the contemporary phase of the debate, however, this judgment has been reversed or at least subjected to serious doubt. It has become quite common, even among sceptics, to point out the disproportionate advance made in recent years by morals and religion on the one hand and science and technics on the other, and to plot graphs to demonstrate the explosion which occurs in history when the "power-curve" (as Arthur Koestler calls it) shoots up and the "spiritual curve" plummets down. It has become quite common to debate, in deadly seriousness, the possible effects of the present widespread feeling of religious meaninglessness upon courage, politics, morals, and even the artistic imagination.

Statements by Paul Tillich, C. E. M. Joad, Erich Heller, Carl Jung, and Arnold Toynbee may be taken as fairly typical. In *The Courage to Be* (1952) the philosopher-theologian Tillich argued that religion supplies the feeling of purposefulness upon which man's courage and vitality, and hence his civilization, ultimately depend. Conversely, the loss of a religious center to life leads to acute anxiety and hence to reduced courage and even despair. Man, of course, is born to anxiety, but in some ages of history he is more aware of his anxiety, is more pathologically anxious, than in others. These great "ages of anxiety" come at the end of eras when accustomed structures of power and belief are disintegrating. The period of the decline of Rome was such an age, likewise the Reformation when Martin Luther and others lived in mortal fear of the wrath of God.

The contemporary age, however, is the age of anxiety *par excellence*. It suffers from what Tillich calls "the anxiety of emptiness and meaninglessness" which is aroused by the loss of a religious center to life. In consequence of the decay of religious belief in modern times there is no answer to the meaning of existence, no meaning to participate in. This situation of "total doubt," and hence unbearable anxiety, has had marked and grave effects on western civilization. It accounts for the negativity of the art, literature, and philosophy of the twentieth century, which at its best, as among the existentialists, can only exhibit the "courage of despair." It explains the political fanaticism of the times —the great mass flight of people from themselves to the collectivist systems which impose answers to all the problems of existence. By such flight, says Tillich, "meaning is saved, but the self is sacrificed." The only way to restore the "courage to be," and civilization too, is to rediscover the religious meaning of life. Other Christians who have developed substantially the same thesis are the Russian exile and self-styled "religious philosopher" Nicolas Berdyaev and the Swiss theologian Emil Brunner, the latter in his Gifford lectures significantly entitled *Christianity and Civilization* (1948). Both Berdyaev and Brunner focus on the disastrous effects on civilization of the breakdown of the idea of man's creation in God's image. When this idea faded with the humanist and positivist movements of modern times—so it is argued—man lost his essential dignity, and his humanity turned dialectically into the inhumanity of modern machine-civilization. Like Tillich and many others, Berdyaev also contended that man's cosmic loneliness drove him into the arms of the totalitarian systems, and that the positivistic limitation of knowledge to sense perceptions in the space-time world dried up man's creative and imaginative faculties.

In *Decadence* (1948), another book about the decline of the West, the philosopher C. E. M. Joad ascribed the troubles of modern civilization to what he calls "the dropping of the object." By "the object" he means absolutes, objective values (truth, beauty, goodness, God) which are located in an order of reality not subject to time and space. The dropping of the object therefore means the denial of absolutes which now appear to be subjective only, the inventions of men rather than the gods. When this occurs in history, as in the present age, the human ego swells up and proudly imagines that it creates everything and that nothing is impossible to it. At the same time, however, it necessarily turns in on itself and becomes morbidly subjective, for it lacks objective standards, "creeds and codes," by which to be guided. In other words, whenever in history the Titans aspire to be gods, the gods cut them down and nemesis confronts hubris. All the symptoms of decadence in the present world—the extreme subjectivism of modern literature and its preoccupation with the abnormal and primitive, the worship and aggrandizement of the state, the absence of a common culture—trace back to this loss of belief in a non-natural world of objective values. Contrariwise, says Joad:

It is only in so far as men accept the existence of this immaterial world [i.e., a religious or metaphysical view of the universe] in their theory and seek to increase the degree of their awareness of and contact with it in practice, that the human mind advances in respect of knowledge, the human character in respect of goodness and the human spirit in respect of the perception and love of beauty.[10]

In *The Disinherited Mind* (1952) Erich Heller, literary scholar and critic, tests the effect of unbelief specifically on

[10] Cyril E. M. Joad, *Decadence: A Philosophical Inquiry* (London, 1948), pp. 248-49.

the artistic imagination, and like Joad he finds it to be devastating. Great literature, which is one of the manifestations of a great civilization, depends, he thinks, upon a commonly accepted belief in the meaningfulness of the world, its interpenetration by transcendence, its symbolic nature pointing beyond itself. The modern world, however, has no such belief. Minds are spiritually disinherited and without certainties. Lacking any supranatural center for holding the world together, artists and writers are thrown back on their own naturalistic resources, and judging by the history of modern literature, the result is sheer chaos—the chaos of Franz Kafka, for instance, who unlike Goethe finds himself in a world without spirit. Between the time of Goethe and Kafka, says Heller, "reality has been all but completely sealed off against any transcendental intrusion." Kafka, representative of the modern mind, epitomizes spiritual uprootedness, the loss of any strong conviction except that of damnation. Thus, chaos has replaced the sense of order transcending disorder which is so marked in writers like Shakespeare and Goethe. Heller is only one of many contemporary scholars and writers who have addressed themselves to this particular aspect of the problem. Others who have done so are Thomas Stearns Eliot, notably in his essay on "Religion and Literature" in which he argues the corruption of modern literature by "secularism," and Professor Basil Willey, of the University of Cambridge, in his studies of the intellectual background of modern English literature.

Those erstwhile Freudians, Carl Jung and Otto Rank, have also been profundly concerned about the civilization-religion problem and have subjected it to lengthy and close analysis. That is to say, as psychologists they are concerned to study the effects of unbelief not only on individuals but also on groups and societies. Why is western civilization in such a parlous state today? How can we account for the uncontrollable upsurges of psychic energy in the contemporary era, the seizures of whole peoples, the mental epidemics, the general destructiveness? If pressed in the matter, Jung might admit that political and economic movements had something to do with it. Basically, however, he would trace its dynamics back to man's inner life, and especially to his lack of religious orientation since the eighteenth-century Enlightenment. According to Jung, the void thus created has had unfortunate social consequences, for a society can function effectively only if its individuals are provided with meanings—meanings, moreover, which satisfy not only the intellectual but also the intuitive or religious side of his psyche—in which he can have a living faith. Only then can his psychic energies go out into the world and into socially productive enterprises. Otto Rank similarly attributes the negativity of the present "psychological era" of western history to a universal absence of spiritual experiences which transcend individuality.

The historian Arnold Toynbee gathers up all or most of these threads of argument and weaves them into a vast historical canvas. Like the others he believes that western civilization is "on trial" and that its trial traces ultimately to a "schism in the soul" as well as to a "schism in the body social." If it would save itself—so he argued, for instance, in an essay entitled "Does History Repeat Itself?"—it must therefore strive, not merely to effect world government in politics, and some compromise between free enterprise and socialism in economics, but also, in the life of the spirit, to "put the secular super-structure back onto religious foundations." To be sure, in another essay on "Christianity and Civilization" and particularly in the last four volumes of *A Study of History*, Toynbee has shifted his emphasis from the civilizations to the churches, preferring now to think of the former as paving the way for the latter in history.

However, he still holds that religion in turn shapes civilization. In the volume on the Universal Churches he expressly rejects the theory, formulated by Gibbon and Sir James Frazer, of the churches as "cancers" which eat away the tissues of civilization. On the contrary, "in seeking God," says Toynbee, "man is performing a social act," and indeed without the fruits which the higher religions supply, civilizations cannot long endure. Among these fruits are a belief in human fellowship and hence power to overcome discord in human society, a solution to the problem of the meaning of history, and the means of exorcising the peril inherent in the worship of man-made "isms." Both Toynbee and another well-known historian Christopher Dawson (in *Religion and Culture*, 1948) talk about a return to religion in the West as the "indispensable condition of human survival."

One does not have to go so far as this to perceive that Toynbee and the other participants in the great religion-civilization debate have raised an important historical problem. However, what they do not always perceive, or at least do not always clearly articulate, is that the objective aspect of the problem necessarily hinges on the subjective. The relationship between religion and civilization is one problem. But the deeper problem, what one might call the problem within the problem, is the extent to which, and also the form in which, it is possible for contemporary Europeans, and more especially the intellectuals, to have any sort of religious conviction. One of the debaters who sees this subjective aspect of the problem clearly is the English commentator on political and foreign affairs, Barbara Ward. Miss Ward agrees wholeheartedly with the others that the attenuation of religious faith in a society has grave consequences for its civilization:

Even the most doubtful must confront the fact that totalitarian government in its extremest form has returned when the waning of religion left the altars of the soul empty and turned men back to the oldest gods of all—the idols of the tribe. Nor is it easy to conceive of any means other than religious faith for preserving a genuine division of power in society; for if a man is no more than the creature of his environment, and a product of his social order, on what foundations can he base claims and loyalties which go beyond the social order? [11]

She then goes on, however, to warn that "faith will not be restored in the West because people believe it to be useful. It will return only when they find that it is true." Hence, the real question is: Can "modern man" accept such a possibility in view of the rise of scepticism during the last four hundred years?

This, it seems to me, is the real nub of the problem. To put it in other words, "modern man"—concretely, the sort of men interviewed by Rowntree and Lavers and analyzed by Jung, whose number is legion—is the heir of a great tradition, let us call it *the sceptical tradition*, which at crucial points challenges another great tradition, the religious Judaeo-Christian tradition, of the West. In the present epoch a large and increasing number of Europeans have expressed a desire to return, as the hero of Arthur Koestler's recent novel *The Age of Longing* puts it, to "the sheltering womb" of the religious tradition, or at least to something approximating it—partly for reasons of psychic health, partly because they suspect that it may be essential to "civilization" to do so. Unfortunately for many of them, however, this new "will to believe," as it might be called, con-

[11] Barbara Ward, *Faith and Freedom* (New York: W. W. Norton, 1954), p. 265.

flicts with their world view. Whenever they take it into their heads to "return," the shades of all the great sceptics, Pierre Bayle and Voltaire, Ernest Renan and Sigmund Freud and the rest, rise up around them and persuade them, with considerable success, that they cannot go back. This is the religious dilemma of "modern man," and it cannot be solved, as Miss Ward rightly observes, simply by utilitarian arguments.

3.

Obviously, this is an existential problem for many Europeans today. However, it is also a historical problem. By this I do not mean that the historian can solve it or that the solution lies mysteriously concealed somewhere in the historical record. I simply mean that history, and more especially intellectual history, can show how and why scepticism has come to be a particularly thorny problem in the present epoch, and at the same time record some of the more striking attempts currently being made to find a solution to it. That is to say, the historian (who else?) can put the problem into a historical context and thereby illuminate if not solve it. In particular, he can point to the role of tradition in creating the problem in the first place.

It is perhaps not sufficiently realized how important a role tradition plays in conditioning the way people think and behave, both as individuals and as members of a group or society. Tradition is at least as important a conditioner as geography and climate, class interest, or the general economic and political situation. This theory of conditioning by tradition does not make man a "product," but it does presume that the traditions which he ingests through his education or by suggestion from his general mental climate

set up in his mind certain powerful biases. Once well established and with the weight of tradition behind them, these
biases are not easily dislodged. They lie, as it were, at the
bottom of the mind and continue to influence men's thinking even after men discover a powerful wish to dislodge
them. No doubt they act on the whole as a conservative
force, prejudicing men to preserve and transmit some idea
that has been tested and found good over a period of historical time. However, it is a curious thing about some traditions that they also act as censors inhibiting men from
finding solutions to their problems by a simple return to a
status quo ante. Where such traditions are operative, solutions are found—if they are found at all—not by going
back, at least not all the way for this would be psychologically impossible, but by grafting something new on the
old and tried.

The sceptical tradition is, I believe, of this latter type.
In any event it is clearly one of the most important traditions in modern European history—and one of the most
neglected. Other traditions, such as the classical tradition,
the romantic tradition, the Christian tradition, the humanistic tradition, the scientific tradition, the conservative,
liberal, democratic, and socialist traditions, have found their
historians. To my knowledge, however, no one has properly identified and charted the course of the sceptical
tradition down to the present.[12] And this is a serious gap,

[12] There are, of course, many monographs on particular phases of the
subject. John M. Robertson's *A Short History of Freethought Ancient
and Modern* (first edition 1899; second edition, rewritten and enlarged,
1906) was a pioneer work of a more general sort and included a review
of previous general studies. My study differs from Robertson's both with
respect to point of view and coverage. Despite his claim to scientific
objectivity, Robertson wrote from the nineteenth-century rationalist
point of view. He also covered both more and less territory. He went
back to the ancient and even primitive world whereas I have chosen to
commence at about the seventeenth century, though with a few glances

for, as has already been indicated, the contemporary religious problem is simply unintelligible—and perhaps ultimately insoluble—without full awareness of it.

The purpose of this book is to begin the work of filling this gap—to fill it completely would obviously require volumes—by sketching the course of the sceptical tradition in broad outline from the seventeenth century to the present; to show how and by whom it was generated, and how it grew and gained momentum up to and including the present "crisis" which Jung, Tillich, Joad, and others so vividly describe. This sketch will commence with another great crisis in western religious history, viz., the epoch of the French Revolution, which witnessed the first concerted effort in the modern West to dechristianize a whole society and to institutionalize scepticism. The plan then calls for going back into the eighteenth-century Enlightenment in order to account for the revolutionary experiment (although, as we shall see, the Enlightenment does not fully explain it), and for going back farther still in order to put Enlightenment scepticism in turn in its historical setting. Having explored these reaches we shall then face round to the post-Revolutionary epoch and eventually work down into the country of Darwin, Nietzsche, and Freud, finally returning to the point where we began in this chapter.

In the course of this study we shall identify four main types of scepticism, or four principal phases through which the sceptical tradition has developed over the past four hundred years. Doubtless, these phases are to a certain extent nothing but phrases, or "ideal types" as Max Weber would say, which do not altogether do justice to the com-

---

farther back. Also, of course, his study came down only to the end of the nineteenth century, whereas a third or more of my study deals with the twentieth century. I also venture to say that his study, though considerably longer, is less analytical than mine.

plexity of the data. Furthermore, there is nothing ineluctable about the number four, nor are the four phases always clearly distinguishable from one another. However, to mark such phases and to describe them by phrases is not only convenient, and ultimately unavoidable for making generalizations, but to do so also has the distinct advantage of pointing up the somewhat oscillatory as well as cumulative character of the sceptical tradition. As in the scientific tradition, there is a sense in which each generation of sceptics feeds upon the cumulative experience and experiments of the past. But the sceptical tradition is more like a political tradition, say the liberal tradition, in the sense that it seems periodically to undergo real qualitative changes. Thus, scepticism at mid-century in our own epoch is not quite the same thing as scepticism in the mid-eighteenth century, and there are nuances and overtones to, for instance, Friedrich Nietzsche's scepticism that were utterly lacking in Voltaire's or Pierre Bayle's. Perhaps the phases can be best understood as main currents of thought to which there are always exceptions and which indeed never more than approximately delineate the scepticism of any given individual. The second of these phases, but the first to be identified, is the Enlightenment, of which Voltaire is the chief prototype, and his "Crush the Infamous Thing" ("*Écrasez l'infâme*") the great slogan. As we shall see, the distinguishing marks of this Enlightenment scepticism were anticlericalism, antidogmatism, even anti-Christianity, but not necessarily antireligion, at least as the term "religion" is understood in this book. (See the excursus at the end of this Introduction for a definition of terms.) It will be argued, however, that this second phase would not have been possible without an initial or preceding phase in which philosophic and scientific sceptics, most of whom were sincere Christians, prepared the way for religious scepticism by dismantling traditional conceptions of nature and knowledge. Leading prototypes of this first phase, as we shall designate it, are Boyle and Bayle, the sceptical chemist and the sceptical historian, and perhaps more particularly the former because he combined scepticism with a deep Christian conviction, which Bayle did not. Hence, the symbol chosen for this first phase is the great mechanical clock at Strasbourg which Robert Boyle so often used to analogize his view of nature. The third phase, which covers the nineteenth century, centers in Nietzsche's obsequies for God which though conducted by a madman were not madness but, on the contrary, a very sober and ultimately true representation of the state of mind of many nineteenth-century intellectuals and of many other people as well. Sceptically speaking, the "Death of God" was much farther to the left than Voltaire's "*Écrasez.*" Arthur Koestler's *The Age of Longing* symbolizes a fourth phase, the twentieth-century or, more precisely, contemporary phase in which scepticism combines in a new way with "longing" for the God who is dead or for a God who is not yet born.

At the end, after having identified the four phases, I shall want to get off the straight historical track and speculate a little on how certain contemporary intellectuals, chiefly laymen, seem to be trying to solve the scepticism-religion problem—in terms of a sort of "Layman's Religion"—and also venture a few remarks, as many others have done, on the civilization-religion problem. This last seems to me to be a legitimate field of speculation for the historian who wants to know not only what the facts are but also what they may possibly mean for his generation. It is too easily assumed, I think, that such matters are the province of the religious leader, philosopher, or creative writer. But surely the historian, with his long view of time and his awareness of cultural change and the power of tradition, can also contribute something useful to the discussion.

Excursus on the Idols of the Market Place

"Words," said Sir Francis Bacon, "put all things in confusion, and lead men away to idle controversies and subtleties, without number." Words are therefore among those "idols" which take such root in the human mind "that truth can hardly find entrance" therein.[18] Since this is so—and clearly it *is* so—there is need, before proceeding farther, for a brief excursus on the definition and possible meanings of the principal terms employed in this book. What, precisely, do the terms "religion" and "scepticism" signify? Or what is more to the point: Of all the possible significations of these terms, which ones does this writer choose to employ as he surveys their history and conflict over several centuries?

The chief point that Bacon wished to establish in his celebrated attack on the Idols of the Market Place was that words—e.g., words like "fortune," "*primum mobile*," "witch"—do not necessarily correspond to real things in nature and hence often obscure the truth. He might have added that one very important reason for the confusion surrounding the meaning of words is that words themselves have a history. This is obviously the case with such frequently-used words as "science," "reason," and "nature," but it is equally true of the words "religion" and "scepticism" whose meanings not only change with the times but also connote some rather different ideas at any one time. In order to avoid total confusion an author must therefore at the very least make clear what *he* means by his terms

[18] Francis Bacon, *Novum Organum*, Aphorisms XLIII, LIX-LX.

even though his definitions cannot possibly satisfy everybody. And that is the intention of this excursus: not to try
to list all possible definitions, but only to supply working
definitions, with which the reader does not have to agree,
but which will let him know what this writer means when
he uses the terms.

A.

"Religion" is a more elusive term than is generally appreciated, even by the *Oxford English Dictionary*. In contemporary usage it has at least two types of meaning which
would seem to be diametrically opposed to each other, or
almost so. On the one hand, there is what may be called
the dogmatic, or ecclesiastical type which is affirmed by
most of the traditional churches. On the other hand, there
has grown up beside it, almost imperceptibly, a radical
new type which reflects the secular spirit of the modern
world. Neither of these types exhausts the meaning of the
word religion as it will be used in this book. It will be
argued, in fact, that the first is only a species of a larger
genus, and that the latter is a false type (false in the sense
that it is a misnomer) which is better designated by the word
"faith" than "religion." Stated in other words, the first is
too narrow whereas the second is too broad, so broad indeed
that it jettisons the old meaning of the idea, robs it of its
uniqueness, and reduces it to categories of secular life.

The dogmatic, or ecclesiastical, type requires little expli-
cation since it is so generally familiar. Perhaps its most
general characteristic is its distinction between "sacred,"
or religious, and secular aspects of life. The "sacred" refers
to the supernatural—specifically, to belief in a supernatural
God who communicates truth to man by some kind of "revelation" which is "above reason" if not necessarily "contrary

to reason." However, as explicated by Roman Catholics and many Protestants, religion also tends to be identified with "the true religion," i.e., with a particular revelation, with the dogma and theology of a particular church, and even to some extent with its ecclesiastical forms, ritual, and imagery. Thus, John Calvin, though he taught that God has implanted in all men a "seed of religion," nevertheless distinguished between idolatries and superstitions, and what he often called "the true religion" (*vera* or *legitima religio*), which was the religion that the Christian God taught man in his Word. "For where there is no certain knowledge of God, there is no religion." [14] Obviously, religion as defined in this way tends to assume an exclusive and even superior attitude toward other sects, and moreover to lock up a large segment of religious knowledge in some form of verbal credo.

The second or secular type goes to the other extreme and destroys completely the old distinction between sacred and secular. Religion now becomes simply devotion to an ideal, whether "religious" in the traditional sense or secular, anything in fact which enables the individual to lose himself in a larger "good," and the group or community to find purpose and meaning. "Any activity in behalf of an ideal and against obstacles and in spite of threats of personal loss because of conviction of its general and enduring value is religious in quality," said John Dewey.[15] It was on the basis of this sort of definition that the historian Carl Becker, for instance, could describe the faith of the eighteenth-century *philosophes* in man's natural goodness and the good life on

---

[14] John Calvin, *Opera*, in *Corpus Reformatorum* (Brunswick, Germany, 1869-96), Vol. XLII, p. 331. "Nam ubi nulla est Dei cognitio certa, nulla est etiam religio, et pietas prorsus exstincta est, et fides abolita."

[15] John Dewey, *A Common Faith* (New Haven: Yale University Press, 1934), p. 27.

earth as "the religion of the Enlightenment." In common parlance today communism is similarly said to be a religion, as is nationalism, which Carlton Hayes has called "a veritable religion" for vast numbers of persons in the contemporary world. According to H. G. Wells in *The Open Conspiracy*, "subordination of self" is "the essence of religion," the sort of subordination, for instance, that would be required to realize the ideal of the coming world community. Not only the social reformer and the political zealot but also artists and scientists become thereby religious men, providing they are properly devoted to an artistic vision or the pursuit of scientific truth. In the words of the English Hegelian philosopher Bernard Bosanquet:

The religious consciousness has no special or exclusive connection with the supernatural, the other world, or even the divine. It is essentially the attitude in which the finite being stands to whatever he at once fears and approves, in a word to what he worships. . . . In short, then, wherever man fairly and loyally throws the seat of his value outside his immediate self into something else which he worships, with which he identifies his will, and which he takes as an object solid and secure, at least relatively, to his private existence—as an artist in his attitude to beauty, or as a man of science to truth—there we have in its degree the experience of religion, and, also in its degree, the stability and security of the finite self.[16]

Now, as already indicated, when the word "religion" is used in this book it will sometimes refer to the first of the above types but never to the latter. The position taken here is that religion is not reducible—at least not completely or fundamentally—to something else, to, say, a humanist or secular faith or even the pursuit of beauty and truth, legitimate and valuable as they may be. The attempt to

[16] Bernard Bosanquet, *The Value and Destiny of the Individual* (London, 1913), pp. 235, 240.

define religion in this way is, as Bosanquet's younger contemporary T. E. Hulme once observed, the result of the
modern compulsion to explain everything in naturalistic
categories, the modern "shrinking" from any idea of "discontinuity" between physical and vital things on the one
hand and religious things on the other.[17]

Following Hulme's concept of "discontinuity" we shall
maintain that religion is something *sui generis*. To adopt
a similar formulation by the anthropologist Bronislaw Malinowski, it refers to the "sacred" as opposed to the "profane"
domain of human life, i.e., to those aspects of the world—
the riddle of human existence, "the transcendental value and
sense of human life," the problem of death, etc.—which
science, at least up to now, has been unable to illuminate
and with respect to which most "profane" or secular faiths
are mute. Malinowski distinguished sharply between "religion" in this "sacred" sense, which he discovered in all the
primitive communities he studied, and the modern "pseudo-
religions" of nationalism, racism, and dialectical materialism;[18] and so shall we in this book, without, however,
intending to say anything more for the present than that
they are *different*.

To state this proposition in slightly different terms, the
distinguishing mark of "religion" as here defined is its
awareness and concern for the *metaphysical* overtones of
human life. On the philosophical side this metaphysical
sense involves probing into things unseen, things which
clearly cannot be accounted for, at least not entirely, in
terms of the ordinary space-time order of science and poli-

[17] T. E. Hulme, *Speculations* (London, 1924). See especially the notes
on "Humanism and the Religious Attitude."
[18] Bronislaw Malinowski, *The Foundations of Faith and Morals*
(Oxford, 1936), p. 62. See also his *Magic, Science and Religion* (Garden
City: Doubleday, 1955), p. 17.

tics; asking and trying to get answers to the great metaphysical questions of "formal and final causes," life and
death, time and timelessness. On the psychological side it
involves the experience of "mysteries" which, as Rudolf
Otto said, are "quite beyond the sphere of the usual, the
intelligible and the familiar," [19] and which shake the foundations. This peculiarly religious form of cognition or experience may or may not crystallize into creedal belief and
membership in a historic church. With Calvin it obviously
did, but with a man such as Goethe it did not. Yet on this
definition Goethe too was a religious man because of his
consciousness of an unseen and meaningful reality which,
though it penetrated, was yet not identical with the space-
time order. On the other hand, Karl Marx does not qualify
as a religious man because of his stated disbelief in anything
beyond the visible natural order; nor does an agnostic like
Sir Leslie Stephen, who thought that if there were such an
order man could know nothing about it. That which binds
Calvin and Goethe together under the rubric of religion, and
which clearly excludes Marx and Stephen, is a sort of symbolic view of the world. Though in different degrees and
with different emphases, for Goethe was a pantheist, both
men saw "nature" as a symbol which reflects and at the
same time points beyond itself to a wider reality. Calvin
would certainly have disagreed with Goethe's statement
that "to have a positive religion is not necessary." But he
might have agreed with another of the great German's
reflections that "true symbolism [Goethe's own symbol-
ism] is present where the specific represents the more general, not as a dream and shadow, but as a living momentary
revelation of the inscrutable." [20]

[19] Rudolf Otto, *The Idea of the Holy*, trans. John W. Harvey (London, 1923), p. 26.
[20] Goethe, *Wisdom and Experience*, pp. 47, 259.

B.

The word scepticism can also be an idol unless it is carefully defined. Scepticism in its most general sense implies "doubting" as well as "inquiring." However, there are obviously different kinds and degrees of doubting and it is essential to establish at the outset precisely what kind of doubting we shall be dealing with in this book. Moreover, a point which the *Oxford English Dictionary* misses entirely, the doubting of the sceptic is in many cases accompanied by some form of believing. Doubting, that is to say, is often only the negative side of the sceptic's mental outlook; the sceptic, paradoxical as this may sound, may be and often is a person who believes very strongly in something. Blaise Pascal was therefore not far from the mark when he said, in one of his *Pensées,* that "there never has been a real complete sceptic."

Scepticism, as we shall use the term, refers primarily to religious rather than philosophical and scientific doubting. To be sure, these tribes sometimes coalesce, yet there is a historical distinction between them. The philosophical sceptic in history is by no means invariably a religious sceptic, nor vice versa. Hence, a history of philosophical scepticism would necessarily follow somewhat different lines from the present work. Philosophical scepticism, at least as it descends from the Pyrrhonists of ancient Greece, is a counsel of epistemological but not necessarily religious despair. According to the classic statement of the position by Pyrrho and Sextus Empiricus, "nothing can be known with certainty" since the only means that man has of knowing, viz., his sense impressions and his reason, are essentially unreliable. The interesting thing is, however, that in history philosophical sceptics are not uncommonly to be found among the defenders of traditional religion. Such, for example, was the case with the Frenchmen Michel de Montaigne and Pascal and the English poet John Dryden, all of whom supported dogmatic Christianity by Pyrrhonistic arguments. Following his master, Sextus Empiricus, Montaigne, in his famous "Apology for Raimond Sebond," denied the competence of the human reason to obtain truth. But then, instead of drawing the expected conclusion, he used his "What do I know?" as the basis for a philosophy of religious faith. He depicted man as all the more fit thereby "to harbour within himself divine knowledge; suppressing his own judgment to leave more room for faith; neither disbelieving nor setting up any teaching contrary to the common observances; humble, obedient, docile, zealous, a sworn enemy to heresy." [21]

The tribe of religious sceptics on the other hand does not invariably take its stand on this sort of philosophical scepticism, although it has sometimes done so. On the contrary, as we shall see, it has usually preferred to affirm rather than to deny the powers of reason, and to criticize religion on rational as well as empirical and moral grounds. In any case, what is in doubt among the members of this tribe, the tribe with which this book deals, is precisely the religious tradition, or certain aspects of that tradition (for obviously some sceptics do not press their doubts nearly so far as others). To this tribe belong, in spite of wide differences among them, the so-called "Averroists" of the middle ages, the infidels and unbelievers of the Renaissance, the "libertines" of the seventeenth century, the deists as well as theists of the Enlightenment, and the whole horde of freethinkers, agnostics, materialists, rationalists, and secularists of more recent vintage. It is a heterogeneous tribe, bound together only by a common "reaction against some phase

[21] Michel de Montaigne, *Essays,* trans. E. J. Trechmann (New York: Random House, 1946), pp. 431-32.

or phases of conventional or traditional doctrine in religion." [22] Patently, it includes the widest possible variety of moods and attitudes. In some of its members righteous indignation predominates, in others triumphant doubt and a sense of emancipation, and in still others sheer indifference or else the reverse, a longing for a religious faith which seems intellectually unattainable. Although, doubtless, specimens of all or most of these attitudes are to be found cheek by jowl in every period, there does seem to be a kind of historical progression to them, in the sense that one attitude succeeds another or at any rate becomes more conspicuous than in a previous epoch.

The final point to be insisted upon in our definition is that scepticism, or the sceptic, usually has a positive as well as a negative side. Most of the religious sceptics who appear in these pages will be found either to have had a strong faith in something—remnants of religious orthodoxy perhaps, or one of those quasi- or pseudo-religions already mentioned —or to be seekers or inquirers after such a faith. Doubting is only one part of their mental spectrum; believing or the will to believe is usually at least as important a part. Hence, this study will concern itself not only with what the sceptic doubts and why he doubts but also with what, if anything, he substitutes for the religious faith he has abjured. The only point at which this thesis might be said to break down is in the present century when an appreciable number of

[22] This is John M. Robertson's definition for "freethought" (see *A Short History of Freethought Ancient and Modern* [New York: G. P. Putnam's Sons, 1906], Vol. I, p. 9). His "freethought" is practically synonymous with my "scepticism." I have preferred scepticism to freethought because the latter term, it seems to me, is somewhat dated, whereas the former not only has a longer history but is still in general use today. Moreover, "freethought" is no less free from ambiguity than "scepticism," for there are obviously different kinds of freethinkers just as there are scientific, philosophical, and religious sceptics.

sceptics, the heirs by now of a sceptical tradition of long standing, would appear to be without any faith whatsoever, living by a philosophy of meaninglessness. In reality, however, even these twentieth-century sceptics long for a faith, and, as we shall see, many of them have made a persistent effort to discover a faith—even a religion—appropriate to their mental condition.

CHAPTER I

"Crush the Infamous Thing"

1.

On the morning of November 10, 1793 (or the twentieth
Brumaire of the Year II, according to the new Revolutionary calendar), there took place in the Cathedral of Notre
Dame of Paris an extraordinary religious event. This was
the Festival of Liberty and Reason, proclaimed three days
before by the mayor of the city. As the spectators, officials
of the Commune and Department of Paris together with a
great concourse of plain citizens, entered the cathedral,
they saw, some doubtless with astonishment, the insignia of
Christianity covered up and their place taken by the symbols of a strange new religion. Rising up in the nave was an
improvised mountain, at the top of which perched a small
Greek temple dedicated "To Philosophy" and adorned on
both sides by the busts of philosophers, probably Voltaire,
Rousseau, Franklin, and Montesquieu. Halfway down the
side of the mountain a torch of Truth burned before an
altar of Reason. Then ensued a bizarre ceremony which
culminated in the emergence from the temple of a beautiful
woman, an actress of the Paris Opera, dressed in red, white,
and blue garments, who personified Liberty. The spectators
proceeded to render homage to Liberty by stretching out

their arms to her and singing a hymn, the words of which were written by Marie Joseph Chénier:

> "Come, holy Liberty, inhabit this temple,
> Become the goddess of the French people."

Soon thereafter the Constitutional Convention decreed that Notre Dame should be known as the Temple of Reason.[1]

Despite its superficiality, hasty contrivance, and indeed evanescence this new cult of reason was an important landmark in the history of religion in the West. It was important chiefly as a symbol, for as an institution it lasted scarcely a year, hounded to death by Robespierre's charge of "fanaticism." It was a symbol, first of all, of Voltairean scepticism which scored Christianity as an "infamous thing," to be crushed (*"Écrasez l'infâme"*: "Crush the infamous thing") and replaced by a religion imbued with "reason," "virtue," and "liberty." For the architects of the new cult, Voltairean in spirit, aimed not merely to assert the prerogatives of the state against the historic Church; nor to subordinate the Church to the state as the National Assembly had recently done with the Civil Constitution of the Clergy; nor yet to restore Christianity to its original purity, in the manner of the Christian humanists of the Renaissance or the Protestants of the Reformation; but actually to dechristianize France—the first but obviously not the last such attempt in a European nation—by disestablishing the Church and substituting for it, as several spokesmen for the Department and the Convention have recorded, a new cult "drawn from the bosom of nature" which would "be henceforth the national religion." Thus, the cult of Brumaire symbolized a would-be revolution in religion which ran parallel to the revolution in politics and the distribution

---

[1] For a full account of this Festival see A. Aulard, *Le Culte de la Raison et le Culte de l'Être Suprême* (Paris, 1909), chap. 5.

of property. At its deepest level it symbolized nothing less than a crisis in French religious belief.

If the cult of Brumaire were an isolated event, it would not be symbolic of much of anything, least of all of a crisis in belief. Such, however, was not the case. It was in fact only one of many anti-Christian "sects," as the Constitutional Bishop Grégoire called them, which sprouted up during the Revolutionary epoch. It was not even the first, for it had been preceded by several cults to "reason" and "nature" in the provinces, notably in Clermont and Nevers, and by a sort of Voltairean cult when in 1791 the National Assembly ordered the interment of the great sage's remains in the new civil Pantheon, formerly the Church of Sainte-Geneviève. After Brumaire there followed in succession, to mention only the best known, innumerable cults of reason, similar to the cult in Paris and less artificial; the cult of the Supreme Being initiated by Robespierre and celebrated on June 8, 1794 (twentieth Prairial of the Year II), with great pomp and circumstance according to the plans of the painter Jacques Louis David; the *culte décadaire* of the Directory which made compulsory throughout France a patriotic service to be held every tenth day (on the *décadi* or Republican Sunday) and led by municipal officers and commissioners of the Republic; and a number of private cults such as the cult of Theophilanthropy, which was founded by the Parisian bookseller Chemin and which included in its membership politicians, men of letters, and ex-priests. A considerable literature grew up around these cults, including a host of catechisms and manuals prescribing orders for public and even private worship.

To be sure, these cults were not cut equally from the same cloth. Some were more conservative than others, some more secular than religious. Generally speaking, they fall into three main types which, however, blur into one another. Brumaire and Prairial represent what may be called the deistic type, although historically the latter arose in opposition to the former. Robespierre, largely for political reasons, tried to make out that Brumaire was atheistic, but the evidence scarcely supports his accusation. "Reason," in the ceremony at Notre Dame and elsewhere, appears to have signified in some vague way, perhaps as an emanation from deity, the god of the deists. At least it was understood to do so by many of its friends and even enemies, as can be seen, for example, from the opening statement of a "Republican Credo" which appeared in 1793 in support of Brumaire: "I believe in a Supreme Being, who has created men free and equal, who has made them to love and not hate one another, who wishes to be honored by virtues and not by fanaticism." Compare these lines with the decree announcing Robespierre's cult: "1. The French people recognizes the existence of the Supreme Being and the immortality of the soul. 2. It recognizes that the cult worthy of the Supreme Being is the practice of the duties of man, etc." [2] The difference is one of degree only. Robespierre, following Jean Jacques Rousseau rather than Voltaire, wished to make quite clear to Europe, understandably shocked by the affair at Notre Dame, that France was not atheistic but, on the contrary, warmly sympathetic to religion. The religion in question, however, was deism—a sort of state deism which would replace the old Christian establishment.

Even these ostensibly deistic cults tended to lose their identity in a second type which some contemporaries boldly labelled "the religion of the Republic," or the Fatherland. This nationalistic faith, as it ought properly to be called, had been building since the early days of the Revolution

[2] For the fuller texts of these two "credos," see *ibid.*, pp. 106-111, 273-74.

when citizens participated in quasi-religious ceremonies on July 14, the new national holiday celebrating the fall of the Bastille. Without much doubt it was strongly mixed with deism in the thinking which inspired the cult of Brumaire. For had not Marie Joseph Chénier, author of the hymn for the day, got up in the Convention only a few days before and advocated just such a "religion"?

Wrench the sons of the Republic from the yoke of theocracy which still weighs upon them. . . . Freed from prejudices and worthy of representing the French nation, you will know how to found, on the débris of the dethroned superstitions, the one universal religion, which has neither sects nor mysteries, whose only dogma is equality, whose orators are the laws, whose magistrates are the pontiffs, and in which the great family burns incense only before the altar of *la Patrie*, common mother and divinity.[3]

But the purest example of the nationalistic type of cult was the *culte décadaire* which was established, as previously noted, by the Directory as part of a deliberate program of secularization. This was an exclusively civic cult without any suggestion whatsoever of deism, dedicated to the *Patrie*, and inculcating instruction in those virtues and arts, agricultural and mechanical, which were deemed useful to the Republic.

Most of the cults register the stirrings of still a third faith, more comprehensive than nationalism, more important, at least for the future, than deism. This was the "Religion of Humanity," a neologism invented not long before by Tom Paine, signifying a universalist faith in man, and in man's ability to create, with or without God's assistance, a new "Kingdom of Man" on earth characterized by happiness, social justice, and peace. There were elements of this faith in Robespierre's decree which, after affirming France's be-

[3] *Ibid.*, p. 35.

lief in the Supreme Being, went on to announce a long list of festivals to be celebrated on the *décadis* throughout the year. Significantly, there were to be festivals, not only to "the Supreme Being and Nature," "the French people," and "Love of country," but also to "the Human race," "the Benefactors of humanity," "Posterity," and "Happiness," all appropriately capitalized. This universalist faith also shines through the catechism or *Manual* of the Theophilan-thropists, who might better have called themselves Philan-thropists, and Condorcet's apocalyptic sketch of the *Progress of the Human Mind,* which was also composed during the Revolution. On the surface, Theophilanthropy appears to be just another deistic-nationalistic mishmash. In sub-stance, however, it was as much a cult to man as to the Su-preme Being and the Fatherland. It prescribed belief in the existence of God and the immortality of the soul, primarily because this "double belief" was "necessary to the conserva-tion of societies and the happiness of individuals." "For," continued the *Manual,* "an aggregation of men who do not recognize God and who believe that their crimes are forever buried in the tomb, will soon become a band of ferocious beasts." In other words, its emphasis was on social utility rather than religion. It further prescribed two duties above all others, namely duties toward one's fellow men and the *Patrie,* in that order; and it defined "the good" as "that which tends to conserve man or to perfect (*perfectionner*) him." Running all through the book is, indeed, a paean of praise to man and man's power. In the morning prayer recommended for private worship, for instance, the em-phasis soon shifts from praise of God to praise of man. "I do not ask of thee, O Father of Nature, the power to do good. For thou hast given me this power, and along with it, a conscience in order to love the good, reason to know it, and freedom to choose it." [4] There is much praise, too, of human work which, like the labors of the ant, can lay up stores for the winter, and even more, achieve the abundant society and "all the pleasures."

Thus, there were shades of difference among the cults, and yet there was a basic similarity too. Patently, they all stood in common opposition to the Christianity of the priests. Even Robespierre, more the follower of Rousseau than Voltaire, looked upon "the infamous thing" with almost as little favor as "atheism." "Fanatics," he said, addressing himself to the priests in his famous harangue on the Supreme Being, "do not hope for anything from us; ambitious priests, do not expect that we shall work to establish your empire. Let us leave the priests and return to divinity." [5] In this anti-Christianity, the cults merely reflected what was in the air from 1792 on. As is well known, the Convention jettisoned the Christian calendar, implying thereby that the advent of the French Republic, and not the advent of Christ, marked the real turning point of history. The Christian Sunday gave way to the republican *décadi;* holidays were named, not for Christian saints as of yore, but for natural objects, chiefly vegetables which symbolized "Nature" and the agricultural wealth of the nation. Citizens began to give up their Christian names, and there were burnings of saints' relics and ecclesiastical documents. We might say, then, that the cults, and the events surrounding them, consummated and institutionalized the sceptical movement of the eighteenth century—what we have desig-

[4] *Manuel des Théophilantropes ou Adorateurs de Dieu et Amis des Hommes,* Auxerre, L'An VI, pp. 22-3, 26-9, 10-11. See also Albert Mathiez, *La Théophilanthropie et le Culte Décadaire* (Paris, 1904), pp. 91-101.

[5] Quoted in Aulard, *Le Culte de la Raison et le Culte de l'Être Suprême,* p. 272.

nated the second phase of the sceptical tradition, which was not so much antireligious as anti-Christian.

The cults, it is true, collapsed with Napoleon's Concordat with the Pope which restored Roman Catholicism as the state religion of France. Doubtless, it is also true that the mass of French people never warmed up to them, that even in their heyday they were "aristocratic," as Robespierre dubbed the cult of Reason, or bourgeois in the allegiance they commanded. Yet they left their mark all the same, even among the masses whom they helped to dechristianize, and even in the face of the religious reaction which followed. This is the conclusion of M. Mathiez, an anticlerical, to be sure, but one of their most eminent historians. "Doubtless," he wrote in 1904, "all the symbolism of the revolutionary cults is well past, but not the spirit which animated them." [6] This also is the conclusion of Crane Brinton who has rightly observed that the Revolution undermined the nexus of loyalties, including the religious loyalties, of the old régime.

[By 1799] Frenchmen had ceased to feel the authority—and a true authority must be *felt*, that is, emotionally incorporated as a projection of the individual's personality—of the God of St. Paul, St. Louis, and even Louis XIV. We have all of us today been so much affected by this abandonment of the Christian God, we are all of us such good children of the eighteenth century, that only by a difficult leap of the imagination can we live again even for a moment in the old world of ideas. . . . Remnants of such ideas still exist among us, but recognizably as remnants, not as parts of a completely unified system. [7]

[6] Mathiez, *La Théophilanthropie et le Culte Décadaire*, p. 609.
[7] Crane Brinton, *A Decade of Revolution, 1789-1799* (New York: Harper and Brothers, 1934), p. 281.

2.

Unquestionably, much of the anti-Christian animus observable in revolutionary France can be attributed to the chain of political events from 1789 to 1794. Relations between the clergy, especially the parish priests, and the other two estates were, on the whole, quite cordial during the first months of the Revolution. By joining with the Third Estate, the clergy indeed made possible the conversion of the old Estates-General into the new National Assembly, and the Assembly was grateful. However, this honeymoon came to an abrupt end when, on the one hand, the Pope denounced the Revolution and, on the other, the Assembly, badly in need of money, nationalized church property and upset the church "constitution." The Civil Constitution of the Clergy, enacted into law on July 12, 1790, made the breach irreparable. For Pope Pius VI probably had no alternative but to condemn as "heretical and schismatical" a law which made the French clergy popularly elected officials and salaried employees of the state. Henceforth, the Roman church, and by implication Christianity itself, became identified in people's minds with opposition to the Revolution, and the rift between Church and Revolution widened when the nation had to fight for its life against internal and external enemies believed to be inspired by the Pope. There is some truth, then, in the contention that the cult of Reason was an "arm of war," adopted by ardent Revolutionaries as an instrument of national defence.

Nevertheless, the Revolutionary experiment in dechristianization is unthinkable except against the backdrop of the eighteenth-century intellectual movement known as the Enlightenment, or the Age of Reason. It is perfectly true, of course, that the "philosophers" of the Enlightenment (the *philosophes*) did not advocate the immediate over-throw of the ecclesiastical establishment; they were far too wary of the unenlightened herd, far too cognizant of the social utility of even an "infamous" religion, to want root-and-branch disestablishment. All they appear to have wanted, at least for the present, was toleration of other religions and a purified national church whose priests would teach good morals instead of bad dogma. Yet by their open scepticism and ridicule of Christian mysteries they provided the mental climate in which dechristianization could grow, and they primed the cultists with arguments, as their frequent references to Voltaire, Rousseau, the Abbé Reynal, and other *philosophes* clearly show.

At any rate, it is clear that the Revolution was preceded by a century of talk about "crushing the infamous thing." "In those years," says Carl Becker, "God was on trial. The affair was nothing less than the intellectual *cause célèbre* of the age." [8] The jurors from whom the philosophers demanded a verdict of "guilty" included not only members of their own lodge, the intelligentsia, but the educated classes in general. One of the significant things about the new "philosophy" in France was that it emerged from the closets and libraries, the schools and colleges, to make noise in clubs and assemblies, in salons and coffee houses. Generally speaking, it did not descend to the marketplace, for it was fearful of rousing the passions of the uneducated rabble and thus disturbing the social order. But it went out of its way to convince the educated classes, and with considerable success.

Of course, by no means all the jurors, perhaps not even a majority, returned a verdict of "guilty." Christianity did not lack defenders, some of whom, like the Abbé Bergier

[8] Carl Becker, *The Heavenly City of the Eighteenth-Century Philosophers* (New Haven: Yale University Press, 1932), pp. 73-4.

in France and Bishops Berkeley and Butler in England, could match wits with the best of the sceptics. For lack of evidence to the contrary, it must be assumed that most bourgeois families continued to accept the old beliefs and to worship in the accustomed manner. Yet there must also have been many bourgeois like the lawyer Thibaudeau who went to church but who admired the philosophers and was actually a deist (Thibaudeau's son, who reports his father's religious views in his *Memoirs,* himself left the Church and later sat in the Revolutionary Convention); or like Mme. Roland who as a young woman ran the whole gamut of religious experience from Catholicism to stoicism to deism. In the atmosphere of the Enlightenment even pious people must have been assaulted at times by genuine doubt of the traditional religion. "In modern times," the historian Edward Gibbon observed, "latent and even involuntary scepticism adheres to the most pious dispositions." Probably M. Aulard was not far from the mark when he observed that on the eve of the Revolution there was in France "a small minority of unbelievers and a large minority of indifferent people." [9] Thus, while scepticism cannot be said to have been predominant in 1789, it had made serious inroads, thanks to the Enlightenment, among the socially and politically effective classes not only in France, although it was certainly more in evidence there, but also in England, Germany, and Italy.

The case for the prosecution often seems superficial and even invincibly ignorant. Lord Morley, himself a sceptic, said of Voltaire that he seldom saw the "ground ideas" against which he was fighting; "he never knew the deeper things of Catholicism." Yet for all that, the indictment was a powerful one, and deadly effective. Frequently couched

[9] A. Aulard, *Christianity and the French Revolution,* trans. Lady Frazer (Boston: Little, Brown, 1927), p. 37.

in the most insulting language, it relied as much upon mockery and abuse as upon cool logic. The prosecutors cordially hated "the infamous thing." It was charged with being unnatural, unreasonable, and absurd, as well as infamous, immoral, and fraudulent. When the prosecution rested its case it left no doubts in the minds of at least some of the jurors that the world would be a better place without dogmatic Christianity, and indeed revealed religion in general.

The indictment—prepared by the French *philosophes,* but with the assistance of English deists, German professors, and Italian anticlericals—rested on three principal arguments. The first was a pragmatic argument: by their fruits ye shall know them, and the fruits were mostly rotten. Christianity, it was said, had failed as a social institution. A reservation was sometimes made in Christ's favor, but there could be little doubt about the institution which called itself by his name. What was being said about its fruits can be learned quickly enough from sampling Voltaire's *Philosophical Dictionary,* which was published in a convenient pocket-size edition, and his treatise *On Toleration.* The *Dictionary* commenced with a castigation of sleek abbés who lived off the fat of the land, and ended with a slap at the theological virtues. In between were articles on intolerance, liberty of the press, religious prejudices, and superstition. According to Voltaire, the Christian church not only lived like a parasite off society, but actively promoted social discord by fanning the flames of religious hatred and persecuting heretics, many of whom were peace-loving and productive citizens. *On Toleration* defended one such heretic, the Huguenot merchant Jean Calas, who was tortured and broken on the wheel after being falsely charged by religious fanatics with strangling his son to prevent him from turning Catholic. As Voltaire wrote to a friend shortly thereafter, France was now more than ever "the country of the Saint Bartholomew massacre," and he, for one, resolved "to seek vengeance." The Church, he said, was also the foe of intellectual progress. Delving back into history, Voltaire discovered that this had always been so. From Charlemagne to Louis XIV, Christianity (in the *Essay on Customs* he included Protestantism in his indictment) seemed to him to be the great foe of western civilization, promoting superstition instead of reason, war instead of peace. What he was challenging was nothing less than the historic assumption that morality, as well as learning, depended upon Christianity. Not himself an atheist, he yet preferred a society of atheists to a society of religious fanatics. "I do, it is true, expect more justice from one who believes in a God than from one who has no such belief; but from the superstitious I look for only bitterness and persecution." [10]

The second argument of the indictment questioned Christian credentials. Did God himself found Christianity, as the Bible and church tradition maintained? Is the Bible the Word of God and are the miracles reported by it authentic? If so, then the pragmatic argument meant no more than that men had corrupted what God had made good, and what had once been good could presumably be made good again by purification and reform. The prosecution, however, maintained a naturalistic theory of the origin of positive religions. The crudest version of this theory was the imposture theory which, as we shall see, had descended without much modification from the Middle Ages. "All religion was born of the desire to dominate," declared the embittered *curé* Jean Meslier, an extract of whose *Testament* Voltaire caused to be published after Meslier's death. Battening on men's ignorance and fears, impostors (priests and tyrants) invented religion "to lull to sleep the people

[10] Voltaire, *Dictionnaire Philosophique*, article "Athée."

in fetters"—clearly, Karl Marx was not the first to hold that religion is the opiate of the people. Voltaire's own theory was somewhat more subtle. He assumed that religious people were sincere, at least some of the time. Therefore the religions of the world were the product, not so much of "mental lying," which was what Tom Paine charged in *The Age of Reason,* as of mental sickness. Christianity, Judaism, and Mohammedanism originated not only in imposture but also, and more deeply, in "superstition" which gave rise to "enthusiasm" and "fanaticism." It is to this "rage of the soul," and not primarily to hypocrisy, that society owes the massacre of 9,718,800 innocents in Christian history.

Having disposed of the question of origins, the prosecution next proceeded to debunk the Bible upon which much of the authority of Christianity, both Catholic and Protestant, presumably depended. To understand the biblical criticism of the Enlightenment it is necessary to have in mind the extreme bibliolatry which had grown up chiefly since the Reformation. This bibliolatry is nowhere more forcefully stated than in John Calvin's *Institutes of the Christian Religion.* In the Bible, according to Calvin, God had opened his sacred mouth and spoken truths which were beyond the power of human conception. It therefore excelled, indeed it differed qualitatively from all other writings. It exceeded all other books in antiquity. It recorded marvelous prophecies and miracles. Properly understood, it agreed beautifully in all its parts. As one of Calvin's English Puritan followers put it, the Bible was "the rule and canon of all truth," comprehending not only theology but wisdom on all subjects whatsoever. It was even appealed to sometimes as a textbook of natural science.

For Voltaire, however, and for many of his contemporaries, the sheen had completely worn off the Bible. It was a book like any other book, or rather worse than most books. If God wrote the Bible, then clearly he did not know much chronology or geography or physics. He also apparently approved deeds which violate the moral code of every nation on earth: witness the crimes of David whom, said Voltaire, the Bible counts as "a man after God's own heart." Were the prophecies of the Old Testament fulfilled in the New? As a matter of fact, as even an indifferent scholar could see, the prophecy from Isaiah, for example, referred, not to the virgin birth of Jesus, but to a young woman in the days of Ahaz, king of Judah. Were there indeed no contradictions in the Bible? Come now, what about the many discrepancies between the Gospel accounts? The Bible also contained errors of historical fact, as witness Luke's story, which antiquarians deny, of a census of the whole earth when Mary was with child. "For if there is a single lie in a sacred book, can that book be sacred?" [11]

In such manner, step by step, the prosecution sought to destroy all the credentials of Christianity. The *coup de grâce* was administered by exposure of the biblical miracles, especially the great miracle of the Resurrection, to critical examination. As the historian William Lecky has noted, there had been a tendency ever since the time of the Protestant Reformation to push authentic miracles farther and farther back in time. The Protestants had denounced as fraudulent all miracles perpetrated by the Roman Catholic church of the Middle Ages. In 1748 Conyers Middleton, librarian of Cambridge University, questioned the miracles of the preceding age of the great Church Fathers. Finally, the Enlightenment attacked the apostolic miracles themselves, that final bastion upon which Christian apologists felt confident that they could always fall back, if worse came to worst.

[11] This paragraph is a paraphrase of the arguments put forward in Voltaire's satirical *Questions of Zapata* (1767).

After the prosecution had done its utmost, only one miracle remained standing, and this was not the special miracle of the Resurrection, which the English deist Thomas Woolston labeled a "sham" and an "imposture," but the universal miracle of natural law.

The argument, as it was developed by Woolston, Peter Annet, Voltaire, David Hume, Samuel Reimarus, Tom Paine in *The Age of Reason*, and many others, was partly empirical, partly rationalistic. "A wise man proportions his belief to the evidence," said the Scottish philosopher David Hume, and the evidence for the biblical miracles was not such as a rational man could accept. "A miracle is a violation of the laws of nature": even Hume (at least in his essay *Of Miracles*) assumed a rule of law, a uniformity of nature, in which, *a priori*, miracles simply could not occur. The presumption therefore was that miracles were either the perpetrations of crafty priests or the products of overenthusiastic brains. Evidently, the day had passed when men could be persuaded of the divine inspiration and the miracles of the Bible upon an authority higher than human reason, "even from the secret testimony of the Holy Spirit," as Calvin expressed it, or from Church tradition, as a Catholic would argue. And the day had not yet come when such phenomena could be accounted for in terms of history or psychology, at least not on any profound basis. In the essentially rationalistic criticism of the Enlightenment, the Bible was either divinely inspired or it was not. If it was not, as reason or common sense seemed to show, then it must be a fraud or a superstition. Lacking historical perspective, the philosophers did not go behind the letter to reconstruct the mental climate in which the Bible was written. How, therefore, could they possibly be sympathetic to it?

Ultimately, Lord Morley notwithstanding, the prosecution did get down to the "ground ideas" of Christianity. To anyone who takes the trouble to follow the trial to its end, it becomes increasingly evident that Voltaire and his contemporaries were attacking, not merely the social and moral record of organized Christianity, nor merely its credentials, but the very system of the universe upon which it was based. This system was, frankly, incredible in the light of modern science and modern experience. The God of Moses and Christ, theological explanations of the workings of nature, special revelations to chosen people, the Christian idea of the nature and destiny of man, even the Christian virtues—all of these ideas came under severe attack in the course of the trial. Obviously this third argument was the most serious and the most telling of all the arguments for the prosecution, and it is necessary therefore to dwell upon it at somewhat more length than the first two arguments.

3.

At this point, however, it is well to take note that Enlightenment scepticism had a constructive as well as a destructive side. The trial of Christianity focuses attention on the destructive side, and later critics have mistakenly inferred from this, as from the parallel attacks on economic, political, and social aspects of the old régime, that the Enlightenment was all negation. "To tear away, was, indeed, all that the philosophers, for the most part, aimed at," John Stuart Mill wrote in his essay on Samuel Taylor Coleridge; "they had no conception that any thing else was needful." This is a serious misconception. If the Enlightenment was, on the whole, anti-Christian, it was emphatically not, on the whole, antireligious, although in the final upshot we may indeed find that it was relatively unreligious. Most of the philosophers were deists (or theists), which is to say that having convicted the old religion, they tried to build a new religion to take its place.

Of course, they denied, and indeed they did not imagine, that they were creating anything new. Like the Protestants of the sixteenth century they claimed to be restoring the good old religion from which the traditional religions of the world had derived or degenerated. This religion was "as old as the creation." As the English lawyer and deist Matthew Tindal wrote in 1730, "there is a religion of nature and reason written in the hearts of everyone of us from the first creation; by which all mankind must judge of the truth of any instituted religion whatever." [12] The way to resurrect this *Ur*-religion was obviously not to consult the Scriptures of a particular religion but rather the "original" document inscribed in everyman's heart; or alternatively to dig out the pure metal which mixed itself in all the religions of the world. Voltaire thought that this mine was more openly worked in China than in Christendom, and Tindal found specimens of the pure metal in the maxims of Confucius as well as the Sermon on the Mount.

Actually, of course, deism was a new religion, or at least it differed in important respects from the traditional religion. It represented an honest attempt to bring religion up to date, to make it square with the latest science, and to put an end to the wars and mutual intolerance of the religious sects. It was, by definition, a religion of "nature" as opposed to supernature or revelation—for most deists, a supernature which impinged upon and sometimes suspended the invariable order of nature was simply a contradiction in terms. It was a religion of "reason" as opposed to faith. Voltaire said of faith, in the *Philosophical Dictionary*, that it "consists in believing things because they are impossible." "What is faith? Is it to believe what appears to be evident? No: it is evident to me that there is a Being necessary, eternal, su-

---

[12] Matthew Tindal, *Christianity as Old as the Creation* (London, 1730), pp. 50-51.

preme, intelligent; that is not of faith, that is of reason."
Clearly, in deist thought, reason and faith did not teach the
same things, as they had done in St. Thomas Aquinas; on
the contrary, they contradicted each other. Deism was also a
universal, indeed the only truly catholic religion as opposed
to the religion of the sects which depended upon special
revelations to chosen peoples and which by that token contradicted each other and made religious warfare inevitable.
Finally, it was a simple religion based upon a very few fun-
damentals, as opposed to the complexity of the dogmatic
religions.

The best way to appreciate the differences between this
Enlightenment deism—we are speaking here of rationalistic
and not emotional deism—and Christianity is to compare
their respective credos at vital points. Says Tom Paine in
that catchall of eighteenth-century deistic beliefs, *The Age
of Reason:* "I do not believe in the creed professed by the
Jewish church, by the Roman church, by the Greek church,
by the Turkish church, by the Protestant church, nor by any
church that I know of. My own mind is my own church." [13]
Like the Christians, Paine and the deists believed in "one
God," but he was emphatically not the God of the Nicene
Creed. Actually, they often preferred the term "Supreme
Being" or "Eternal Cause" to "God" because the latter term
connoted the deity of Moses and the special revelations.
The existence of the Supreme Being seemed to them incon-
trovertible, not because the Bible or the Church told them
so, but on wholly rational grounds. The arguments were
the familiar cosmological and teleological arguments, i.e.,
deductions from the observed effect and order of nature to
a first cause and designer. Cleanthes, the deist in David
Hume's *Dialogues concerning Natural Religion,* voiced as
clearly as any the famous argument from design. "Con-

[13] Thomas Paine, *The Age of Reason,* Part I, chap. 1.

sider," he said, "anatomize the eye, survey its structure and contrivance, and tell me, from your own feeling, if the idea of a contriver does not immediately flow in upon you with a force like that of sensation. The most obvious conclusion, surely, is in favour of design; and it requires time, reflection, and study, to summon up those frivolous though abstruse objections which can support infidelity." [14] Atheism was an absurdity, a pejorative word in the deist's vocabulary, given his assumptions about nature and the validity of *a posteriori* deduction. The great machine of the world so obviously argued an intelligent designer.

So far most Christians would have agreed with the deists except that to the rational or natural proofs they would have added supernatural proofs, and possibly also an ontological argument. It is at the point of the deity's attributes rather than his existence that the divergence between the credos begins to be clear-cut. Here the deist usually took an agnostic position. "The theist [deist]," said Voltaire, "is a man firmly persuaded of the existence of a Supreme Being"—but—"the theist *does not know* how God punishes, how he rewards, how he pardons; for he is not presumptuous enough to flatter himself that he understands how God acts." [15] Voltaire himself rang changes on this theme throughout his works, notably in *The Ignorant Philosopher*. Man, he said, is "ignorant" of everything that transcends the observed order of nature. He can infer from this order that God is, but not what He is. Underlying such statements we can sense an extreme antimetaphysical bias. To most deists, and to a theist like Voltaire, metaphysics and theology represented vain speculation, an unwarranted departure from the rule of clear and distinct ideas laid down by Descartes. "All the metaphysicians, all the theologians

[14] David Hume, *Dialogues concerning Natural Religion* (1779), Part III.
[15] Voltaire, *Dictionnaire Philosophique*, article "Théiste" (italics mine).

of antiquity, were necessarily charlatans who could not agree. The very word indicates this: *metaphysics*, above nature; *theology*, knowledge of God. How can we know what is not natural? How can man know what God has thought and what he is?" [16]

With delightful inconsistency the deists did often let slip affirmations of the righteousness and justice, the goodness and power of God. Here too, however, it was with a difference. The Supreme Being of their mind's eye was not so personal nor so powerful as the Christian "God the Father Almighty." He might distribute rewards and punishments in an after life, but in this life He had better things to do than to concern Himself with individuals, with the fate, for instance, of Sister Fessue's sparrow or cat. Petitionary prayers could not be offered to Him, at least with any hope of success. He provided for the universe in only a general, not a particular way. Uniform natural laws limited Him in what He could do. The metaphysic of nature which the deists assumed (for despite their antimetaphysical bias they clearly had a metaphysic) made it difficult if not impossible for them to conceive of an intimate relationship between man and God, such a relationship, for example, as the old father-child metaphor implied. All that man could now be sure of was a "general Providence" which sustained the universe.

The most radical feature of the deist credo, however, was its anthropology. The keystone of Christian anthropology was original sin, and no doctrine was more anathema to the deists, and indeed to the Enlightenment as a whole. It was an obsession with Voltaire. He excoriated it again and again, in his diatribes against the "sublime misanthrope" Blaise Pascal, in many articles of the *Philosophical Diction-*

---

[16] Voltaire, *Dieu et Les Hommes*, quoted in Norman Torrey, *The Spirit of Voltaire* (New York: Columbia University Press, 1938), p. 276.

ary, in fact whenever and wherever he had the opportunity. "We are told that human nature is essentially perverse, that man is born diabolical and wicked. Nothing could be farther from the truth." "Man is not born wicked; he becomes wicked as he becomes sick." Even so Voltaire calculated that not one man in a thousand could really be called wicked, and even that one was not wholly so. Monstrous to suppose that most women and children were wicked; entire nations of the world, the Chinese, the peoples of Siam and Japan, had not known war for over a hundred years. Voltaire blamed the priests in general, and St. Augustine in particular, for spreading this "heresy." Rather than to apprise each individual of his wickedness we ought to say to him: "You are born good; see how frightful it would be to corrupt the purity of your being. . . . Remember the dignity of man." [17] The revolutionary thing about this emphasis on the dignity rather than the wretchedness of man was that it rendered the Christian doctrine of the Atonement superfluous. Man no longer needed the atoning work of Jesus Christ to be saved. Salvation was by works, not by faith; the deist was an arch-Pelagian. As Voltaire contemptuously remarked, "the mystery of original sin is the object of faith, not of reason."

The deist also reinterpreted the last article of the Christian credo. He too believed in "one catholic church," but his catholic church was not identical with the church of the Christian apostles, nor indeed with any of the sects. He broadened the conception of the Church to include the wise men of all countries from Peking to Paris. His God was, in the words of the poet laureate of the movement (who, incidentally, managed to be a Roman Catholic as well as a deist)

[17] Voltaire, *Dictionnaire Philosophique*, article "Méchant"; see also "Péché Originel."

> Father of all! in ev'ry age,
> In ev'ry clime ador'd,
> By saint, by savage, and by sage,
> Jehovah, Jove, or Lord! [18]

In the final analysis a doubt remains as to just how genuinely religious the deists of the eighteenth century really were. On the one hand, as the above argument shows, they did get down at last to the "ground ideas" of religion; in fact, they could not leave them alone but were perpetually wrestling with them and debating with one another about them. On the other hand, there is, after all, something to Lord Morley's contention that they "never knew the deeper things of Catholicism." The deists had no deep understanding of the traditional concepts of sin and grace, nor any interest really in the salvational problem. This lack of understanding explains why they could not comprehend the genesis of the great positive religions of the world except on a hypothesis of imposture or ignorance. Whether this alone gives us the right to label them unreligious is a moot point, but when we also detect in them a serious attenuation of the metaphysical sense, with which all genuine religion would seem to be bound up, we have some cause to be suspicious. Madame de Staël was not far from the mark when she observed, some years later, that the philosophy which attributed all ideas to sensations and whose first principle was "not to believe anything which cannot be proved like a fact or a calculation" cut the ground out from under genuine religion.[19] She referred, of course, to the Lockean philosophy (or to an exaggerated version of the Lockean philosophy) to which all the deists were more or less addicted and whose famous metaphor of the sailor's line epitomized their antimetaphysical bias and

---

[18] Alexander Pope, *Universal Prayer*.
[19] Madame de Staël, *De l'Allemagne* (1813), Part III.

hence their lack of religious sensibility. The sailor, John Locke had said, needs to know the length of his line, but he cannot expect to fathom with it "all the depths of the ocean." Analogously, let men cease to extend their inquiries beyond their capacities, to loose their thoughts "into the vast ocean of Being." This same Locke, in the fourth book of this same *Essay concerning Human Understanding,* expressed a deep suspicion of religious "enthusiasm" in general. Doubtless he had good reason to do so in view of the extravagant claims to special religious insights made by so many sectarian enthusiasts of the seventeenth century. But the eighteenth-century attack on enthusiasm (see, for instance, Voltaire's article on "enthusiasm" in the *Philosophical Dictionary*) was so extreme as to be tantamount to a repudiation of all prophetic insight and fresh religious experience. "Reason must be our last judge and guide in everything," the great Locke had said, and his disciples of the Enlightenment, following suit, distrusted all religious knowledge which was not based upon reason—meaning by reason, not the intuitive or Platonic reason, but the discursive reason.

Actually, the deists came close to reducing religion to ethics. "To do good—that is his worship." In so characterizing the theist, Voltaire might almost have been paraphrasing Locke's statement that "our business here is not to know all things, but those which concern our conduct." This was to supply a new pragmatic test, almost a new definition of religion. Religion is what it does.[20] Its truth ultimately devolves, not upon theoretical criteria, but upon its moral effects, i.e., the individual's private character and his efforts to be useful in promoting the public good. The tendency

[20] See Ernst Cassirer's illuminating remarks on this point in his *Philosophy of the Eighteenth Century* (Princeton: Princeton University Press, 1951), chap. 4.

of the rationalistic movement in religion from the seventeenth century on was to make religion (the first commandment) supplemental to ethics (the second commandment). The deists and so-called supernatural rationalists were agreed that virtue was the principal part of worship. The only question between them was whether, to be virtuous, men needed the light of revelation as well as natural reason. Locke thought that they did, that the candle of reason burned too dimly to give them the illumination they needed to perform their moral duties; he still had some sense, albeit a decayed sense, of the effects of original sin. For Voltaire, on the other hand, reason was sufficient to make man "do good."

From the available evidence we might hazard the conclusion that the deists were unreligious, not by temperament, but because their intellectual convictions would not permit them to be religious. One suspects that in another climate some of them, Voltaire, for instance, and even Denis Diderot, would have been noted for their piety. Voltaire had the makings of a mystic. In a letter of 1736 to his confidante, Mme. du Châtelet, he wrote, for instance, of he charm of philosophy which lifts the sagacious mind above envy. "Tranquil, high in the heavens which have surrendered to Newton, it knows no longer whether it has any enemies. . . . Yes, in God's bosom, far from this mortal body, the spirit seems to listen to the voice of the Eternal." [21] But the point is that Voltaire did not often let himself go in this fashion, and he never mistook such visions for cognitive truth, for as a good Lockean he was convinced of the severe limits of human knowledge. Diderot too pulled himself up short when his religious sensibilities threatened, as they sometimes did, to overwhelm his intel-

[21] Quoted in Torrey, *The Spirit of Voltaire*, pp. 254-55. Torrey is the chief proponent of this idea of Voltaire's incipient mysticism.

lect. He never watched religious processions, he wrote in 1765, "without being moved and shaken deep down inside me, without tears coming to my eyes. There is in all that something great, sombre, solemn, melancholy." But then he added hastily, "My friend, if we love truth better than beauty, let us pray to God for the iconoclasts." [22]

4.

In the final analysis, deism failed historically as a substitute for traditional Christianity. It did not survive as one of the great religions of the western world. It failed to capture the imagination of the masses, despite the herculean propagandist efforts of some of the Revolutionary cultists and of popularizers like Tom Paine. Even more significant, it failed even to hold the intellectuals. Thus, its permanent achievement was primarily to leave a legacy of doubt about religion as it had been traditionally conceived.

Like the Roman Empire, deism declined and fell principally for internal reasons. It was too abstract to engage men's hearts, too prosaic to arouse for long their sense of wonder. True to the analytical spirit of rationalism, it thought to dispense with the religious symbols upon which most mortals depend for mediating their relationship with the Beyond. It also suffered from excessive vagueness, with the consequence that no two deists thought alike nor could they easily gather together in a church for common worship. But most important of all, deism was hoist by its own petard. As events proved, rational and empirical arguments could be turned with deadly effect against deism itself as well as traditional Christianity. Thus, Voltaire discovered reasons for doubting some of the fundamental premises of

[22] Denis Diderot, *Salon of 1765,* quoted in Lester G. Crocker, *The Embattled Philosopher* (Lansing: Michigan State College, 1954), p. 62.

deistic belief. Diderot espoused deism only to abandon it for a materialistic interpretation of nature. David Hume ruthlessly subjected deistic theology to empirical tests and found it wanting. By the second half of the eighteenth century many erstwhile deists, and others too, had moved on to an extreme sceptical or even atheistic position. The lady philosopher whom Horace Walpole reported as saying of Voltaire, "Il est bigot, c'est un déiste," appears to have been one of a growing number.

By 1765, when Walpole reported this tidbit to the poet Gray, Voltaire himself had already begun to have his doubts about deism—at least the optimistic deism of Leibnitz and Alexander Pope. He had already written his troubled *Poem on the Lisbon Disaster* which, although it literally ended on the word "hope" (*espérance*), attacked the idea of divine providence. How, in the face of the great Lisbon earthquake in which thousands of innocents perished, could one hold that "whatever is, is right"? Voltaire could no longer accept complacently even the general providence of the deists. Deism, he seemed to be saying, offered no better explanation of the problem of evil than orthodox Christianity: "earth's the seat of woes: we strive in vain its secret source to find." It might even be, he suggested in passing, that the material universe had defects which permanently thwarted God's will. Who knew? Voltaire was obviously in a quandary.

The sceptic from Scotland needed no earthquake to shake him loose from deism's fallacies. He simply sat back and watched the empirical argument spin out to its logical conclusion in religious problems. When he had done, he had proved to his own satisfaction at least, not only that there was no empirical evidence for miracles, but also that we have no experience of how our cosmos was produced nor any empirical validations of a future life. Doubting that

causes could be known from their effects, or even that the
effects (the design of nature, for example) were necessarily
what the deists said they were, Hume inexorably cut down,
as the German philosopher Immanuel Kant did after him,
the favorite cosmological and teleological arguments of the
deists. "Our ideas," says Philo-Hume in the *Dialogues concerning Natural Religion*, "reach no farther than our experience. We have no experience of divine attributes and
operations." Moreover, is the universe really such a perfect
machine as most deists suppose? Such experience as we do
have reveals excesses and defects which not infrequently
involve individuals in ruin and misery, and which would
seem to infer therefore a good deal of "inaccurate work-
manship" on the part of the maker. Thus, in the *Dialogues*
the "careless sceptic" Philo undermines Cleanthes' deism as
well as Demea's orthodoxy. To the big religious questions
Philo gives the agnostic answer: "I do not know." "All
religious systems," he concludes, "are subject to great and
insuperable difficulties. . . . But all of them, on the whole,
prepare a complete triumph for the *sceptic*. . . . A total
suspense of judgment is here our only reasonable re-
source." [23]

The French materialists, those remarkable men who
dined and debated far into the night at the table of the
notorious Baron d'Holbach in Paris, swung much farther
to the religious left than even Voltaire or Hume, and it is
interesting to see why they did so. Denis Diderot, who had
the most troubled and original mind of the Holbachian
circle, wrestled with religious and ethical problems all his
life. Originally intended for the priesthood, he rejected
Christianity for the usual eighteenth-century reasons; because it was fanatical and obscurantist and because it was
based upon imposture. For a time he appears to have con-

[23] Hume, *Dialogues concerning Natural Religion*, Parts II, VIII, IX.

sidered deism favorably, at least as a buttress to good morals. But by 1749, when he wrote his first major work *The Letter on the Blind,* Diderot had rejected deism in turn. He ended up in D'Holbach's camp, as a convinced scientific naturalist.

What principally turned Diderot against deism was the new current of biological and geological thinking in the 1740's,[24] and thereon hangs a tale of great significance to which we shall want to return in later chapters. The historical vogue of religious and sceptical modes of thought is inextricably tied to the fate of the systems of nature with which they are allied. Traditional Christianity, for instance, began to lose face as the old Aristotelian-Ptolemaic cosmos became outmoded. And now deism too became less attractive as the Newtonian picture of nature was challenged. Newtonianism postulated a static machine-universe of primarily mathematical properties, which required a Supreme Being to create and sustain it. But suppose that nature was more like an organism than a machine, composed essentially of living rather than dead matter, creatively active, capable therefore of constantly producing new forms, and self-sustaining. A polyp when cut into pieces could generate new polyps, it was reported; muscles when severed from the body continued to show irritability; life itself could apparently be generated spontaneously from water in a sealed flask. These were some of the thoughts that were running through Diderot's head between 1749 and 1770. As an avowed empiricist, he ought perhaps to have made quite sure of his facts before he constructed a new system of nature. But the important thing to note is that he and the Baron and La Mettrie and other materialists had begun to

[24] For the biological "discoveries" of Tremblay, Needham, and Haller, and their effect on Diderot's thinking, see Aram Vartanian, *Diderot and Descartes* (Princeton: Princeton University Press, 1953), chap. 4.

see in their mind's eye a possible alternative to Newtonian nature, a vibrant, creative nature which could do all the things that the deist God could do and which therefore made God unnecessary. "O Nature!"—D'Holbach prayed to her as though she were God—"Sovereign of all beings! And you her adorable daughters, virtue, reason, and truth! Be ever our only Divinities!" [25]

Along with this dogmatic atheism went, of course, a scepticism about absolutes of any sort in the universe. The deist, even so halfhearted a deist as Voltaire, believed in God after all and in a permanent order of nature guaranteed by God. But for Diderot everything in nature, including man's ethical ideas, was in a state of flux. Toward the close of his life, to be sure, he postulated, not unlike Rousseau, an intuitive feeling of absolute right and wrong in man. In many of his mature works, however, he argued not only that man's ethical ideas are relative to the structure of his body (thus, the blind man's morality as well as his knowledge is likely to be different from that of the man of normal sight), but also that they are relative to his changing experience and social needs. Thus, he proclaimed a sort of evolutionary and materialistic ethic, completely divorced from religious absolutes or indeed absolutes of any kind.

Jean Jacques Rousseau reacted against the materialism of the Holbachian circle, but it is important to note that he did so in the name of a deism substantially different from the deism of Voltaire—which is proof, if further proof is needed, that eighteenth-century deism was a house divided against itself. Up to a certain point Rousseau, to be sure, argued like any other rationalistic deist. The notorious

[25] Baron d'Holbach, *Système de la Nature* (1770), Part II, chap. 14.

"Profession of Faith of the Savoyard Vicar," [26] for example
—which not only the French Parlement but also the city
councils of Geneva and Berne ordered to be publicly
burned and its author arrested—contained all the familiar
arguments about the bad moral effects of the exclusive
churches, the same objections to ecclesiastical authority, the
same agnosticism about the nature of God, the same demand for credible evidence of prophecies and miracles, the
same emphasis on ethics; and on the constructive side it
advanced the same rational proofs for the existence of God
and made the same plea for a simple religion of nature upon
which all men could agree. Yet the tone of this remarkable
confession was noticeably different from that of the *Philosophical Dictionary* as well as Diderot's *D'Alembert's
Dream* or D'Holbach's *System of Nature*. It was different
in two respects. In the first place, despite its deference to
"reason," it preferred in the final analysis to base religion
on "feeling." "Feeling precedes knowledge," the Vicar says
to his young protégé Émile. "The decrees of conscience are
not judgments but feelings. Although all our ideas come
from without, the feelings by which they are weighed are
within us." "Too often does reason deceive us; we have
only too good a right to doubt her; but conscience never
deceives us; she is the true guide of man; it is to the soul
what instinct is to the body." "I feel God in myself." Thus,
Rousseau's test in religion is ultimately subjective as Voltaire's was objective, his deism at bottom emotional rather
than rationalistic. Toward Christianity in particular, moreover, Rousseau maintained a more reverential attitude than

[26] The "Profession de Foi du Vicaire Savoyard" is embedded in Part IV
of *Émile*, Rousseau's well-known book on education. In my opinion, it
has been mistranslated as "The Creed of a Savoyard Priest," for it was
not really a creed but rather a confession, compounded half of scepticism
and half of Rousseau's religious "feelings."

the deists of the "*écrasez*" school. His doubt, he says, is "reverent doubt," his scepticism "unwilling scepticism." Admittedly, says the Vicar, the Bible "is full of incredible things, things repugnant to reason, things which no natural man can understand or accept." But at the same time it "speaks to my heart," and he prefers Jesus to Socrates. In the end he advises Émile to go back to the religion of his fathers, avoiding the extremes of atheism and fanaticism in the interest of public order and "in our present state of uncertainty." This was the position arrived at nearly two hundred years before by Michel de Montaigne. If to the evidence of the "Profession of Faith" is added that of the *Social Contract*, in which Rousseau argued for a "civil religion," it is easy to see why in religion as in politics he has been claimed by many diverse groups. He is harbinger of the religious revival, the Civil Constitution of the Clergy, and the cult of the Supreme Being all rolled into one.

Thus, by the time of the Revolution there were many varieties of deism; and what is more germane to the present argument, deism, of whatever variety, never quite filled the hearts and minds of the philosophers of the Enlightenment. During the Revolution, as we have seen, it still had its advocates, and attempts were made to give it an institutional form; the cult of Reason, it might be said, tried to institutionalize the rationalistic deism of Voltaire; Robespierre's cult of the Supreme Being, the emotional deism of Jean Jacques. But by that time there were many who professed deism but halfheartedly, and not a few others who had obviously dispensed with it entirely. Thus, the chief religious legacy of the Enlightenment was probably, after all, the *écrasez*, the negative prosecution of the faith of our fathers, and not a positive faith in the great Watchmaker.

5.

Yet the Enlightenment was a great Age of Faith, one of the greatest, and it is essential to the thesis of this book to realize that this was so. But faith in what, if not faith in deism? Clearly, what inspired the philosophers as a group and galvanized them into purposeful action was a belief in man. This belief, which, as we have seen, lay at the heart of the Revolutionary cults, might or might not combine with a belief in some sort of God; in the eighteenth century it usually did, but belief in God was not really essential to it.

This humanistic—and essentially secular—faith had two main strands. In the first place, it signified belief in man's power: his moral capacity to grow in virtue, his rational capacity to read the laws of nature and thus to harness nature to his use; his ability also to engineer society as well as physical nature, and ultimately to reduce all life and all history to a rational plan; in a word, to accomplish in time what had previously been considered to be the work of eternity, to carve out on earth a great kingdom or empire of man, morally better and intellectually superior to anything that had gone before. A mighty faith, this, and differing substantially from the humanism of the Renaissance from which it partly derived. The humanistic enthusiasm of the Renaissance had been tempered by the conviction that fate rules half our actions, or a little more than half, as Machiavelli had said. But the Enlightenment proposed to take fate by the throat and eliminate it from human affairs except for certain unavoidable vicissitudes of personal life and the final intrusion of death. It takes no great perspicacity to see that what was being forged in the eighteenth century by the likes of Diderot and D'Alembert, Helvétius and Condorcet, was the working faith of the "modern" western

world. It was the faith of the engineer, or, as Arthur Koestler would say, the "commissar" who looks upon the universe as a machine whose motions he can learn to predict
and control. To be sure, not all the philosophers adhered to
this faith all the time or in equal degrees. There was not one
of them, unless it was Condorcet, who did not have his bad
moments when he doubted man's freedom of will, and
despaired of enlightening the masses and engineering evil
out of the world. Yet, on balance, a man such as Voltaire
was an optimist about man, though not an optimist of the
Leibnitzian type for which "everything that is, is right";
and Diderot, who had a healthy respect for "fate," both
cosmic and environmental, was, after all, the heart and soul
of the *Encyclopedia of the Arts, Sciences, and Crafts*.

This twenty-eight volume *summa* of rational and empirical knowledge was the age's greatest symbol of the new
humanistic faith in man's power. To begin with, unlike St.
Thomas Aquinas' *Summa Theologica*, it focused, not on
God, but on man. In the "Preliminary Discourse" Diderot's
co-editor, the mathematician D'Alembert, pays lip service
to God who, he says, "must hold the first rank among
spiritual beings by virtue of his nature and by the need
which we have of knowing him. Below this Supreme Being
are the created spirits of which Revelation teaches us the
existence. Next in order comes man. . . ." Having said
this, however, D'Alembert repeatedly complains of the
"despotism of theology," and in his great "map" of human
knowledge he relegates theology and religion to a comparatively minor place, clearly subordinate to the "science of
man" and the "science of nature." [27] This humanistic focus
is also unmistakable in many of the articles. "It is the presence of man that gives interest and meaning to the existence

---

[27] *Encyclopédie, ou Dictionnaire raisonné des Sciences, des Arts, et
des Métiers* (Paris, 1751-65), Vol. I, pp. xvi, xxiii-xxiv.

of living things," said Diderot in his article "Encyclopedia."
"In this work, why not give to man the place that is allotted
to him in the universal scheme of things? Why not make
him the center around which everything revolves?" And in
another article it was stated that the philosopher's chief
business should be the study of human society: "civil society
is, so to speak, a divinity for him on earth; he burns incense
to it, he honors it by attention to his duties and by a sincere
desire not to be a useless or embarrassing member of it."

The engineer's mind pervades the entire work. Reading
between the lines, the reader can sense the transformation
of a society and the emergence of the modern mentality.
There were, of course, many articles on theology, some of
them quite cautious and even orthodox, but the main interest was obviously shifting to political and social reform,
physical science, and the practical arts. Philosophy, that is
to say, was being redefined as knowledge useful to man, as
opposed to the "vain" speculation of theology and metaphysics. Who are the most useful people in the community?
Not the ecclesiastics and idle nobility, surely, nor the
"proud reasoners" and "useless contemplators" who fill our
cities, but those people, including the industrial craftsmen,
who are getting things done, who are hard at work on useful projects designed to make men happy. In the spirit of
Francis Bacon, Diderot tried to break down the ancient distinction between the liberal and mechanical arts, and in so
doing voiced, as D'Alembert also voiced, a new conception
of work. This distinction, he wrote in his article on "Art"

has produced a bad effect by degrading some very estimable
and useful people, and by strengthening in us I do not know
what natural laziness, which has already disposed us only too
much to believe that to give constant applications to experiences and particular objects, sensible and material, was to dero-
gate from the dignity of the human mind. . . . [the result has

been] that we have praised a great deal more the men occupied in making us believe we were happy, than the men occupied in making us so indeed.[28]

True to his teaching, Diderot visited the shops, rubbed shoulders with the craftsmen, and inspected the latest machines which he then proceeded to immortalize in the wonderful plates which adorn the *Encyclopedia*. Clearly, Diderot's real dream, at least while he was at work on his *magnum opus*, was of a human happiness effected in large part by scientific and technological progress.

Diderot's friend and sometime antagonist, the tax collector Claude-Adrien Helvétius, further glimpsed the power available to man through education and the manipulation of the social environment. His doctrine, as he outlined it in his posthumously published treatise *On Man* (1772), stemmed from the Lockean epistemology: man's mind, as Locke had conclusively shown, is like a blank sheet of paper (*tabula rasa*) at birth, without innate ideas, character, or prejudices; the outside environment, through the senses, impresses upon it such ideas as it comes to have; *ergo*, change the environment, educate man differently, subject him to different laws, and he will be a changed man. "Education makes us what we are"; "a different government gives by turns, to the same nation, a character noble or base"; "the almost universal unhappiness of man, and of nations, arises from the imperfections of their laws, and the too unequal partition of their riches." The prospect opened up by such aphorisms was dazzling in the extreme. Some of the philosophers, conspicuously Diderot, boggled at Helvétius' egalitarianism, but they shared his faith in the efficacy, if not necessarily the omnipotence, of education and legislation. Behaviorism, the manipulation of the human mind,

[28] *Encyclopédie*, Vol. I, p. 714. See also on this subject D'Alembert's remarks in the "Preliminary Discourse," *ibid.*, p. xiii.

was as endemic to the budding faith of the engineer as was the idea of power over physical nature.

During the Enlightenment, however, belief in man's power happily combined with belief in man's dignity. This was the second strand of the new humanistic faith. Carried to its logical extreme Helvétius' behaviorism would have reduced man to a machine, an object devoid of moral worth or dignity. But in the thought of the Enlightenment behavioristic logic was counter-balanced by humanitarian considerations. Man's power was not conceived as an end in itself but rather as a means to an end, namely the melioration of the human lot or, as a utilitarian like Helvétius expressed it, "the greatest happiness of the greatest number." We can hardly fail to note in the philosophers, especially the French, an extraordinary sensitivity to human suffering and a veritable passion for social justice. Self-styled rationalists, they were filled with "the holy enthusiasm of humanity" which the Abbé Raynal urged upon the kings of Europe. This again was humanism with a difference, for few Renaissance humanists had had the vision of a general happiness measured in terms of legal security and improved living conditions for all. Nor was it simply a borrowing from Christianity, a secularized version of Christian charity, as has so often been claimed. Eighteenth-century humanitarianism differed from traditional Christianity in its indignation at the existing social order and in its belief that that order could be altered for the better. Two new words, "beneficence" (*bienfaisance*) and "humanity" (*humanité*), both popular among the philosophers and used more or less as synonyms, epitomize the difference. The Abbé de Saint Pierre coined the word "beneficence," he said, to take the place of the old word "charity," so misunderstood by the Christians who persecuted their opponents. "I have been looking out for a word which would clearly remind us that it was our duty to do good to others, and I have found nothing that better conveys what I have in mind than the word beneficence." [29] Beneficence, in contrast to charity, emphasized, not primarily almsgiving, which implied acceptance of the status quo, but a vigorous assault on society's abuses. It was also frequently construed to mean the displacement of piety, or the selfish motive of personal salvation, by unselfish labor for the happiness of the human race in this world. The philosophers had no monopoly on humanitarian reform in the eighteenth century, but they were in the vanguard of the movement and clearly played a larger role in it than the clergy.

The Marquis de Condorcet described "the new philosophy" precisely in terms of this new humanitarian humanism. In the eighteenth century, and not before, he said, there arose a class of men who never ceased to protest with indefatigable energy against "all the crimes of fanaticism and tyranny"; invoking the name of nature "to bid kings, captains, magistrates and priests to show respect for human life; laying to their charge, with vehemence and severity, the blood their policy or their indifference still spilled on the battlefield or on the scaffold; and finally, taking for their battle cry—*reason, tolerance, humanity*." [30]

In the name of humanity Montesquieu and Voltaire, among others, demanded recognition of the "natural rights," or civil liberties of the individual; liberty of the body as well as the mind, protection against an outmoded and inhumane criminal code, equality of taxation, abolition of the last vestiges of serfdom which represented for Vol-

[29] Quoted in Paul Hazard, *European Thought in the Eighteenth Century*, trans. J. Lewis May (New Haven: Yale University Press, 1954), pp. 170-71.

[30] Marquis de Condorcet, *Sketch for a Historical Picture of the Progress of the Human Mind*, trans. June Barraclough (New York: Noonday, 1955), p. 137.

taire "the rubbish of a ruined gothic edifice." The Milanese philosopher Cesare Beccaria wrote a justly famous *Essay on Crimes and Punishments* (1764), the Abbé Raynal an immensely popular *History of the Indies* (1770), which attacked Christian inhumanity toward the Indians and Negroes of the New World and demanded the abolition of slavery. Beccaria's book contains the kernel of the humanitarian philosophy. "I owe everything to French books," he wrote to the French translator of his treatise. "They first developed in my soul feelings of humanity which had been suffocated by eight years of a fanatical education" (like so many of the philosophers Beccaria was educated by the Jesuits). To create "the maximum of happiness" and "the minimum of misery" should be the aim of good legislation, he wrote; the greatest virtues are "humanity, benevolence, and toleration of human errors." Yet for centuries tyranny and fanaticism had succeeded in imposing upon society an arbitrary and senselessly cruel system of justice. In the spirit of Voltaire, Beccaria particularly deplored "a certain class of crimes which has covered Europe with blood, and raised up those horrid piles, from whence, midst clouds of whirling smoke, the groans of human victims, the crackling of their bones, and the frying of their still panting bowels, were a pleasing spectacle, and agreeable harmony to the fanatic multitude," [31] i.e., crimes committed in the name of God. Beccaria called for a complete renovation of European laws according to the principles of humanity. He had visited the prisons of Milan, and he hoped for a day when "compassion and humanity shall penetrate the iron gates of dungeons."

These two strands of the new humanistic faith, confidence in man's power and yet tender feeling for man's

[31] Cesare Beccaria, *An Essay on Crimes and Punishments* (London, 1770), pp. 158-59.

dignity, united to form a new conception of history not dreamed of in Christian philosophy. This was the "new doctrine," as Condorcet labeled it, of "the indefinite perfectibility of the human race." Turgot, Price, and Priestley, he said, were its first and most brilliant apostles. But his own sketch, composed, ironically, at the height of the revolutionary Terror, and when he himself, as a Girondist, was under sentence of death, was its supreme expression— Benedetto Croce has rightly called Condorcet's *Progress of the Human Mind* the "last will and testament" of the Enlightenment. Human history, Condorcet thought, had taken a catastrophic turn for the better in the seventeenth and eighteenth centuries. Up to the time of Descartes, Newton, and Locke, history was the scene of an epic struggle between light and darkness, philosophy and religion, with the palm of victory usually going to the latter. With the discovery, however, of a sure method of discovering truth (Lockean empiricism) and concomitantly of enlightened ideas of politics and human rights, and with the spread of scientific knowledge and techniques, light slowly began to prevail. From this point on in his narrative Condorcet's language becomes truly apocalyptic. Never again, he said, could the human mind lapse back into the state of error and fanaticism from which it had at length emerged. In the foreseeable future, thanks to the power of reason and the discovery of new knowledge, mankind would rise to unprecedented heights, to perfectibility, in fact. "No bounds have been fixed to the improvement of the human race. . . . The perfectibility of man is absolutely indefinite. . . . Everything tells us that we are approaching one of the grand revolutions of the human race." In the "tenth epoch" to come the sun would shine upon free men only, and the worst inequalities between nations and within each nation would be modified. Science would augment the food

supply, and machinery would increase production and reduce labor. It was reasonable to suppose that even disease
would be checked and the life span greatly increased. What
if crimes and injustices did still pollute the earth? The philosopher was consoled by the thought that this would not
always be so, that in future mankind would be freed from
its chains, released from the empire of fate. What did it
matter if his contemporaries treated him unjustly? Posterity
would give him his true deserts. In Condorcet's famous last
words:

It is in the contemplation of this picture . . . that he finds his
true recompense for virtue. The contemplation of this picture
is an asylum in which the memory of his persecutors does not
follow him, an asylum in which, living in imagination with
mankind re-established in its rights and in its true nature, he
can forget mankind corrupted and tormented by greed, fear,
envy. It is in this asylum that he truly lives with his fellows,
in a *heaven* which his reason has created, and which his love
of humanity embellishes with the purest joys.[32]

This was quasi-religious language, and it suggests that
Condorcet and his sceptical contemporaries were consciously seeking a substitute for the traditional religion
which they had impeached and found guilty. In the case
of men like Condorcet and Diderot the substitute was a cult
of pure humanity or a cult of posterity.[33] "Posterity," said
Diderot in a famous epigram, "is for the philosopher what
the other world is for the religious." In this cult (it was,
of course, a purely private cult without ecclesiastical trap-
pings) the human race took the place of God—not the

[32] The translation is Carl Becker's, in his *Heavenly City of the Eighteenth-Century Philosophers*, pp. 150-51.
[33] See Becker's remarks on "The Uses of Posterity," *ibid.*, chap. 6,
also R. R. Palmer, "Posterity and the Hereafter in Eighteenth-Century
French Thought," *Journal of Modern History* (June, 1937).

human race as presently constituted, still imperfect and
fallible, but the human race as it would be in the future,
endowed with all the attributes of the old God, timelessness, wisdom, and justice. *This* humanity would judge men
and confer upon them individually such immortality as
they deserved in the form of fame or glory. To deserve
such fame, or, to put it another way, to receive the accolade
of history, men must be virtuous, i.e., they must labor, not
to achieve personal salvation in the old religious sense, but
to make the Humanity of the future come true. They must
lose themselves in the cause of Humanity; they must exhibit
"beneficence."

Not all the philosophers were as consistently sanguine
about Humanity as Condorcet. Even Diderot, as has been
intimated, oscillated between historical optimism and pessimism. It was not uncommon, even in the Enlightenment, to
view history, especially the history of governments, as a
"world in flux." [34] It was not uncommon—witness Voltaire
and D'Alembert as well as Diderot—to deplore the decline
of the fine arts, literature, and taste from the high standards
set by the ancients and the age of Louis XIV. Environmentalism obviously cut both ways: some of the very
things that supposedly denoted progress, the advance of
commercial prosperity and luxury, for instance, and even
the analytical spirit, might, and did, harm the arts and reduce poetic inspiration. Moreover, Condorcet and Jean
Jacques were decidedly *avant-garde* in their belief that
enlightenment could spread to the masses. Nevertheless,
optimism was in the air. Progress might be slow, it might
even be temporary, yet there were things that men could
do to make the world a better place to live in. "Hope"—

[34] On this point, and on Enlightenment pessimism in general, see Henry
Vyverberg, *Historical Pessimism in the French Enlightenment* (Cambridge: Harvard University Press, 1958).

the hope of a secularized Humanity—is writ large, not only in Condorcet's *Sketch*, but in the *pensées* of most of the philosophers.

Thus, the century ended with a great efflorescence of new faiths. But the greatest of them all, greater than deism, greater than the cults of reason and *La Patrie*, was this cult of Humanity, for in a sense it underlay and subsumed all the other cults. From the Christian standpoint this was the arch-heresy, for it not only put man at the center of the universe, but it assumed that if "heaven" were ever to come on earth it would be due to man's reason and ingenuity alone.

This phase of the sceptical tradition, which coincided with the Enlightenment and the French Revolution, thus had a constructive as well as destructive side. Voltaire struck the destructive note with his slogan, "crush the infamous thing." Christianity, the traditional religion of the western peoples, underwent a blistering attack which undoubtedly scored heavily among the educated classes, particularly in France. Simultaneously, however, there started up a great ground swell which we shall call the Great Substitution. Conscious of their loss, men sought substitutes. For some, deism sufficed, at least for a time. Probably the majority of the sceptics continued to believe in God in some shape or form. But the big new thing to note is the profound shift of consciousness from the theistic to the humanistic plane, which expressed itself in the new humanism. Deists and theists, as well as materialists and atheists, shared in this vision of power which in the next century would threaten to eclipse not only Christianity but religion in general. This vision, however, as well as the "*Écrasez*," had its roots in the thought of preceding centuries, especially the century of Boyle and Bayle, to which we therefore turn next.

CHAPTER II

The Strasbourg Clock

1.

Whether Robert Boyle, the "Skeptical Chemist," ever actually saw the famous astronomical clock at Strasbourg is not known. If he did see it, it must have been when he was a young boy, possibly during a side trip from Geneva where he and his brother Francis studied with a Protestant master of that city from 1639 to 1641. In any event this clock, constructed in 1574 according to the plans of a Strasbourg mathematician, evidently made a deep impression on the great English scientist, for in after years he repeatedly used it as an analogy for "nature." Nature (or the world), he wrote typically in one of his treatises, is not as the peripatetics or Aristotelians "vulgarly" conceive it, that is to say, as a puppet whose "almost every particular motion" derives from its artificer's pulling upon its wires or strings. On the contrary, nature

is like a rare clock, such as may be that at Strasbourg, where all things are so skillfully contrived, that the engine being once set a moving, all things proceed, according to the artificer's first design, and the motions of the little statues, that at such hours perform these or those things, do not require, like those of puppets, the peculiar interposing of the artificer, or any intelligent agent employed by him, but perform their functions upon particular occasions, by virtue of the general and primitive contrivance of the whole engine.[1]

In a word, nature seemed to Boyle to behave like a "machine" or "automaton," a "watch" or a "clock," a "self-moving engine," all of which variants appear in his printed works. He also frequently referred to atoms as "the alphabet of the universe" by means of which it was possible not only to read the fundamental properties of nature but also to explain, by their permutations and combinations, nature's endless variety.

These two metaphors of the clock and the atomic alphabet, particularly the clock, were quite common in intellectual circles by the late seventeenth century. They implied a radically new conception of nature, a "new philosophy" which Boyle sometimes called the mechanical, sometimes the corpuscular philosophy. "Is it not evident in these last hundred years," John Dryden wrote in 1668, "(when the study of philosophy has been the business of all the Virtuosi in Christendom), that almost a new Nature has been revealed to us?" [2] As we shall see, it is almost impossible to understand the religious scepticism of the eighteenth-century Enlightenment without reference to this "new nature" which was constructed by Galileo, Descartes, Sir Isaac Newton, and Robert Boyle, among others, in the seventeenth century. The majority of these scientists, it should be noted, were pious Christians, or at any rate intended no break with the churches to which they were affiliated. In other words, they foresaw but dimly if at all the religious consequences of their scientific virtuosity. This combination of "faith" and "reason" was more or less characteristic of the initial phase of the sceptical tradition to

[1] Robert Boyle, *Works* (London, 1772), Vol. V, p. 163.
[2] John Dryden, "An Essay of Dramatic Poesy," in *Essays,* ed. W. P. Ker (Oxford, 1926), pp. 36-7.

which we shall address ourselves in this chapter, and which precedes and in large part explains the more radical phase already considered in the first chapter.

The point to be noted here is that the "new nature" exploded many of the main features of the older, in large part Aristotelian, conception of the world with which Christianity was traditionally identified. The traditional conception, still virtually intact among the majority of educated Protestants as well as Roman Catholics at the end of the sixteenth century, was animistic rather than mechanical. That is to say, it projected a universe in which mind or spirit was ceaselessly at work, drawing and prodding creatures to their initially appointed ends, on occasion even suspending the "law of nature" for special ends. In scholastic thinking, a cause must contain more than its effect, hence all effects were referred back to the final or First Cause who was God. However, the Christian God not only created the cosmos and its laws but, subsequent to the creation, continued to provide for it, not only in a general but in a very particular way. He established it in the first place as a teleological hierarchy, stretching from macrocosm to geocosm to microcosm, from the angels to man to brute nature, each with its appointed goal or task. Thereafter he sustained and governed it, not directly, but by means of agents. Thus, he appointed spirits and intelligences to move the heavenly bodies (which in current physical theory needed the presence of a constantly impelling force), to send comets as presages, to cure disease, etc. The general features of this animistic system are clearly delineated in such a book as Richard Hooker's *Laws of Ecclesiastical Polity*, written during the 1590's. Hooker's universe, like that of St. Thomas Aquinas, was a universe of law and order, but the law and order was teleological, not mechanical. According to this Elizabethan philosopher and divine, "the law whereby the Eternal himself doth work" stood behind all cosmic and earthly laws. Thus, the real explanation of all phenomena was metaphysical. God was both the final and efficient cause of everything that happened in nature. Nature pursued no independent course of its own; nature constantly leaned on supernature. "Those things which nature is said to do, are by divine art performed, using nature as an instrument," said Hooker. Why did bodies move or grow? "Nothing can move unless there be some end," continued Hooker, following the "arch-philosopher" Aristotle, "the desire whereof provoketh unto motion," and all things in the world coveted the highest cause which was God. Were God to remove his hand from the world it would surely collapse. "There is no kind of faculty or power in man or any other creature which can rightly perform the functions allotted to it, without perpetual aid or concurrence of that Supreme Cause of all things." Moreover, God had created nature to be not only teleologically subordinate to himself, but also to man—as Hooker indicated when he observed that "God assigned Adam maintenance of life," or when he asked what would become of man "whom these things now do all serve" if God were to withdraw his "concurrence." [3]

A man like Hooker, able to enter imaginatively into such a conception, must have felt that he lived in a world saturated with Providence. He must have felt the pressure of Providence at all times and in all places. Everywhere he looked he saw signatures of the Lord God, spirits doing God's bidding. Another way of saying the same thing is that it was a world saturated with metaphysical and ethical values. There was no dualism between man and nature. Nature was created, at least partly, for man's moral edification.

[3] Richard Hooker, *Of the Laws of Ecclesiastical Polity*, Book I, Parts I-III.

The heavens, of a different order from the sublunary world, were an abiding proof to man that there was something unchangeable and permanent in the universe, and upon this "proof" he could build an immutable ethic. Plants and animals furnished him with examples of human virtues and vices, winds and storms corresponded to tempests in the soul. It was a universe of qualities as well as quantities. It was a meaningful if mysterious universe in which man could know his place and goal. It was a universe in which he could feel himself to be at the very center, metaphysically as well as physically.

Now Boyle, to be sure, still lived half within this animistic and teleological world. In the section just before the passage cited above, he was very careful to explain that he did not deny "providence, of which nature is the grand instrument." He accepted God's "ordinary and general concourse" of the universe, and in another treatise on "final causes" he went out of his way to assert God's ability, "whenever He thinks fit, to suspend, alter, or contradict those laws of motion, which He alone at first established, and which need his perpetual concourse to be upheld"— in a word, miracles. Yet his use of new metaphors and his rejection of Aristotelian puppetry indicate that he was also feeling his way toward a "new nature." These two conceptions of nature, the old Aristotelian-Christian and the new corpuscular-mechanical, existed side by side in Boyle's mind. But in other, bolder minds the latter took precedence, so that before the end of the century educated men had been presented with a picture of a "nature" more or less emptied of teleology, possessed of primarily mathematical properties, operating according to regular and necessary natural laws, explicable largely in terms of physical rather than metaphysical causes. Even Boyle, so anxious to preserve God's providence, explained natural effects in terms of "second causes," i.e., prior or local motion of some sort or the combination of atoms. To account for the motions of the Strasbourg clock, one did not need to resort to final causes. Assuming God's general concourse, he said, "the phenomena I strive to explicate may be solved mechanically, that is, by the mechanical affections of matter, without recourse to . . . substantial forms, or to other incorporeal creatures."

How this "new nature" arose in men's minds may be deduced from another of Boyle's innumerable statements about watches. Only a very dull inquirer, he said, could rest satisfied with being told that a watch is an engine made by a watchmaker or that it works because it is endowed with a soul; the true inquirer wants to understand "the mechanism of a watch," the structure of its spring, wheels, and balance, and how these parts co-operate in order to make the needle point out the true hour of the day. What this and similar statements (of which there were many in the seventeenth century) argue is, as has often been observed, a vast shift of interest from metaphysics to physics. People were becoming more interested in "how" things worked rather than "why." Why this shift of interest? Partly, no doubt because scientists and philosophers were looking for certainty in human knowledge at a time, following the Renaissance and Reformation, when so many traditional intellectual authorities were in doubt. Partly also, however, because these men were set down in a bustling, increasingly urban and commercial society which demanded answers to pressing physical and technological problems. Metaphysics might tell the world about God but it obviously could not deal with projectiles, ships, sanitation, water supply, cultivation, and the like. It is interesting to observe that both René Descartes and Boyle were keen students of the mechanical engines and "automata" constructed in their day. They argued analogously from these machines to the world-machine and in so doing dreamed of reducing nature to a quantitative and predictive system and thereby becoming its lords and possessors. Understandably, metaphysics came to be relegated to a less conspicuous position in the hierarchy of knowledge. As another seventeenth-century scientist, Robert Hooke, explained it, the business of the Royal Society (England's first chartered scientific academy) was to improve knowledge of natural things and not to meddle in "divinity" or "metaphysics."

The sceptical implications of the new nature are fairly obvious in hindsight. By and large the "virtuosi" (scientists) protested that science, far from endangering Christianity, actually enhanced it, by revealing the glory of God in his creation. Seen in this light the study of nature was as much a religious act as attending church or reading the Bible. "There is no inconsistence," Boyle insisted in *The Christian Virtuoso*, "between a man's being an industrious virtuoso, and a good Christian." And to implement this and similar statements he founded the Boyle Lectures for the purpose of reconciling Christianity and the new science. Dr. Richard Bentley and Dr. Samuel Clarke, both divines and both supporters of Newtonian science, were among the earliest Boyle lecturers. Nevertheless, a good many people were apprehensive, even in Boyle's day, lest science degenerate into Hobbist materialism, or at the very least into deism, and in the long run their fears proved to be not wholly unfounded. The classical scholar Meric Casaubon put his finger on one of the principal points when he wrote to an acquaintance in 1669 that if great care were not taken, men whose attention was fixed on "matter and secondary causes" "may in time and by degrees forget that there be such things in the world as *Spirits*, substances really existing and of great power, though not visible . . . ; forget I say that there is a God." [4]

What was chiefly in dispute at this time, however, was not God's existence but his power. In the great metaphysical debates between Cartesians, Newtonians, and Leibnitzians there was never any question of the existence of God, or of God's original creation of "matter" and the laws of motion. There was general agreement that a mechanical nature, not less than an animistic nature, required, as Sir Isaac Newton put it, a First Cause "which certainly is not mechanical." But the machine concept did raise serious questions about God's continuing activity in nature. It did so for several reasons. In the first place, as we have already seen, it depreciated "final causes," preferring wherever possible to explain an event by "second," or natural causes. And on the new assumptions about nature it was possible to go quite far with this naturalistic type of explanation. For example, the new law of inertia made it unnecessary to invoke spirits to account for the motion of a body, for it was now presumed to be "natural" for it to move in a straight line until affected by another force. The machine concept also took all the "qualities" and values out of nature, with the result that it was no longer easy to see divine-ethical signatures in it, nor, indeed, to grasp its teleological significance for man. Thus, divine activity in nature was significantly reduced if not eliminated.

It is a fascinating thing to watch this *reductio* proceed, almost ineluctably it would seem, from Galileo to Newton and Leibnitz. Some thinkers carried it much farther than others. Boyle must be listed among the conservatives, though not the ultraconservatives. The Strasbourg clock

[4] Quoted in Louis Bredvold, *The Intellectual Milieu of John Dryden* (Ann Arbor: University of Michigan Press, 1934), p. 59, note 33.

notwithstanding, his God still resembled somewhat the providential deity of traditional religion. Newton was slightly to the left of Boyle. Though he insisted more than once on God's power—he called him "Lord God," and in his opinion, no being, however perfect, "without dominion" could be said to be "Lord God"—actually, he restricted God's activity in the daily cosmic economy to preventing the fixed stars from collapsing together in the middle of space, and to overcoming noted irregularities in the motion of planets and comets.[5] This last was the basis for the German philosopher Leibnitz's sneer that Sir Isaac Newton and his followers had "a very odd opinion concerning the work of God." According to these gentlemen, said Leibnitz, the machine of God's making is so imperfect "that he is obliged to clean it now and then by an extraordinary concourse, and even to mend it, as a clockmaker mends his work."

"According to my opinion," Leibnitz continued, "the same force and vigour remains always in the world, and only passes from one part of matter to another, agreeably to the laws of nature and the beautiful pre-established order. And I hold that when God works miracles, he does not do it in order to supply the wants of nature, but those of grace." [6]

Samuel Clarke, who crossed swords with Leibnitz on Newton's behalf, replied in words which, while not altogether fair to the German, cut to the very heart of the problem.

The notion of the world's being a great machine, going on without the interposition of God, as a clock continues to go without the assistance of a clockmaker, is the notion of ma-

[5] See Edwin A. Burtt, *The Metaphysical Foundations of Modern Physical Science* (Harcourt, Brace and Company, 1927), chap. 7.

[6] *A Collection of Papers which passed between the late Learned Mr. Leibnitz and Dr. Clarke* (London, 1717), pp. 5-7.

terialism and fate, and tends (under pretence of making God a *supra-mundane intelligence*) to exclude providence and God's government in reality out of the world. And by the same reason that a philosopher can represent all things going on from the beginning of the creation without any government or interposition of providence; a sceptic will easily argue still farther backwards, and suppose that things have from eternity gone on as they now do without any true creation or original authors at all, but only what such arguers call all-wise and eternal nature.[7]

Thus, Clarke represented Leibnitz as the champion of a still more radical conception, namely that of God as a "supra-mundane intelligence." Galileo and Descartes had the same conception, though they differed profoundly from Leibnitz in other respects. In Galileo's mechanical system God was required only to create the original atoms, and Descartes, assuming an initial bestowal by God of matter and motion, tried to account for the present constitution of the universe by a purely mechanical theory (his famous vortex theory). Of Descartes, the Christian Blaise Pascal said very much the same thing that Clarke said of Leibnitz: "I cannot forforgive Descartes. In all his philosophy he would have been quite willing to dispense with God. But he had to make Him give a fillip to set the world in motion; beyond this, he has no further need of God." [8] Still farther to the left were Clarke's "sceptics," such a man, for example, as the Jewish philosopher Benedict de Spinoza who identified God with nature which he conceived as an objective mathematical order, operating wholly by necessary laws, indifferent to man, without beginning or end.

Thus, by Voltaire's time a new God, or rather a number of new gods, had been born, all of them as the result of the

[7] *Ibid.*, pp. 15-17.
[8] Blaise Pascal, *Pensées*, no. 77.

"new nature" visualized by the scientists. To use Alexandre Koyré's expression, a "God of the Sabbath," who finished his work and found it good, had displaced the "Work-Day God" in whom Boyle and Newton still half believed. Or as Samuel Clarke had said, the conception of a king who ruled threatened to give way to the conception of a *"roi fainéant"* who reigned but did not rule. And once men like Diderot and D'Holbach had seized the idea of a nature capable of renewing and transforming itself, even the *"Dieu Fainéant"* could be dispensed with as a necessary hypothesis. This reductive movement developed simultaneously with the movement already noted with respect to miracles (see p. 49). The tendency in both cases was to push God's activity farther and farther back in time, leaving "nature" to operate without benefit, or relatively without benefit, of divine providence.

Of course, for most seventeenth-century thinkers there remained the internal world of thought which according to Descartes' dualistic theory was not subject to mechanical laws, and upon which God could still presumably exert a direct influence. But by this same Cartesian dualism the internal world was now sealed off from the external world, with the consequence that it was next to impossible to feel, as Hooker had felt, the old correspondence between man and nature. In the new theory, man was clearly no longer a microcosm reflecting and participating in a teleological order of nature. Moreover, as time went on, the new mechanical nature began to erode man's inner citadel, as in the so-called associationist psychology of Thomas Hobbes and his successors, in which the human mind itself was reduced to terms of secondary causality. At the very least, for a man conversant with the new theories, the world of nature must now appear to be indifferent, to go its own way independently of any human or ethical purpose. It so appeared, for example, to the French sceptic Pierre Bayle and to Spinoza, both of whom were contemporaries of Boyle and who lived and wrote in the comparatively free atmosphere of Holland. Did comets appear in the heavens as divine messengers of doom to mankind? No, concluded Bayle in his *Miscellaneous Thoughts on the Comet of 1680;* on the contrary, "it is necessary to believe that comets are the ordinary works of nature which, without regard to the happiness or misery of mankind, are transported from one part of the heavens to another by virtue of the general laws of motion. . . . Whence it follows that none of them are presages." Was it God's will that a stone should fall from a roof in order to kill a particular man? Nonsense, said Spinoza; "there is no need to show at length, that nature has no particular goal in view, and that final causes are mere human figments."[9]

This is the point of view that informs Voltaire's article on "Providence" in the *Philosophical Dictionary.* "Sister Fessue" represents the old conception of nature when she says that "Providence takes visible care of me" and that God had brought her sparrow back to life because she had said nineteen *Ave Marias.* "The metaphysician" has the new nature in mind when he replies to her that God does not concern himself about either her or her sparrow. "I believe in a general Providence, my dear sister, from which has emanated through all eternity the law that governs everything . . . ; but I do not believe that a particular Providence changes the economy of the world for your sparrow or your cat." [10] Voltaire's metaphysician was a deist whom the "new nature" of Galileo, Descartes, and Newton had

[9] Pierre Bayle, *Pensées Diverses sur La Comète,* Sect. 56; Benedict de Spinoza, *Ethics Demonstrated in the Geometrical Manner,* Part I, Appendix.

[10] Voltaire, *Dictionnaire Philosophique,* article "Providence."

taught not to believe in a particular providence and particular miracles.

The machine idea, symbolized by Boyle's Strasbourg clock and summarized by Voltaire's metaphysician, was not the only feature of the new nature calculated to sow seeds of scepticism. It was only the most conspicuous. Scarcely less unsettling was the infinity-plurality idea, preached by the Italian renegade monk Giordano Bruno at the end of the sixteenth century and accepted by many scientists and amateurs of science in the seventeenth century. This was the idea, as Bruno expressed it, that "this world is merely one of an infinite number of worlds similar to this, and all the planets and stars are infinite worlds without number composing an infinite universe." [11] Strictly speaking, the idea was not new. It had been avidly discussed by medieval Schoolmen as well as the Greeks, and by no means always unsympathetically. However, it achieved a special prominence in the seventeenth century, undoubtedly because the new astronomy seemed to support it. In this connection the decisive document was not the *De Revolutionibus Orbium Celestium* (1543) of Nicholas Copernicus, which postulated only the immeasurability but not the infinity of the universe, but the *Sidereus Nuncius* (1610) of Galileo. When the great Italian scientist looked through his telescope and saw new "planets," "stars innumerable," and a moon like the earth, he seemed to confirm scientifically the metaphysical speculations of Bruno. Paradoxically, however, the chief support for the idea continued for some time to come from metaphysics rather than science, specifically from the idea of God's plenitude, and its corollary, the principle of sufficient reason. This idea, expounded at

[11] Giordano Bruno, *De immenso et innumerabilibus* (1591), quoted in Preserved Smith, *A History of Modern Culture* (New York: Henry Holt and Company, 1930), Vol. I, p. 44.

length by Bruno and derived from Greek and scholastic sources, stated simply that since God's essence was infinite, so also must the universe be infinite and filled with an infinity of worlds and beings; moreover, if there was a reason why the place occupied by our planet should be filled, so there was equally good reason for filling all the other places in the universe capable of occupancy. Significantly, this argument crops up frequently in popular treatments of the subject like Fontenelle's *Plurality of Worlds* (1686).

It is not hard to see why the infinity-plurality idea was disquieting to men of settled religious opinions. In the first place, it not only contradicted Plato and Aristotle, but also the Bible. "The position (say some) is directly against scripture; for St. John, speaking of God's works, says he made the world in the singular number, and therefore there is but one." [12] More importantly, it seemed to deprive man, to a much greater degree than the heliocentric theory of Copernicus, of his central place and unique value in the universe. It also struck at the doctrine of the Atonement, as the Lutheran theologian Philip Melanchthon had pointed out in the early sixteenth century. Were there creatures in the universe other than the sons of Adam? If so, did they, too, have to be saved, and did this mean that there were redemptions other than the one supreme redemption by Jesus Christ? Finally, the idea appeared to some to endanger the idea of creation itself. This aspect comes out very clearly in the debate between Samuel Clarke and Leibnitz. Clarke argued that the idea of infinity logically included the idea of the eternity of the world.

[12] John Wilkins, *The Discovery of a New World* (1638), in *Works* (London, 1802), Vol. I, p. 17. Wilkins himself refuted this position and devoted his *Discovery* to showing "that it is probable there may be another habitable world in the moon."

If the material universe cannot be finite . . . ; then (I say) it follows evidently, that God neither can nor ever could set bounds to matter; and consequently the material universe must not only be boundless, but eternal also, both *a parte ante* and *a parte post*, necessarily and independently of the will of God.[13]

By no means all religious people shared these misgivings. There were some like Bishop John Wilkins who boldly asserted that "a plurality of worlds does not contradict any principle of reason or faith," others like the Cambridge Platonist Henry More who reveled in the idea of infinity which he thought greatly enhanced the glory of God. Nevertheless, judging by the many and heated controversies over the subject it seems clear that the infinity-plurality idea, like the machine idea, was a source of growing scepticism.

In general, if "new philosophy" (the new science) did not "call all in doubt," it did raise doubts. It did so chiefly in two ways. Most important, as we have seen, it presented a new conception of nature which was profoundly upsetting to men who, like John Donne, had been reared on the Aristotelian-Christian conception.

> And new Philosophy calls all in doubt,
> The Element of fire is quite put out;
> The Sun is lost, and th'earth, and no man's wit
> Can well direct him where to look for it.
> And freely men confess that this world's spent,
> When in the Planets, and the Firmament
> They seek so many new. . . .[14]

When Donne penned these lines in 1611 the new cosmology of Copernicus, William Gilbert, Galileo, and even Bruno had already begun to provoke lively discussion in European

[13] *A Collection of Papers*, etc., pp. 319-21.
[14] John Donne, *The First Anniversary*, lines 205-11.

intellectual circles. Donne did not see all its implications nor did it make him into a sceptic or atheist; in fact, he was currently undergoing a conversion from Roman Catholicism to Anglicanism, and would soon take holy orders and be made Dean of St. Paul's, London. But he had the wit to see that "new philosophy" turned the cosmos upside down, and that the new cosmology posed problems for Christians. By Boyle's time if not before, it was raising doubts which helped to lay the groundwork for the type of scepticism exhibited by Voltaire and the deists.

New philosophy also concealed a second source of scepticism which escaped Donne, namely the empirical or experimental method of knowledge, elaborated chiefly by British philosophers from Francis Bacon to Newton and Locke. The impact on religion of the "inductive method," as Bacon called it, was, however, more delayed and indirect. The fact that it aroused no furious theological debates in the seventeenth century, as did the "new nature," makes its influence extremely hard to chart. Nevertheless, it might be said that just as there was a line running from the clock conception of nature to Voltaire's "theism," so a line ran from the new empiricism to David Hume's agnosticism, and indeed to the agnostic positivism of Auguste Comte in the nineteenth century. As is well known, the empirical, or experimental, method emphasized the discovery of new knowledge by means of observation (sense perception) and experiment. It disparaged ancient authorities, reverence for whom, as Bacon said many times in his *Novum Organum*, kept men back "as by a kind of enchantment from progress in the sciences." It also emphasized the tentativeness of knowledge, for the discovery of new phenomena made necessary the continual framing of new hypotheses. It was suspicious of metaphysics, meaning by metaphysics the "vain" search of scholastic philosophers for essences and forms, the underlying nature of things. Its chief psychological effect was undoubtedly to nurture a sceptical frame of mind, which took little on trust, which was on the whole quite nominalistic, and which demanded facts or sensible evidence for the objects of investigation. The association between the new empiricism and scepticism is as clear as day in Locke's *Essay concerning Human Understanding* (1690). Locke did not doubt the existence of self or of God, whom he thought could be known either by intuition or demonstration. However, in the realm of so-called "sensitive knowledge," i.e., ideas received from external or internal sensation, he doubted that the human mind could penetrate beyond the perception of particular instances to knowledge of their nature, substance, or "hidden causes." Thus, beyond a few more or less certain truths, the mind had to be content to live with uncertainty or probability. And Locke hedged even probable knowledge round with a number of exacting tests: the number, integrity, and skill of witnesses, contrary testimonies. Translated into religious terms what this empiricism meant—at least for Locke—was that one should be extremely careful about accepting claims to metaphysical truth. Locke specifically warned against relying on the opinion of others. "If the opinions and persuasions of others . . . be a ground of assent, men have reason to be Heathens in Japan, Mahometans in Turkey, Papists in Spain, Protestants in England, and Lutherans in Sweden." [15] He pleaded therefore for an expression of mutual ignorance and charity.

We should do well to commiserate our mutual ignorance, . . . and not instantly treat others ill, as obstinate and perverse, because they will not renounce their own, and receive our opinions. . . . For where is the man that has incontestable

[15] John Locke, *An Essay concerning Human Understanding*, Book IV, chap. 15, Sect. 6.

evidence of the truth of all that he holds, or of the falsehood of all he condemns; or can say that he has examined to the bottom all his own or other men's opinions? [16]

Most of the seventeenth-century empiricists, including Locke, were sincere Christians. Nevertheless, in the long run empiricism too took its toll of traditional theology, as can be seen even more clearly in the scepticism of David Hume. Hume took Locke's arguments and carried them to their logical extreme. Ruthlessly applying the empirical criterion to traditional theology, he argued that men had no reliable evidence for miracles, personal immortality, or even the idea of a First Cause. It is perhaps worthy of note that even in his own lifetime Locke was accused of scepticism and infidelity, specifically of denying the existence of spiritual substance (which was palpably false), and of nominalism which Bishop Stillingfleet pointed out was irreconcilable with the doctrines of the Trinity and the Incarnation. With more justice Stillingfleet might have charged the empiricists with spreading the habit of doubt which, once it had commenced in one sphere, could scarcely be expected not to cross over into other spheres including the theological. Even more dangerous for orthodoxy was empiricism's constant demand for sensible evidence and its simultaneous depreciation of other kinds of knowing, also the very obvious damper that it put upon spiritual and metaphysical exploration. Among other things, empiricism had the effect of forcing Christian apologetics back upon an empirical line of defence, that is to say upon external signs and miracles which, however, were already becoming suspect on other grounds, as we have seen.

[16] *Ibid.*, Book IV, chap. 16, Sect. 4.

2.

The new science was probably the most important single source of scepticism in the early modern period. However, it was neither the only nor the earliest source, for the sceptical tradition was well established before the new science began to take hold. We must now try, therefore, to identify some of the other sceptical influences which ran parallel with, and in some cases antedated, the scientific revolution.

Judging by the frequent and often hysterical attacks upon them there would appear to have been a not inconsiderable number of atheists, libertines, "*esprits forts,*" and deists in the early seventeenth century. These labels, all of them, save atheism, of quite recent vintage, were loosely used to designate persons who scoffed at religious credulity and were impatient with traditional dogmas or moral rules. Undoubtedly, the books exaggerated their number and influence, such a book for example as the Abbé Mersenne's *Impiety of the Deists* (1623) which claimed that there were fifty thousand atheists in Paris alone. Yet the references to them were so frequent and the number of defences of Christianity against them so numerous that one simply cannot doubt their infiltration of the cultivated classes. It was commonly said that they flourished chiefly in Italy, proverbially the land of both superstition and atheism. But, clearly, by now scepticism had migrated north of the Alps to reside also in the cities and universities of the north. In one of his last books, ostensibly a defence of Christianity against "atheism," the Italian monk Tommaso Campanella provides us with a classification of the various types of sceptics whom he claimed to have encountered during his lifetime in both Italy and France.[17] There were, first of all, he says, the hypocrites who despite doubts preferred to stay within the fold of the Church, either because they feared persecution or else were loath to give up prebends and honors. Then there were the pure sceptics who denied the possibility of knowing the truth because of the existence of so many different religions and theological schools. The real "plague of this age," however, was the "libertines" who denied every Christian belief and taught that religions were invented by astute men in order to keep the masses in obedience. Finally, there was a small group of very rare philosophers—Campanella said that he knew only four in the present generation and only twenty-five in the whole history of thought—who believed in a natural religion of which the historic religions were but partial reflections. These were, of course, the deists of whom Campanella himself may have been one, though of a very curious kind.

Significantly, Campanella, though a passionate defender of Galileo, does not associate any of these current forms of scepticism with the new science. Where, then, did they come from? Campanella thought, quite rightly, that libertinism in particular descended from the medieval tradition of heterodox Aristotelianism which had flourished, most recently, at the University of Padua. But this was by no means the whole story, nor was deism currently so rare a phenomenon as Campanella made out. Lord Herbert of Cherbury, Campanella's English contemporary and sometimes called the "Father of Deism," furnishes some additional hints in his *De Religione Laici* (*Of a Layman's Reli-*

[17] For a full description of Campanella's classification of sceptics in *Atheismus Triumphatus* (1636), see G. Spini, *Ricerca dei Libertini. La teoria dell' impostura delle religioni nel seicento italiano* (Rome, 1950), pp. 75-92.

gion) which was published just nine years after Campanella's *Atheism Vanquished*. In the opening paragraph of
this book, Herbert posed what seemed to him to be "a very
serious question."

What, namely, shall the layman, encompassed by the terrors
of divers churches militant throughout the world, decide as to
the best religion? For there is no church that does not breathe
threats, none almost that does not deny the possibility of salvation outside its own pale. Many faiths or religions, clearly,
exist or once existed in various countries and ages, and certainly there is not one of them that the lawgivers have not pronounced to be as it were divinely ordained; so that the Wayfarer finds one in Europe, another in Africa, and in Asia, still
another in the very Indies. . . . What Wayfarer, then, born
in an unfortunate land or age, shall save himself? How, especially, shall he protect himself if every man's individual dogmas
about necessary and excellent truth are so proposed as to damn
all the rest? [18]

And elsewhere Herbert speaks of "the multitude of sects,
divisions, sub-divisions and cross-divisions in the schools"
which "hopelessly distract the wits of the learned and the
consciences of the unlettered."

Here, then, in two books by an Italian and an Englishman
we have a number of hints as to the main nonscientific
sources of early seventeenth-century scepticism. With his
Italian background Campanella very naturally stresses the
heterodox Aristotelian-Paduan tradition. Out of a different
background Herbert points to three additional strands. First,
by his reference to Africa, Asia, and the Indies he hints at
the effects which an increasing knowledge of the extra-
Christian cultures, culled from commercial contacts and
the literature of travel, was beginning to have on European

[18] Lord Herbert of Cherbury, *De Religione Laici*, trans. Harold R.
Hutcheson (New Haven: Yale University Press, 1944), p. 87.

religious thought. Second, he alludes to the chaos of beliefs engendered by wide reading in the pagan philosophies, including Greek scepticism, about which Europeans learned a good deal during the Renaissance. Naturally, however, the factor that loomed largest to the Englishman Herbert was the "multitude of sects" spawned by the Reformation, each claiming the truth and hence throwing all truth in doubt. Let us pursue each of these strands in a little more detail.

The tradition to which Campanella pointed was of medieval vintage. Contrary to popular supposition there was plenty of scepticism in the Middle Ages, and some of it was quite radical. Heterodox Aristotelianism, or "Averroism" as it was often called after the Arab philosopher Averroes (1120-1198), was one of its most radical manifestations. This Averroism chiefly flourished where there was a confluence between Christian, Arab, and Jewish learning. From books written against it by Thomas Aquinas and Albertus Magnus, and from its condemnation by the Bishop of Paris in 1277, we know that it was strongly represented in the Faculty of Arts of the University of Paris in the thirteenth century. Petrarch testifies to its vitality in Venetian Italy in the following century. At the University of Padua, which became its chief locus, it maintained a vigorous and continuous life right down to the time of Campanella. Moreover, its influence was not restricted to the universities. The proceedings of the Inquisition bear witness that it also impregnated the thought of monks and priests as well as rich and cultivated laymen. How many of the latter were affected it is, of course, impossible to say, but Petrarch talks, doubtless with exaggeration, of a new crop of "religious men" (i.e., men belonging to a religious order) who preferred "that frantic dog Averroes" to St. Augustine and even Christ, and of people "adoring Aristotle" and sneering at Christ "at every street corner." [19] The medieval myth of the Three Imposters (Christ, Moses, and Mohammed), attributed variously to Averroes, the Emperor Frederick II, and others, may be evidence that a sort of vulgar Averroism had reached out to even wider circles.

Averroism, in the sense used here, was a mélange of ideas derived from various sources. One source was, of course, Aristotle as interpreted by Averroes, whose commentaries became available to the West in the thirteenth century. Other sources were astrology, which was a recognized science in the Middle Ages, anticlericalism, and, in the case of the sixteenth-century Italian philosopher Pietro Pomponazzi, also Stoicism. This heterodox Aristotelianism or "Averroism" has been aptly described as "the crisis of the Christian understanding, tottering under the massive irruption of pagan knowledge." [20] In general, it stood for a naturalistic interpretation of religion and ethics, with a strong dash of anticlericalism. It was not atheistic. But wherever possible it sought a naturalistic explanation of things, thus excluding God, far in advance of the scientific revolution, from the everyday economy of the universe. The universe was depicted as the reign of eternal nature and natural laws, admitting no miracles, demons, or angels. Religion was explained, not as a supernatural, but as a natural and social phenomenon. According to the astrological interpretation, the religions of the world originated, waxed, and waned according to a favorable or unfavorable conjunction of the stars, and were thus involved like everything else in nature's process of generation and decay. According to the social interpretation, popular religion, the religion which

[19] For Petrarch on the Averroists see *The Renaissance Philosophy of Man*, ed. Ernst Cassirer, *et al.* (Chicago: University of Chicago Press, 1948), pp. 93-4, 140-43.
[20] Fernand Van Steenberghen, *Aristotle in the West*, trans. Leonard Johnston (Louvain, 1955), p. 237.

proclaimed miracles and future rewards and punishments, was merely a *lex* or law invented for the sake of the vulgar who could not be expected to understand the workings of nature and who had somehow to be restrained from evil-doing. The myth of the Three Imposters embodied this latter interpretation in its crudest form: Jesus, Moses, and Mohammed were rascals or imposters who were more astute than other men and capable therefore of imposing on the ignorance of the vulgar.

Averroism as a specific body of teaching died out as Aristotle went out of fashion and astrology was debunked. Nevertheless, it survived as an undercurrent in the libertin-ism of the seventeenth century, as Campanella reports, and even in the eighteenth century. One of the carriers of the tradition was the great French sceptic, Pierre Bayle, whose *Critical and Historical Dictionary* included long articles on Averroes, Pomponazzi, and the latter's disciple Zabarella, in which ideas like the eternity of matter, the mortality of the soul, and the independence of morality from religion were inevitably rehashed. The imposture theory likewise never died out. There are frequent allusions to it in litera-ture from the sixteenth to the eighteenth century when, indeed, it was often featured in books like Jean Meslier's *Testament*, extracts of which Voltaire published, and in the two books, one in Latin and one in French, that actually circulated under the title of *The Three Imposters*.

Lord Herbert of Cherbury, as has been said, pinpointed several other, more modern sources of scepticism. Of two of these, one might be said to have projected the mind out-ward in space and the other backward in time. But both together, the discovery of other civilizations overseas and the "revival of antiquity," had the effect of broadening men's horizons and of weakening the claims of Christianity, or of a particular Christian church, to a monopoly of religious truth. For instance, from the spate of travel books published in the seventeenth and early eighteenth centuries —over five hundred volumes appeared on the Orient alone between 1660 and 1740—western Europeans gradually became aware, to a degree never before possible, of non-Christian civilizations, not only Mohammedan but also Indian and Chinese, which had achieved a high level of wisdom and morality without benefit of Christian revelation; civilizations, moreover, some of which appeared to have arrived independently at beliefs in monotheism, the immortality of the soul, even the resurrection of the body and prophets born of virgins, and which claimed, as Herbert said, to be "divinely ordained." To be sure, European expansion overseas offered a magnificent opportunity for missionary enterprise of which the Christian churches did not fail to avail themselves. At the same time, however, it planted seeds of real doubt. It threw some men into total confusion, as La Bruyère observed in his *Characters*, apropos of the *"esprits forts"* of the seventeenth century: "Some men complete their demoralization by long voyages, and lose whatever shreds of religion remained to them: everyday they see a new religion, different customs, different ceremonies." [21] It taught others the lesson of religious relativity, and inspired still others to deistic speculation. The idea of the relative goodness of all religions was not, of course, new. It had been exemplified long before in the story of the Three Rings, which probably originated at about the same time as the Three Imposters and which Giovanni Boccaccio developed in *The Decameron*. This story could only have flourished in a milieu like fourteenth-century Italy where Christians had learned, by continuous cultural interchange with Mohammedans and Jews, to respect and tolerate their religious rivals. As Boccaccio told

[21] La Bruyère, *Oeuvres* (Paris, 1865), Vol. II, p. 238.

the story, Melchizedek the Jew explained to Saladin that the three great religions were so alike to one another that "the true might not be known," even as the three sons who inherited identical rings from their father could not tell which was the genuine article. The relativistic idea was given a new twist in the post-Columbian age. Now the religions of the earth were depicted as relative to climate and region, producing their own peculiar customs and wisdom. Michel de Montaigne did so, for example, in several of his essays. Supposedly upon receipt of reports from a mariner about the civility of the Brazilian Indians, Montaigne concluded that "we have no other level of truth and reason but the example and model of the opinions and usages of the country we live in. There we always see the perfect religion, the perfect government, the perfect and accomplished manner of doing all things." [22] By the early eighteenth century this sort of observation had become fairly common. A statement by the Comte de Boulainvilliers in his *Life of Mahomet* is typical. "Every nation," he said, "has its customs, consecrated by use" which "are independent of the notions and different practices that other people have upon the same subject"; thus, Confucianists, Mohammedans, and Christians alike "could not draw better conclusions from their premises than those which they have followed." [23]

Possibly the chief intellectual effect of the literature of overseas travel, however, was to promote deistic thinking to which a good many Europeans were already addicted for other reasons. The intellectual discovery of China, which began in the late seventeenth century, was particu-

[22] Montaigne, *Essays*, "On Cannibals."
[23] Comte de Boulainvilliers, *The Life of Mahomet* (London, 1731), p. 178. See Paul Hazard, *La Crise de la Conscience Européenne, 1680-1715* (Paris, 1935), Vol. I, chap. 1 for additional evidence of the relativistic idea.

larly decisive in this respect. Ironically, it was chiefly the Jesuits who out of their missionary experience purveyed new information about China to Europe. In a series of impressive works, of which Father Couplet's book on Confucius (1687), Father Louis Le Comte's *Memoirs on the Present State of China* (1696), and Father Du Halde's *Description of China* (1735) are only the best known, the Jesuits depicted China as a happy and virtuous land, and the Chinese religion as a high type of deism which was not fundamentally incompatible with Christianity. Their Franciscan and Dominican rivals accused them of tolerating idolatry and minimizing revelation, and strove to prove that the Chinese were in reality atheists and materialists. Thus, two pictures of China came to stand side by side. Both pictures, however, provided ammunition for the sceptics. If on the one hand one accepted the Franciscan picture, then it could be maintained, as Pierre Bayle, for example, maintained, that virtuous atheistic societies could and did exist and that morality was not therefore necessarily dependent on religion. If on the other hand one preferred the Jesuit picture, then it could be argued not only that Christianity was not unique but that in some respects Chinese "deism" was preferable to Christianity, notably in its lack of dogma and in its superior social effects. Voltaire, who got his first knowledge of China from his Jesuit teachers at the school of Louis-le-Grand, took this second line. A great Sinophile, he saw in the land of Confucius a civilization equal to that of Europe and a religion superior to Christianity. The religion of the "wise Chinese," he taught, was a tolerant deism which Christians would do well to imitate: a religion without superstitions or absurd legends, conspicuously lacking in dogmas which insulted religion and nature; a simple cult uniting all people in the worship of God, in contrast to Christianity which was hopelessly divided, as he said, be-

tween the schools of St. Thomas and St. Bonaventura, Luther and Calvin, Jansen and Molina.[24] Doubtless, Voltaire
read into Confucianism what he wanted, but there can be
little doubt that he and others were confirmed in their
deistic convictions by the new knowledge of exotic religions, chiefly the Chinese.

The "revival of antiquity" inside Christendom had similar effects. During the Renaissance, educated Europeans
were deluged by a veritable flood of pagan philosophical
systems. Hence, they had now to absorb, not only a heterodox Aristotle and Averroes, but also a heterodox Cicero,
Pliny, Lucian, Lucretius, Plutarch, and Zeno, among others.
They also had to contend with Greek philosophical scepticism, or Pyrrhonism, which reached them through several
translations of the works of Sextus Empiricus. Some idea of
the bewilderment caused by this "racket of philosophical
brains" may be gathered from a passage in Montaigne's
"Apology for Raimond Sebond" in which the great French
sceptic juxtaposed no less than twenty-seven ancient views
of the nature of God.

Thales, the first who inquired into this matter, regarded God as
a spirit, that made all things of water. . . .
Pythagoras made God a spirit, diffused through the nature of
all things. . . .
Empedocles declared the four elements, of which all things are
made, to be gods. . . .
Plato varies in his belief. . . .
Aristotle says at one time that it is the mind, at another the
world. . . .
Zeno, the Law of Nature. . . .
Aristo thinks the form of God to be incomprehensible. . . .
Diagoras and Theodorus flatly denied that there were gods. . . .[25]

[24] Voltaire, *Dictionnaire Philosophique*, article "Chine."
[25] Michel de Montaigne, *Essays*, trans. E. J. Trechmann (New York:
Random House, 1946), pp. 439-41.

Montaigne also frequently quoted the Latin poet Lucretius, disciple of Epicurus, who, as is well known, advanced a materialistic conception of the universe and argued against Providence.

What was one to make of this almost infinite variety of opinions? How could one reconcile them, either with one another or with Christianity? Montaigne himself answered this question on two levels and in so doing epitomized two quite common reactions to the classical revival. In the first place, he took the pessimistic line that the human reason was obviously incapable of arriving at truth, that man must reconcile himself to living in doubt and perpetual suspension of judgment. He therefore quoted with approval the "profession of the Pyrrhonians" which is "to waver, to doubt, and to inquire; to be sure of nothing, to answer for nothing"; and he denounced "Dogmatism" which, he said, "will not allow us to be ignorant of that of which we are ignorant." [26] This was, as it were, a first Montaigne, whose philosophical scepticism often seems to imply a religious scepticism. However, in the same essay Montaigne also used Pyrrhonism to support a philosophy of religious faith, or fideism. Since "philosophy" could not find the bean in the cake, man's only access to divine knowledge was through faith, meaning by faith the common teaching and observances of the religion established in one's own country. "It is Faith alone," said Montaigne, "that vividly and with certainty embraces the sublime mysteries of our religion." [27] Fideism became the refuge of many seventeenth-century Roman Catholics who found that they could not reconcile faith with reason. It was naturally suspect by the Church which perceived the danger of trying to combine philoso-

[26] *Ibid.*, pp. 428-29.
[27] *Ibid.*, p. 371. See also pp. 431-32.

phical scepticism and religion, and thus of setting up a kind of double truth.

The "racket of philosophical brains," as Montaigne called it, also encouraged religious eclecticism and deism. Obviously, the ancient philosophies and religions, as well as the Christian sects, were in profound disagreement on a great many things; nevertheless, on deeper examination they might be found to agree on certain "common notions" which, when discovered, could provide a basis for universal religious consent. Thus, the fifteenth-century Florentine philosopher, Marsiglio Ficino, discovered a fundamental harmony between Platonism and Christianity and, unlike St. Augustine, regarded Platonism as divinely inspired. Thus, Ficino's younger contemporary Pico della Mirandola found the Truth reflected in all the philosophies of mankind, in the pagan classics, in Arabic and Jewish thought, as well as in patristic and medieval theology. Thus, Lord Herbert of Cherbury perceived five "common notions" underlying all the classical mythologies and religions of the earth: belief in a "Supreme Power"; belief that this Supreme Power should be worshipped; belief that virtue constituted the principal part of divine worship; belief that vices should be expiated by repentance; and belief in rewards and punishments in an afterlife. These common notions, Herbert thought, were the rock upon which "the true Catholic or universal church" was built.

For the church which is built of clay or stone or living rock or even of marble cannot be claimed to be the infallible Church. The true Catholic Church is not supported on the inextricable confusion of oral and written tradition to which men have given their allegiance. Still less is it that which fights beneath any one particular standard, or is comprised in one organization so as to embrace only a restricted portion of the earth, or a single period of history. The only Catholic and uniform Church is the doctrine of the Common Notions which comprehends all places and all men." [28]

Thus was formulated the idea of a natural religion, discoverable in universal consent and by reason, which lay hidden in all the revealed and particular religions of history.

Militating in the same direction was the third factor mentioned by Herbert, namely the multitude of religious sects within Christendom, scarcely one of which did not "deny the possibility of salvation outside its own pale." "The causes of atheism are divisions in religion," wrote Sir Francis Bacon. However, the more immediate reaction to the religious divisions resulting from the Reformation was not so much atheism as latitudinarianism, which was first cousin to deism. Confronted by innumerable claims to exclusive salvation, the moderates of all lands tried to discover a formula which would comprehend all Christians, or at least all Protestants. The criterion for devising such a formula was inevitably "reason," for the locus of the true Church was in dispute, and the Bible, admittedly the rock of salvation, had to be interpreted. Divine revelation, wrote John Locke in the true latitudinarian spirit, "is the proper object of faith: but whether it be a divine revelation or no, reason must judge." [29] And according to Herbert, "reason" expressed itself in "universal consent" ("I accept, then, whatever is universally asserted as the truth"), and contrariwise whatever did not win the universal consent of rational men could not be absolute truth but only speculation, could not therefore be essential or necessary to salvation. Using this criterion the latitudinarians boiled Christianity down to a

[28] Lord Herbert of Cherbury, *De Veritate*, trans. Meyrick Carré (Bristol, 1937), p. 303.

[29] Locke, *An Essay concerning Human Understanding*, Book IV, chap. 18, Sect. 10.

few simple "essentials," often including not much more than belief in Jesus as the Messiah and belief in a righteous life, leaving the "non-essentials" free to the particular church and the individual conscience. Herbert the deist was only carrying this process one step farther when he stipulated his "common notions" as the marks of "the true Catholic Church," pagan as well as Christian, ancient as well as modern.

The concomitant of this irenicism was the deflation of dogma, the demotion of revelation to a position of supplemental importance in religion, and the emphasis on deeds rather than creeds. We have already remarked on the Enlightenment tendency to define religion in terms of what it does. The background of this pragmatic, ethical conception was the religious warfare of the sixteenth and seventeenth centuries during which peaceful men grew weary of the claims and counterclaims of innumerable sects, the ensuing persecutions, and the general decay of "charity." The titles of two books by a late seventeenth-century English clergyman, the latitudinarian Joseph Glanvill, typify the growing ethical emphasis: *The Vanity of Dogmatizing* (1661) and *Catholic Charity Recommended* (1669). "Catholic, universal charity," Glanvill wrote in the latter work, "is a doctrine exceedingly fit for these times, in which divisions, and mutual animosities have produced so many fatal and deplorable effects." "Religion consists not in knowing many things but in practicing the few plain things we know." [30] From Glanvill and Locke it is not such a long step to Voltaire who, in his article on "religion" in the *Philosophical Dictionary*, makes this same point, although, as one would expect, with less "charity" and more irony. He dreamed, he said, that an angel carried him into a desert

[30] Joseph Glanvill, *Catholick Charity Recommended* (London, 1669), p. 29; *An Essay concerning Preaching* (London, 1678), p. 33.

all covered with piles of bones, including "the bones of the Christians who have cut one another's throats over metaphysical disputes." To make a long story short, he eventually encountered, wandering around in this desert, a man of simple mien who appeared to be about thirty-five years of age and whose hands and side were pierced and whose ribs were flayed from lashings. Upon being asked what he had done to be so cruelly persecuted, he replied that he had only tried to teach men what "true religion" was. And what is true religion? "Have I not already told you?" said the stranger. "Love God and your neighbour as yourself."

How all of the above influences, both scientific and non-scientific, meshed to produce a sceptical effect can be seen in the life history of such a man as Pierre Bayle (1647-1706), whom Voltaire called the "advocate-general of the *philosophes*" and whose famous *Critical and Historical Dictionary* (1697) has been labelled the "Bible of the eighteenth century." Bayle was certainly one of the most widely read men of his generation. From an early age he steeped himself in the ancient classics, Plutarch and Cicero being among his favorite authors. Through Montaigne, also a favorite, he became acquainted with Pyrrhonism, a subject treated at length in the *Dictionary*. As we have seen, he was also familiar with the Averroist tradition. At the University of Geneva he encountered the Cartesian philosophy, and later, enough of modern science to share, at least in general, its view of nature and its methodology. Frequent entries in the *News of the Republic of Letters*, a cosmopolitan journal which he edited in Rotterdam, show that he also took considerable interest in the latest travel books and reports of overseas civilizations, including the Chinese. However, the greatest single influence on his thought was unquestionably the religious wars of Christendom of which he and his French Huguenot family were personal victims. Bayle in fact was the victim of both Roman Catholic and Protestant persecution. Twice he was exiled from his native land by Louis XIV's drive to make France "all Catholic." And in Holland where he eventually settled he was repeatedly attacked by that arch-defender of Protestant orthodoxy, Jurieu, and hounded from his professorship in the new municipal academy of Rotterdam. Thus, Bayle was in a position to know firsthand, even better than Lord Herbert, not only the differences between the sects but also the fanatical lengths to which they were willing to go to eliminate those who contested their claims to absolute truth.

This experience eventually turned Bayle into an indignant sceptic. He protested that he was a good Calvinist and he was buried in the French Huguenot church of Rotterdam. But actually his mind was a microcosm reflecting at one time or another most of the beliefs extant in his age. He was successively Protestant, Roman Catholic convert, relapsed Catholic, possibly fideist, possibly even modern Manichee if Jurieu is to be believed. He probably ended as a sceptic who doubted the possibility of absolute truth in religion or philosophy, who hated priestcraft worse than atheism, and who held religion up to the moral test and found it wanting. It would be wrong to call Bayle typical of his age. He was not so typical as, for instance, Boyle or Locke who remained Christian, or even Lord Herbert who was a deist. Nor did he exactly adumbrate the Enlightenment with its predominantly deistic frame of reference. But he shows as well as any man how the events and intellectual currents of the seventeenth century could combine to produce a sceptical cast of mind. And his scepticism did influence profoundly the destructive if not the constructive deism of the Enlightenment.

3.

We do not, however, exhaust Bayle's significance for the history of religion when we say that he was a sceptic. He was also a secular or semisecular man (semisecular because he was, of course, deeply concerned about religious questions even though he might not always answer them in the traditional way). That is to say, he also reflected a mighty cultural movement of which scepticism was but one facet and whose full effects were not to be felt until the nineteenth and twentieth centuries. This movement was secularism—we might call it the Great Secularization of European life and thought—which already by Bayle's time had begun successfully to drive theology out of one sphere of knowledge after another, to set up autonomous "laws" within these spheres, and to limit theology to the comparatively restricted sphere of religious faith and morals (in Bayle's case not even morals escaped the secular juggernaut, for he tried to show that there was no necessary connection between morals and religion). We might think of this movement on the analogy of "Sunday religion," a well-known phenomenon of modern life: one day or one hour of the week in which the Church presumably has its say; six other days, however, in which this "say" is presumed to be simply irrelevant to the mundane activities laymen are engaged in. The history of the Great Secularization is still to be written and in any case it is too vast a subject to treat here in detail. A few examples must therefore suffice to indicate something of its nature and to show how in its way it too contributed to the rise of scepticism.

To appreciate its contribution we may cite by way of contrast the famous tableau by Peter Paul Rubens entitled "The Triumph of the Catholic Faith," executed in 1626-

1628. Like Bayle, Rubens was a baptised Protestant and a convert to Roman Catholicism, but there all resemblance between them ends, for Rubens, basically secular painter though he may have been, remained faithful to Catholicism and indeed dedicated many canvases to her service. In the painting referred to, Religion, seated in a triumphal chair, occupies the central position, and behind her stand three figures who by their attitudes clearly show their subservience to her: Science, represented as young in years; Philosophy, a bearded old man leaning on a staff; and Nature, of ample Rubenesque bosom. Behind these three are two more figures, an American Indian and a Negro who personify the new world recently won to the true religion by the missionaries. The picture obviously symbolizes theology as queen of all the sciences, the new sciences as well as the old.

This was the traditional conception. However, already by Rubens' time and certainly by Bayle's, this conception, temporarily resurgent in the Protestant as well as the Catholic Reformation, was retreating before strong secular forces.[31] Within the decade just prior to Rubens' representation, for example, the young Science had issued two signal declarations of independence from theology. The first was Galileo's famous letter to the Grand Duchess Christina of Tuscany (1615); the second, Francis Bacon's *Novum Organum* (1620). Galileo, as is well known, had been attacked by certain theologians for championing the Copernican theory of the universe, not merely as a mathematical hypothesis but as a physical fact, a position said to be contrary to Holy Scripture. In his retort Galileo expressed complete scorn of his accusers' view "that since

---

[31] It is perhaps worth noting that Henri Busson, in his *La Pensée française de Charron à Pascal* (Paris, 1933), pp. 609-10, uses Rubens' painting as a symbol of the retreat of "incredulity" and the renewal of Christianity in the early seventeenth century.

theology is queen of all the sciences, she need not bend in any way to accommodate herself to the teachings of less worthy sciences which are subordinate to her; these others must rather be referred to her as to their supreme empress." Galileo admitted theology's title to queenship only in the sense that she excelled the other sciences in dignity and ruled over "supernatural things which are matters of faith." He denied her right to interfere in "purely physical matters" which would mean delivering up science to persons who knew nothing about it and thus hindering the progress of knowledge.[32] Bacon similarly noted the "corruption" of science "from the admixture of superstition and theology," which, he said, had indulged in the strange levity, for instance, of endeavoring to found natural philosophy upon the first chapter of Genesis or the book of Job, "thus seeking the dead among the living,"—a preposterous procedure which Voltaire was later to lampoon as "Biblical physics." Bacon and Galileo meant no harm to Christian theology, far from it; but they were determined to free science from theological control, i.e., to secularize it, which also implied, especially in Galileo's case, freeing Nature from final causes and teleology. "It is therefore of great importance," Bacon concluded, "to give to faith no more than the things that are faith's."[33]

Galileo's letter is reminiscent of still another declaration of independence, made almost exactly one hundred years earlier, by another Italian professor. This was Pietro Pomponazzi's *Apology* (1518) in which he defended the unorthodox position he had taken several years before in his book on the immortality of the soul. Like Galileo, Pomponazzi got into trouble with the clergy over these books and nar-

---

[32] *Discoveries and Opinions of Galileo,* ed. Stillman Drake (Garden City: Doubleday-Anchor Books, 1957), pp. 191-93.
[33] Francis Bacon, *Novum Organum,* Aphorism LXV.

rowly escaped condemnation as a heretic. And small wonder, for in effect they proclaimed a philosophy, as Galileo
was later to proclaim a "science," without benefit of clergy.
Carrying on in the Averroistic tradition Pomponazzi taught
a thoroughly naturalistic philosophy: a naturalistic theory
of the universe which excluded the supernatural except as
a Prime Mover, a naturalistic account of the origin of religions, and a naturalistic ethic. Only a few years after the
Church had established the immortality of the soul as an
official doctrine (at the Lateran Council of 1512) Pomponazzi was saying that it could be disproved by reason, and
that a truly high morality ought not to depend on a crude
doctrine of rewards and punishments. In these views he
followed the Stoics and chiefly Aristotle, whose arguments
he stripped down to what he thought was their true, and
unchristian, meaning. To avoid theological reprisals Pomponazzi took refuge in the doctrine of "double truth,"
which the Church had condemned in 1277 and again in
1512. As a Christian, Pomponazzi said, he accepted the
doctrine of the immortality of the soul on faith; but as a
philosopher he could not teach that it was demonstrable
by reason. "A philosopher cannot do this," he declared in
his *Apology;* "especially if he be a teacher, for in so teaching he would be teaching falsehood, . . . and he would be
acting contrary to the profession of philosophy." [34] Thus,
by Pomponazzi's day old man Philosophy had begun to cut
a bold and secular figure, especially in the Italian universities
in Venetian territory which had never had theological faculties. He became even more secular in the next century,
north as well as south of the Alps, as he was influenced, not
only by Renaissance Aristotelianism, but also by the new
scientific (and anti-Aristotelian) rationalism.

[34] Pietro Pomponazzi, *Apologia*, quoted in *The Renaissance Philosophy
of Man*, ed. Ernst Cassirer, *et al.*, p. 275.

Rubens' tableau included no specific symbols for political and economic theory. However, the same secular trend is observable in these spheres as in the spheres of science and philosophy. "The age in which political theory was cast in the mould of religion had yielded," says R. H. Tawney, "to one in which religious thought was no longer an imperious master, but a docile pupil." [35] Proof of this statement is contained in the new philosophy of the secular or "modern" state and the new "political arithmetic" or economic science which clearly implied a double standard of behavior, one operative in public or commercial life and another and different one in private life. "Business and politics are one thing, religious ethics another." "Merchants' doings must not be overthwarted by preachers and others, that cannot skill of their dealings," says the spokesman for business in Thomas Wilson's *Discourse upon Usury* (1572).[36] In proportion as this view gained ground in the sixteenth and seventeenth centuries teleology was banished from politics and economics, significantly at the same time that it was being abandoned as a working concept in natural science. To put it another way, the Church was obliged to climb down from its proud and traditional position as arbiter of man's total life and to confine its influence to the private aspect only, specifically to matters pertaining to faith and private morals.

The classic—and extreme—statement of the new political secularism is to be found in Niccolo Machiavelli and Thomas Hobbes. The general horror in which the Italian "devil" and the "atheist" of Malmesbury were held in the sixteenth and seventeenth centuries should not blind us to their importance in articulating the current secular trend.

[35] R. H. Tawney, *Religion and the Rise of Capitalism* (London, 1933), p. 190.

[36] Thomas Wilson, *A Discourse upon Usury*, ed. R. H. Tawney (London, 1925), p. 250.

Contemplating the realities of Italian politics in his day, Machiavelli, as is well known, came to the conclusion that to be successful the prince must be prepared on occasion to flout religious ethics. "It must be understood," he wrote in a characteristically extreme statement, "that a prince cannot observe all those things which are considered good in men, being often obliged, in order to maintain the state, to act against faith, against charity, against humanity, and against religion." [37] Machiavelli nowhere said that men should behave so in private. On the contrary, he believed that the health of the state ultimately depended not only on the machinations of the prince but also on the "virtue" (*virtù*) of the people, which was contingent upon the everyday adherence to at least some kind of ethical and religious standard. But the new thing in Machiavelli is that he crowded religion out of politics, except in so far as religion could be used as a booster for public morale. It was for this reason, incidentally, that he preferred paganism to Christianity: because it appeared to him to support the qualities most necessary for public spirit, e.g., patriotism, honor, glory in battle, etc., in contrast to Christianity which, he said, emphasized humility, lowliness, and a contempt for worldly objects, and thus "made men feeble."

Hobbes' standard was really not so much double as single. He made the secular state "sovereign" in every sphere of human society. In his theory—designed to solve the problem of order in modern society and particularly in England during the period of the Civil Wars—the state was likened to a "great Leviathan," "that Mortal God, to which we owe under the Immortal God our peace and defence." Like the proverbial monster fish, the Hobbesian state swallowed up everything in its wake, i.e., subordinated to itself all rival jurisdictions, including the ecclesiastical. In his

---

[37] Niccolo Machiavelli, *The Prince*, chap. 18.

chapter on "Power Ecclesiastical" in *Leviathan* (1651) Hobbes made it abundantly clear that "the Kingdom of Christ is not of this world," that "they that have no Kingdom can make no laws," that "preachers therefore have not magisterial, but ministerial power." In other words, Hobbes reduced "Power Ecclesiastical" to the "power to teach." But even this power to teach depended on the will of the sovereign. The legal existence of the Church, its government and even its creed, indeed morality itself could be authorized only by him. Extreme though Hobbes was, he only expressed in somewhat balder terms than his contemporaries the growing secularization of European politics and political theory.

Theology's dominion over historiography was similarly breaking down, as we know from such a work as Bayle's *Dictionary*. Bayle was by no means the first "modern" to write history from a secular point of view (Italian humanists were doing this as early as the fourteenth and fifteenth centuries) or to apply critical tests to historical sources; but he was certainly one of the first to dissolve the traditional distinction between "sacred" and "profane" history. Up to his time secular historians normally stopped short of "sacred" history, i.e., the events described in Holy Scripture and the subsequent history of the Church. Bayle, however, had no compunctions about invading that sphere, stripping it of its providential aura, and in general treating it as though it operated by the same laws as any other history, or indeed nature itself. He expressed incredulity of biblical chronology, he cast doubt on the accuracy of Christian records, he pointed out the similarity between certain biblical and pagan stories, he cut Old Testament heroes like Abraham and David down to human size, he planted doubts about the miracle stories. In his hands "sacred" history from the time of Christ to the Reformation fared, if anything, even worse. His clear inference was that there was nothing providential at all about the record, that if there was such a thing as Providence, Christians should be ashamed of it, that the victory in so-called "sacred" history usually went to the priests and theologians, which is to say, the devil. Bayle, it should be noted, was not the only biblical critic of the seventeenth century; he was only the most frank, the one who more than any other drew profane conclusions. In a sense his criticism was the logical outcome not only of his personal brush with ecclesiasticism but also of the philological labors of scholars like the Protestant Louis Cappel, who discovered that the Bible was not written in the original Hebrew but in Aramaic, and the Roman Catholic Richard Simon, who thought that the Old Testament had been gradually altered by a guild of scribes; also of inferences drawn by laymen like Spinoza and Hobbes, the latter of whom opined that the canon of the Bible was only what had been allowed by imperial mandate in the fourth century. The sum total of this early "higher criticism" was to undermine the verbal inspiration of the Bible, and, as Bayle showed in his *Dictionary*, to secularize sacred history itself.

Thus did the Great Secularization—still a tendency only, to be sure, and by no means a completed process—manifest itself in the various "sciences" in the sixteenth and seventeenth centuries. To appreciate its significance for the rise of religious scepticism, however, we need to realize that it was, at least to some extent, a response to the growing secularization of life itself. It was a response to the growth of the secular state in actual fact, and to the new economic system with its complicated techniques and its impersonal financial mechanism. On a still deeper level it was a response to the changing rhythm of life, as people, ordinary people as well as intellectuals, experienced it in their daily round.

Unfortunately, it is not possible to document this response as we would like, for history records more the conscious thoughts than the unconscious feelings of men. The German historian Bernhard Groethuysen came close to doing this, however, in his important and still little-known work on the origins of the bourgeois world-view in seventeenth- and eighteenth-century France.[38] Drawing largely upon contemporary sermons and pedagogical treatises Groethuysen tried to demonstrate the emergence of a new type of man in European life, the middle-class townsman, who differed from all previous types. The preachers constantly belabored this man, not for denying the creed or ceasing to go to church, but for holding an outlook, a "profane ideology," which made much of the teaching of the Church seem psychologically unreal. He came to have this outlook, not by conscious appropriation of arguments by sceptical philosophers (whose books in any case he rarely read), but by a natural—and largely unconscious—response to the life of business he led. How could he fully appreciate the Church's teaching about death and the priority of the after life when it was his constant endeavor to learn to be at home in this world and to drive out the "irrational"? How could he truly believe in Providence when he had learned to trust in his own strength to rule the future? Everything in his daily life conspired to make him affirm this world and to seek happiness "here." He was "different from the man of earlier times for whom life was intelligible only in terms of transcendental explanations, and to whom it seemed that he could not live without answers to the last questions."[39] He called himself a Christian but he could

[38] Bernhard Groethuysen, *Die Entstehung der Bürgerlichen Welt- und Lebensanschauung in Frankreich* (2 vols.; Halle, 1927).

[39] *Ibid.*, Vol. I, p. xviii.

normally do perfectly well without the transcendental explanations.

This thesis seems to me to have a wider application than even Groethuysen supposed. I have no doubt that some such unconscious transvaluation of values must have been taking place on a broad front not only among people specifically designated "burghers" but among other people as well, and that the scepticism of the intellectuals was itself in large part a response to this "life." I have no doubt, moreover, that Groethuysen was substantially correct when he said that "Herein lies the deep ground of modern unbelief." [40]

4.

To state this proposition in still broader terms: the seventeenth century presided at the birth of a new secular faith which did not so much oppose as simply outflank the old religious faith. This was the faith that later blossomed into the Enlightenment idea of progress. Essentially, as we have seen (see pp. 74 ff.), it was a vision of man's power to meliorate his living conditions, to build an "empire" or "kingdom of man" on earth.

The novelty and essential secularity of this new faith can be appreciated only against the background of a view of history which had been commonplace in Christian circles for over a thousand years. This view was fundamentally pessimistic and providential. Both nature and man were believed to be in a state of decay, to have declined from the pristine state which God had created. God stood in judgment on history and would terminate it, according to the Book of Revelation, at the appointed hour. History, in other words, had no extended future, man no chance of

[40] *Ibid.*, Vol. II, p. 217.

creating a permanent "empire" in time. The decisive event was, of course, the Fall, in consequence of which man became enfeebled in body, reason, and will. Man's Fall caused nature's fall, owing to the close correspondence between microcosm and geocosm. Though traditional, this view received a fresh emphasis in the sixteenth and early seventeenth centuries, with the increased emphasis put upon sin and the need for divine help by the Protestant reformers, and with the bewilderment caused by the decline of the Church and other medieval standards of value. Even the new science contributed to the prevailing gloom by showing that not only the sublunary world but also the celestial world (the macrocosm) was subject to mutability if not corruption. John Donne reflected this view in his *First Anniversary*, as did Godfrey Goodman, soon to become bishop of Gloucester, in his celebrated *Fall of Man, or The Corruption of Nature* (1616), and a host of others.

> The world [lamented Donne] did in her cradle take a fall,
> And turn'd her brains, and took a general maim,
> Wronging each joint of th' universal frame.
> The noblest part, man, felt it first; and then
> Both beasts and plants, cursed in the curse of man.
> So did the world from the first hour decay. . . .[41]

Already in Donne's age, however, a new view of history, which was eventually to become a new secular faith, was rising to challenge the idea of decay. Doubtless, many things conspired to produce a more optimistic view: new inventions such as the compass and printing, better communications, economic and geographical expansion, the progress of luxury, even the new millennial visions of Protestant theorists who because of the recent successes of the Protestant movement preferred now to dwell on the temporal millennium rather than the general debacle predicted

[41] Donne, *The First Anniversary*, lines 196-201.

by the Book of Revelation. But the new science, at first so disconcerting to tender souls like John Donne, would seem to have been the most decisive factor. In the course of the century the new science raised men's hopes by changing their notions about both the macrocosm and microcosm. In the first place, it rejected the notion that what happened in the microcosm (man) affected in any way the macrocosm (nature). As we have seen, the notion slowly but surely took hold that nature was an impersonal order not designed specifically for man's use or tied to his destiny. Hence, even though man might be fallen, this did not argue the fall of nature, and there seemed to be no empirical evidence that nature had fallen, in fact quite the contrary. Moreover, scientists and amateurs of science were beginning to talk with more confidence about the microcosm too, to marvel at man's power and achievements, especially in the "modern" period of history. Hence, while they might continue to believe theologically in original sin and Providence, what they liked most to talk about was man's heroism and his ingeniousness in devising new methods and concepts of knowledge. And why should they not believe in man's power in view of the marvelous new inventions and flights of the human mind, undreamed of by the ancients. Donne's lament that "we're scarce our fathers' shadows cast at noon" simply did not describe what a man like Henry Power, "doctor of physic," knew about the moderns who invented "the experimental philosophy." On the contrary, according to Power:

This is the age wherein all men's souls are in a kind of fermentation, and the spirit of wisdom and learning begins to mount and free itself from those dross and terrene impediments wherewith it hath been so long clogged. . . . This is the age wherein (me thinks) philosophy comes in with a spring-tide. . . . These are the days that must lay a new foundation of a more magnificent philosophy, never to be overthrown: that will empirically and sensibly canvas the phenomena of nature, deducing the causes of things from such originals in nature as we observe are producible by art and the infallible demonstration of mechanics.[42]

Two new metaphors, used repeatedly by the seventeenth-century "Moderns" in their quarrel with the "Ancients," epitomize this new confidence in man and man's quasi-providential role in history. The first affirmed man's intellectual equality with the ancients, the second his superiority in knowledge and method. Both appear side by side in such a work as Fontenelle's *Digression on the Ancients and Moderns* (1688). Fontenelle, champion and popularizer of the new science and soon to become secretary of the Paris Academy of Sciences, first compared the human brain to the size of trees. Trees, he affirmed, are obviously just as large today as they were in the days of Homer, Plato, and Demosthenes; *ergo*, modern brains are equal to ancient brains. "We are all perfectly equal, ancients and moderns, Greeks, Romans, and French" for the reason that "Nature uses a certain paste which is always the same."[43] True, Fontenelle says nothing about Adam's brain, but it is perfectly clear from the metaphor that he did not accept the decay idea, at least as regards human brain power. Nor did Fontenelle's English contemporary, Joseph Glanvill, despite his undoubted belief in the doctrine of original sin. Significantly, Glanvill, also a believer in "modern" progress, emphasized "our decay and ruin by the Fall, particularly those of our intellectual powers" only when he was attacking the philosophy of Aristotle and "School-Divinity" which he considered to be litigious and barren of fruits. When he turned to another kind of philosophy, the natural

[42] Henry Power, *Experimental Philosophy* (London, 1664), p. 192.
[43] Bernard Le Bovier de Fontenelle, *Oeuvres diverses* (La Haye, 1728), Vol. II, pp. 125, 127.

philosophy of his own day, he frequently became rhapsodic. "Methinks those generous Virtuosi, who dwell in an higher region than other mortals, should make a middle species between the Platonical Theoi and common humanity." The constellation of illustrious worthies who compose the Royal Society, he said, "is enough to strike dead the opinion of the world's decay and conclude it in its prime." [44]

Fontenelle's second metaphor compared the collective mind of the race to the mind of a single individual. Just as the old man knows more than the boy, so the present age knows more and reasons better than antiquity. Actually, said Fontenelle, the metaphor is not exact, for the collective man of whom I speak "will have no old age." That is to say, the race, unlike the individual, "will never degenerate, and the sound views of all the good minds through the centuries will always be building upon each other." [45] Fontenelle was, of course, only repeating what Baconians and Cartesians had been saying all through the century. "*Antiquitas saeculi juventus mundi*," Bacon had said in *The Advancement of Learning* (1605). According to Bacon, as to Fontenelle, not only had man's "stock of experience" increased but his methods and instruments of thinking had greatly improved in the modern epoch. And the only thing that would prevent still greater progress in the future, both intellectual and material progress, was that men would "despair and think things impossible." If only they would shake off their excessive reverence for antiquity and realize their own strength, the old "*non ultra*" in knowledge would surely give way to "*plus ultra*."

Of course, these seventeenth-century "Moderns" intended no disrespect to divinity by their preachments about progress. On the contrary, they sincerely thought that

[44] Joseph Glanvill, "An Apology for Philosophy," in *Scepsis Scientifica*, ed. John Owen (London, 1885), pp. 208-209.
[45] Fontenelle, *Oeuvres diverses*, Vol. II, p. 134.

natural philosophy, upon which progress depended, increased rather than diminished a man's religion since it revealed the power and intelligence of the Creator. Indeed, in opposition to his detractors, the scientist's investigation of nature was often depicted as a religious duty or even vocation. "Physics," said Fontenelle, "becomes a kind of theology when it is pursued correctly." [46] At the same time, however, the Moderns clearly delineated a philosophy of history in which, as Professor Butterfield has said, "man could play Providence over himself," and in which God's Providence played a comparatively inconspicuous role. Bacon's favorite word was "power," and he used it to denote two ideas. First of all, there was God's power which natural philosophy revealed in the same way that the study of Scripture revealed God's will. There was also, however, man's power and this was the denotation that he used most commonly. Over and over again, in the *Novum Organum* and elsewhere, he referred to "human utility and power," "the power and dominion of the human race over the universe," and similar ideas. Man, then, was the real hero of history, especially since he had broken loose from thralldom to the ancients, though to be sure he received his power by divine bequest. By means of his power man could establish a veritable utopia on earth, not the sort of utopia or millennium foretold by the Book of Revelation, but a utilitarian "kingdom" or "empire of man over things" in which the emphasis was on the relief of man's worldly estate. Something of the nature of this utopia can be gleaned from the rhapsodic words of one of Bacon's followers.

Should those heroes [the great scientists of the seventeenth century] go on as they have happily begun, they'll fill the world with wonders. And I doubt not but what posterity will find many things that are now but rumors, verified into prac-

[46] *Ibid.*, Vol. III, p. 8.

tical realities. It may be some ages hence, a voyage to the
southern unknown tracts, yea possibly the moon, will not be
more strange than one to America. To them that come after us,
it may be as ordinary to buy a pair of wings to fly into re-
motest regions; as now a pair of boots to ride a journey. And to
confer at the distance of the Indies by sympathetic convey-
ances, may be as usual to future times, as to us in a literary
correspondence. The restoration of gray hairs to juvenility, and
renewing the exhausted marrow, may at length be effected
without a miracle. And the turning of the now comparative
desert world into a paradise may not improbably be expected
from late agriculture.[47]

This faith, as it may be called, was not, of course, full
blown in the seventeenth century. Most of the "moderns"
hedged it round with restrictions of one sort or other.
Fontenelle, for example, believed in the indefinite progress
of scientific knowledge now that man had learned to think
correctly, but he did not believe in progress in eloquence
and poetry, nor in progress in morality and happiness.
While Bacon had a wider view of progress than Fontenelle,
he did not believe in its inevitability or perhaps even in
its indefinite extension. What cannot be missed in this literature, however, is the change in psychological tone, the sense
of new beginnings, almost of salvation by human works.
The idea of decay no longer held the imagination, especially
after the seventeen-forties and seventeen-fifties. Faith in
man's power was now more the focus of imagination, his
power over nature, and his power to achieve something
new and significant in time. Men like Bacon, Henry Power,
and Glanvill might still believe in divine Providence, but
what they talked about mostly was human providence. Bacon was a Christian and Condorcet was not, but the
Englishman's "Kingdom of Man" clearly prefigured the
Frenchman's secular dream of a "Tenth Epoch."

[47] Glanvill, *Scepsis Scientifica,* pp. 156-157.

CHAPTER III

"The Death of God"

1.

Friedrich Nietzche, the nineteenth-century German philosopher, liked to speak in parables. One of his most striking parables is the parable of the madman in *The Joyful Wisdom* (1882). A madman rushes into the market place and cries out: "I seek God! . . . Where is God gone? I mean to tell you! *We have killed him,*—you and I! . . . God is dead! . . . The holiest and the mightiest that the world has hitherto possessed, has bled to death under our knife,—who will wipe the blood from us?" But the crowd in the market place, not understanding his message, berates and mocks him. In agony the madman then exclaims:

I come too early, I am not yet at the right time. This prodigious event is still on its way, and is travelling,—it has not yet reached men's ears. Lightning and thunder need time, the light of the stars needs time, deeds need time, even after they are done, to be seen and heard. This deed is as yet further from them than the furthest star,—*and yet they have done it!* [1]

This remarkable parable was both prophetic and descriptive. It was prophetic in the sense that Nietzsche foresaw a "period of gloom and eclipse" when westerners would

[1] Friedrich Nietzsche, *Complete Works*, ed. Oscar Levy (Edinburgh and London, 1910), Vol. X, pp. 167-69; see also pp. 275-76.

have fully understood what it meant to live in a godless world, a world which, so to speak, had been loosened from its sun. It was also, however, descriptive of what Nietzsche believed to be a fact of supreme historical and cultural importance. He was saying, in effect, that in the nineteenth century the sceptical tradition had moved into a new phase which was both qualitatively and quantitatively different from the previous phases. In this phase the intellectual classes did not seek merely to convict the *Christian* God with the weapons of reason; they drew their knives and assassinated God himself. Thus, for Nietzsche at least, "the death of God" supplanted "crush the infamous thing" as a symbol of the sceptical movement. By his use of the simile of the market place Nietzsche also intimated that the rage had now spread beyond the intellectuals to the masses whom the philosophers of the eighteenth century had been so careful not to arouse with their infidelity. Nietzsche himself, despite his prophecy of a time of troubles ahead, exulted in the deed: deicide, whatever its immediate historical consequences, opened up the horizon and the sea to "free spirits," as perhaps never before in history. But to become worthy of their newly found freedom, he warned, men must themselves "become Gods." By these words, put into the mouth of the madman, Nietzsche may have been thinking of the host of ersatz-religions or faiths which were in fact substituted for religion in the nineteenth century. It seems more likely, however, that he had in mind merely his own "philosophy of power" which became the crown of his philosophic career.

Did Nietzsche's madman read correctly the signs of the times? Of course he exaggerated. Christianity, much less religion, did not literally die in the nineteenth century. This was, in fact, one of Christianity's greatest eras of expansion —outside Europe; and inside Europe, where it was distinctly less successful, it was lacking neither in vitality nor resourcefulness. The dechristianizing movement of revolutionary France had petered out with the accession of Napoleon, and during the early decades of the new century the climate of romanticism supported a genuine religious revival in protest against the sceptical tendencies of the Enlightenment. Later in the century, when the fires of evangelicalism and tractarianism burned lower, liberal Protestantism made a great effort to adjust itself, and not altogether unsuccessfully, to the new wave of sceptical opinion. We should also not fail to note that the nineteenth century produced its share of creative religious thinkers: the great Schleiermacher, for instance, who invented a new "theology of feeling"; John Henry Newman, Rome's greatest convert, and prior to his conversion, a leader of the Oxford Movement; the agonized Søren Kierkegaard who laid the basis for a new existentialist approach to religion; Christian socialists like F. D. Maurice and Charles Kingsley; and others like Samuel Taylor Coleridge and Goethe who, while they did not fit into an orthodox framework, held fast to a religious conception of the universe.

Nevertheless, Nietzsche's madman was right in the main. The evidence is simply overwhelming that, to use another nineteenth-century metaphor, the sea of faith was continuing to recede, faster than ever before, despite everything that the religious parties could do to stem it. The "turning of the balance," as the historian J. M. Robertson has termed the movement toward scepticism, occurred earliest and most openly on the European continent where religion was closely identified with political and social reaction. But England soon caught up. In 1859, John Stuart Mill could still describe his country as "destitute of faith, but terrified at scepticism," in which people felt sure, not so much that the old religious opinions were true, as that they were perhaps still necessary for the preservation of society.[2] But by the seventies and eighties, scepticism in England was not only widespread but largely divested of that "terror" which its supporters might once have felt at the public utterance of their views.

In 1879—obviously Nietzsche was not the only person to observe the "death of God" in the nineteenth century— John Henry Newman, upon receiving notice of his elevation to the College of Cardinals, warned against "the great apostasy" which was taking place in all countries. "Liberalism in religion," he said (by "liberalism" he meant "the doctrine that there is no positive truth in religion, but that one creed is as good as another") was daily gaining force and threatening to ensnare the whole earth. In 1872, the English statesman William Ewart Gladstone had said even more pointedly, in an address to the Collegiate Institution of Liverpool:

I doubt whether any such noxious crop has been gathered in such rank abundance from the press of England in any former year of our literary history as in this present year of our redemption. . . . *It is not only the Christian Church, or only the Holy Scripture, or only Christianity, which is attacked.* The disposition is boldly proclaimed to deal with root and branch, and to snap utterly the ties which, under the still venerable name of Religion, unite man with the unseen world, and lighten the struggles and the woes of life by the hope of a better land.[3]

And lest this evidence be partially suspect as coming from persons closely identified with the religious camp and therefore perhaps overprone to see "apostasy," we have the cor-

[2] John Stuart Mill, *On Liberty* (New York: Dutton—Everyman's Library, 1931), pp. 83-4.
[3] Quoted in J. M. Robertson, *A History of Freethought in the Nineteenth Century* (New York: G. P. Putnam's Sons, 1930), Vol. II, p. 396. Italics mine.

roborative remarks of two prominent men of letters. Like Newman, Matthew Arnold observed a "revolution" in thinking about religion. Clergymen, he observed in the Preface to *Literature and Dogma* (1873), everywhere lament "the spread of scepticism" and the decreasing hold which religion now has on the masses of the people—"*the lapsed masses*, as some writers call them"; and indeed the artisan class, formerly awed by religion, now "seem to have hardly any awe of it at all, and they freely question its truth." "Once vivid faiths," wrote Lord Morley in 1874, "[are now become] very numb. Religion, whatever destinies may be in store for it, is at least for the present hardly any longer an organic power." [4] These are just a few examples of what by the seventies had become a universal observation, and they testify, as does Nietzsche, to the new lengths to which scepticism had gone in the nineteenth century and also to its spread to a wider clientele.

In truth, to perceive this sceptical "revolution" hardly required a man of extraordinary acumen like Nietzsche or Newman. The signs were there for all to read in the neologisms, the changing literary taste, the decline in prestige of clergymen and theologians as well as the decline in church attendance, the changes in public law pertaining to the churches, and, perhaps most convincing of all, the life histories of innumerable individuals who experienced what might be called religious conversions in reverse.

Gladstone himself must have been present at the first meetings of the famous Metaphysical Society[5] when

[4] Matthew Arnold, *Literature and Dogma* (New York: Macmillan, 1873), pp. vi-vii; John Viscount Morley, *On Compromise*, in *Works* (London, 1921), Vol. III, p. 17.

[5] The Metaphysical Society was a typical Victorian debating club, founded in 1869 to debate the great question of the day, religion *vs.* science. As such, it included men of different persuasions, Protestants and Catholics as well as sceptics, some of them among the most illustrious names of Victorian England.

Thomas Henry Huxley, "Darwin's bulldog," was parading his new word "agnostic," invented, as Huxley said, to give him a tail like other foxes. "Agnostic" was but one of many sceptical neologisms. "Positivism," the philosophy, named by the French sociologist Auguste Comte, "to supersede theology in the spiritual direction of the human race," had long been *à la mode,* and in 1851 the freethinker George Jacob Holyoake, casting about for a term less compromising than "infidel" or "atheist," hit on the word "secularist" and helped to found a National Secular Society. While the Metaphysical Society was still holding its debates, men were already talking about the "conflict between religion and science" (the title of a well-known book published in 1874) which Andrew D. White, the first president of Cornell University, later called the "warfare between science and theology."

When in his Liverpool speech Gladstone referred to the "noxious crop" gathered from the press of England, he had particularly in mind three recent books by Herbert Spencer, David Friedrich Strauss, and Winwood Reade. If he had been so inclined, however, and had had the leisure, he might have compiled a truly formidable bibliography of nineteenth-century scepticism, indicating a profound change in literary taste. Such a bibliography would have included, in addition to noted books by men like Strauss and Ernest Renan in the so-called Higher Criticism of the Bible, the two Ludwigs, Feuerbach and Büchner, in philosophy, and interpreters of Darwinism, like Huxley, as well as a great number of lesser titles, such as Charles Bradlaugh's *Freethinkers' Text-Book.* It would have listed novels and poems: Mrs. Humphry Ward's *Robert Ellsmere* (1888), for instance, which Gladstone himself reviewed, and Edward Fitzgerald's famous translation of *The Rubaiyat of Omar Khayyam* (1859), which by the end of the century had become one of the most popular poems in the English language, not merely because of its aesthetic appeal but also undoubtedly because its antitheistic Epicureanism struck a response. It would have cited the new bold periodicals, ranging from the highbrow *Fortnightly Review* under the editorship of George Henry Lewes and Lord Morley, which spelled God with a small "g" (at least in Morley's own articles publicizing the French *philosophes*), to the lowbrow *National Reformer* of Bradlaugh, which carried scepticism to the working masses. Had Gladstone spoken thirty years later he might also have turned his guns on an institution like the notorious Rationalist Press Association, whose object was to reprint in cheap editions the works of outstanding rationalists and freethinkers.

He might also have taken cognizance of the universities, religious tests for entrance to which were abandoned in his own country in 1871, and which were largely secularized in Italy and France by the mid-eighties. Commenting on the theological faculty which had once occupied the place of honor in German universities, Friedrich Paulsen wrote in 1902 that "it is now scarcely mentioned in the same breath with the sciences, the peculiar pride of the present day. Numerous representatives of a scientific radicalism are inclined to exclude it altogether, or to relegate it to the past. . . . Theological students can scarcely avoid meeting with such or similar opinions." [6] Professor Paulsen also remarked on the loss of prestige of the clerical calling, which many were saying had outlived its usefulness, and which, indeed, was having trouble filling its ranks not only in Germany but also in France.

The legal reforms carried through within Gladstone's lifetime were still another barometer of society's growing

[6] Friedrich Paulsen, *The German Universities and University Study* (New York: Charles Scribner's Sons, 1906), p. 384.

secularism. In England, in addition to the aforementioned reform applying to the universities, the secularists succeeded in abolishing the disabilities of nontheistic witnesses, in discrediting the blasphemy laws, and in securing the right of avowed atheists to sit in Parliament. This last, perhaps their greatest triumph, came as the result of the famous Bradlaugh case of the eighties. Bradlaugh, an atheist and elected member from Northampton, refused to take the oath of allegiance required of all members of Parliament, on the ground that it contained the expression "So help me God." The case dragged on for six years until finally, in 1886, Bradlaugh was permitted to take the oath (he had by then indicated his willingness to swear it, on the understanding that to do so did not bind his conscience). Two years later Parliament passed an Affirmation Bill permitting members simply to "affirm" their allegiance. Gladstone, be it noted, had been for a bill of affirmation all along. Defender of the faith, he nevertheless took the position that to exclude atheists did religion more harm than good, and that in any case the House of Commons had no jurisdiction to exclude anyone who had been duly elected. In 1883, he supported "affirmation" in a famous speech which not only revealed his liberalism and common sense but which pointed infallibly to the dominant form that the "death of God" was currently taking in English thought. Not atheism, but agnosticism, he told the House, was "the specific form of irreligion" with which the country had to contend.

[Atheism] is a rare opinion very seldom met with; but what is frequently met with is that form of opinion which would teach us that, whatever may be beyond the visible things of this world, whatever there may be beyond this short span of life, you know and you can know nothing of it, and that it is a bootless undertaking to attempt to establish relations with it.

That is the mischief of the age, and that mischief you do not attempt to touch.[7]

Meanwhile, on the continent even more extreme steps were being taken in the direction of what the French called "the lay state" (*l'état laïc*). This was the period of the *Kulturkampf* or "struggle for civilization" between the Roman church and the secular state. In Prussia, Bismarck's attempt to subordinate the Church to the state ultimately failed, although it had the indirect effect of helping to spread disrespect for religion. In both Italy and France, however, the state was effectually dechristianized, in the former by the Law of Guarantees of 1871, in opposition to which the pope chose to become a "prisoner" in the Vatican, and in the latter by the Law of Separation of 1905 which disestablished Roman Catholicism as the state religion of France. In both countries, as has previously been noted, education was secularized. The Coppino education law of 1877 closed the university theological faculties and introduced compulsory elementary education by the state without religious instruction, except at the request of parents. The famous Ferry laws of the eighties imposed practically a secular monopoly of education in France. The effect of the *Kulturkampf* in general, and of the new education in particular, was to bring up a new generation of young people who were either hostile or indifferent to religion. It was both a symptom and a cause of the growing scepticism of western European society.

What, however, must have been particularly distressing to men like Gladstone and Newman were the conversions in reverse among the intelligentsia which were literally legion in the nineteenth century, and which were a sufficiently important phenomenon to become a theme in litera-

[7] Quoted in John Viscount Morley, *The Life of William Ewart Gladstone* (New York: Macmillan, 1921), Vol. III, p. 20.

ture. These conversions varied a good deal, of course. Some, like that of Cardinal Newman's younger brother, Francis, were from orthodox Christianity to another form of theism, thus following more or less the familiar pattern of the Enlightenment. Others, however, were more drastic, involving the abdication or suspension of any kind of formal religious belief. We can see what Newman meant by "the great apostasy" when we dig down into the life histories of such men as the Frenchmen Auguste Comte and Ernest Renan who abandoned the Catholic faith of their forefathers, Renan while he was actually training for holy orders in the seminary of St. Sulpice; the German David Friedrich Strauss, whose notorious *Life of Jesus* (1835-1836) estranged him from his father and cost him his teaching post at the University of Tübingen; the great Swiss historian Jacob Burckhardt who, upon being confronted as a theological student with the Higher Criticism, gave up all thought of a clerical career; and Englishmen like Charles Darwin who, generally reticent and cautious about religious ideas, finally drifted into scepticism, as we know from his autobiography and letters; the mathematician William Kingdon Clifford who, originally an ardent High Churchman like Gladstone, went on to live by his own motto, "Thou shalt live and not formulize"; Sir Leslie Stephen, brought up as an evangelical Christian, who gave up holy orders and became one of the leading agnostics as well as a leading literary figure of his day; and Charles Bradlaugh whom the arguments of an obscurantist and unyielding Anglican pastor appear to have driven from Christianity at the age of fifteen, and who then became a deist and eventually an atheist. Bradlaugh's case is especially significant, for he represents the appearance of a new type, the working-class sceptic. The son of a solicitor's clerk and a nursemaid, he was entirely self-taught, and earned his way as dragoon and errand boy before becoming the freethinking editor, lecturer, and politician who made it his business to communicate scepticism to the masses. The census on church attendance taken by R. Mudie Smith for the London *Daily News* in 1902-1903 should be read in the light of these "conversions." Smith discovered that only a little over two in every eleven persons attended places of worship in London on Sundays over a period of more than a year. These figures would have to be revised upward for England at large, but there was evidently a considerable falling off in church attendance in the country as well as the towns in the course of the century.

Not only men, but women, too, experienced the conversion in reverse. Perhaps the best known example of a nineteenth-century female "convert" of this type is the novelist George Eliot whose father, a churchman of the old school, threatened to disown her when she determined to give up going to church. As a young woman Marian Evans had been powerfully influenced by evangelicalism and possibly accepted the Calvinist doctrine of election. But reading in the eighteenth-century rationalists convinced her that this was not for her, and by 1843 she had already experienced the sensation of conversion to another way of thinking. "For my part," she wrote to Mrs. Pears, "I wish to be among the ranks of that glorious crusade that is seeking to set Truth's Holy Sepulchre free from a usurped domination. We shall then see her resurrection!" [8]

Another woman, not so scholarly as George Eliot or Mrs. Humphry Ward but no less thoughtful, actually made the conversion in reverse the pivot of a sensational novel. The parable of the hunter and the white bird of Truth (we meet Truth again!) in Olive Schreiner's *Story of an*

---

[8] George Eliot, *Letters,* ed. Gordon S. Haight (New Haven: Yale University Press, 1954-55), Vol. I, p. 125.

African Farm (1883) epitomizes, indeed, the experience of
many a nineteenth-century sceptic, including that of the
authoress herself.[9] A hunter sees in a lake the reflection of a
great silver bird which an old man named Wisdom tells him
is named Truth. The hunter then determines to catch the
bird in a net which he weaves with the thread of his Wishes
on the Shuttle of Imagination and into which he throws the
few grains of Credulity which his father bequeathed to him
at his death. But alas, none of the birds that he ensnares and
locks up in an iron cage "called a new creed"—they sing
songs of a human God and immortality and reward after
death—turns out to be Truth. "The birds you have
caught," says Wisdom, "are of the brood of Lies." He who
sets out in search of Truth must leave Superstition forever
and wander down into the land of Absolute Negation and
Denial. He must then go into the country of Dry Sunshine
where the mountains of Stern Reality will rise before him.
"*Beyond* them lies Truth." The hunter forthwith breaks
his iron cage although the people denounce him for a
lunatic and atheist. He follows Wisdom's advice and after
many years of hard toil carving out steps to climb the
mountain, he dies clasping to his breast a white feather
which at last had fluttered down from the white sky above.
The stranger who tells this parable to the young Dutch
boy, Waldo, sums up Miss Schreiner's moral in language
that would have struck a response in many a nineteenth-
century sceptic's breast.

Do you wonder what I mean? To all who have been born in
the old faith there comes a time of danger, when the old slips

---

[9] The daughter of a missionary of German birth sent out to South
Africa by the London Missionary Society, Olive Schreiner (1862-1920)
developed unorthodox religious views which estranged her from most
of her family. Her novel was a success in England, arousing the interest
of Gladstone himself.

from us, and we have not yet planted our feet on the new. . . .
We have proved the religion our mothers fed us on to be a
delusion; in our bewilderment we see no rule by which to
guide our steps day by day; and yet every day we must step
somewhere. . . . In the end experience will inevitably teach
us that the laws for a wise and noble life have a foundation
infinitely deeper than the fiat of any being, God or man—even
in the groundwork of human nature.[10]

The stranger then hands the boy a book which he says may
give him a center on which to focus his ideas. But "you
must not expect too much," he says. "We of this generation
are not destined to eat and be satisfied as our fathers were;
we must be content to go hungry."

2.

For the purpose of analysis the "death of God"—the critical side of nineteenth-century scepticism—may be boiled
down to a number of characteristic arguments. There were
at least six such arguments which we shall label, for the
sake of convenience, the utilitarian, the scientific, and the
anthropological (referring to the new science of anthropology); the psychological, the economic, and the historical. Obviously, the scepticism of any given individual, a
Karl Marx, say, or a Sir James Frazer, might be, and usually was, a blend of two or more of these modes, although
it might be chiefly noted for one in particular. The first
two, and to some extent the third, resembled modes already
familiar in the eighteenth century, but with significant ad-
ditions and elaborations, as we shall see. The last three,
however, were essentially novel, reflecting new intellectual
currents and helping to account for the more radical tenor
of nineteenth-century scepticism. Under the impact of new

[10] Olive Schreiner, *The Story of an African Farm* (2nd ed.; London,
1883), p. 151.

knowledge and new perspectives, intellectuals were emboldened to reduce religion (not merely Christianity, but all religion) to "opiate" or "myth," to psychological "self-projection" or "reflex" of the economic world; to relegate it to the realm of the "unknowable," or to classify it as a "phase," presumably the most primitive and childish phase, in the evolution of the human mind. The common thread running through all these arguments was that man made religion, and not religion, man. In the words of Ludwig Feuerbach, "Theology is anthropology."

The utilitarian argument, advanced by Benthamites, secularists, and often by socialists, stands in a class by itself, for, unlike the other arguments, it was concerned, not so much with the truth of religion as with its "utility," i.e., its effects on society. Thus, it is reminiscent of the pragmatic argument of the *philosophes* (see p. 46), brought up to date and adjusted to the problems of an industrial society. In brief, it charged that priests and rulers formed an unholy alliance to keep the middle and lower classes down, that, in a word, religion almost invariably threw its weight on the side of political and social reaction. And indeed there was considerable truth to these accusations, at least for the first half of the century. Was not the Roman church the inveterate foe of the French Revolution? What was one to think of Pius IX's Syllabus of Errors which denounced as an error the assertion that "the pope can and should reconcile himself to and agree with progress, liberalism, and modern civilization?" Did not the Prussian Lutheran church likewise condemn political and social democracy? Did not the Anglican bishops oppose the Reform Bill of 1832? Were not Methodist and evangelical leaders opposed to Chartism and trade unions? Did they not teach that poverty was ordained by God? The conclusion seemed ineluctable: if there was to be reform and progress for "the greatest number," religion would have to be shorn of its prestige and power in society.

Jeremy Bentham's *Analysis of the Influence of Natural Religion on the Temporal Happiness of Mankind* (1822) is an excellent summary of the utilitarian argument from the standpoint of a middle-class liberal. Religion, said Bentham, did not meet the test of "utility"; on the contrary, it manifestly injured both society and the individual. It injured the individual by instilling in him fears of endless torment, depriving him of innocent pleasures, and subjecting him to the will of a capricious tyrant. It injured society by creating intolerance of unbelievers and heretics, impeding intellectual progress, and giving power to priests who connive with rulers to plunder the community and maintain the social *status quo*. Deeper still, religion, by inculcating duty to God, subtracts from duty to man and creates an aversion to social improvement. "Our duty to God," said Bentham, "is a deduction from the pleasures of the individual without at all benefiting the species." [11] In a word, the English Utilitarians looked upon religion as "a great moral evil" which consecrated a social order badly in need of liberal reform. James Mill, according to his son, regarded religion

with the feelings due not to a mere mental delusion, but to a great moral evil. He looked upon it as the greatest enemy of morality: first, by setting up fictitious excellences,—belief in creeds, devotional feelings, and ceremonies, not connected with the good of human-kind,—and causing these to be accepted as substitutes for genuine virtues: but above all, by radically vitiating the standard of morals. . . .[12]

The utilitarian type of argument also frequently crops up

[11] Philip Beauchamp (Jeremy Bentham and George Grote), *Analysis of the Influence of Natural Religion on the Temporal Happiness of Mankind* (London, 1822), p. 41.

[12] John Stuart Mill, *Autobiography*, chap. 2.

in the writings of secularists and socialists, though hardly ever in such unadulterated form and, of course, with more express application to the social evils produced by the Industrial Revolution. In a lecture delivered in 1879, Professor Robert Flint of the University of Edinburgh rightly attributed the rise of "secularism" (the movement led by George Jacob Holyoake and Charles Bradlaugh) among the manual workers of England more to "political dissatisfaction" than to rational conviction. The clergy and governing classes, he said, had asked for it by their "blind opposition," in the period after the French Revolution, to political and social progress. Speaking as a Christian, Flint thought that secularism would evaporate if the clergy were to address themselves to the real needs of the lower classes, "so that no man might be tempted to believe that religion is one of the things which stand either in the way of his personal happiness or of justice to his class." [13] The well-known socialist aphorism "Religion is the opiate of the people" also rested partially on this utilitarian base. Regardless of whether religion was true, it had observably bad effects on people: so contended the majority of both "utopian" and "scientific" socialists, though this was obviously not all that they contended. Religion sanctified all the abominations of capitalist as well as monarchist regimes. Religion allied itself with the existing order of property relations which it hoped to preserve by putting the people to sleep with the pipe dream of otherworldly salvation. Religion discouraged social reform, in fact "activity" of any kind, by its otherworldly emphasis. "The mortgage that the peasant has on heavenly blessings guarantees the mortgage that the bourgeois has on peasant lands." [14]

[13] Robert Flint, *Anti-Theistic Theories* (Edinburgh and London, 1879), p. 249.

[14] Karl Marx, *The Class Struggles in France, 1848-50* (New York: International Publishers, n. d.), p. 85.

Hence, for these reasons among others, the "True Socialist" Moses Hess professed a "philosophy of activity" and preferred "morality" to "religion." "Religion" preaches subservience, obsequiousness before authority; "morality," on the other hand, demands "activity," doing something to rectify the ills of capitalist society.[15] And Marx too, though he had no use for Hess's "morality," advocated a philosophy of activity which, in contrast to the otherworldly philosophy of religion, would enable the exploited to change the face of society to their advantage.

As previously intimated, the utilitarian argument almost invariably intertwined, even in Bentham, with arguments impugning the truth of religion. Among these latter none was more pervasive, nor more generally persuasive, than the argument from science. This argument was not new, but it was now more sharply stated and forced to conclusions more damaging to religion than ever before. It can be analyzed into two chief arguments which often interlaced, if somewhat illogically, in the thought of the day. The first of these was epistemological, centering in the new word "agnosticism." The second, more dogmatic in its tendency, was metaphysical, deriving from a new idea of nature which, for many, told overwhelmingly against a religious view of the universe.

"The word Agnosticism," Sir Leslie Stephen wrote in 1876, describes "a form of creed already common and daily spreading." The word was coined by Thomas Henry Huxley, as Stephen duly noted, but the idea had been formulated by an earlier generation, by Auguste Comte, the prophet of French Positivism, and in England by the Mills and Herbert Spencer, not to speak of David Hume.

[15] On Hess, see Sidney Hook, *From Hegel to Marx* (New York: Reynal and Hitchcock, 1936), pp. 194-95.

All of these men were deeply imbued with the spirit of modern science and conceived it to be their personal mission to carry this spirit into the stronghold of religion itself. The heart of the agnostic argument was epistemological.

The Agnostic [Stephen continued] is one who asserts . . . that there are limits to the sphere of human intelligence. He asserts further . . . that those limits are such as to exclude at least what Lewes called "metempirical" knowledge. But he goes further, and asserts, in opposition to theologians, that theology lies within this forbidden sphere. . . . The Gnostic [on the other hand] holds that our reason can, in some sense, transcend the narrow limits of experience. He holds that we can attain truths not capable of verification, and not needing verification, by actual experiment or observation.[16]

Throughout *An Agnostic's Apology* Stephen appealed from "reason" (which, as he used it, was often tantamount to "*a priori* guesses") to "experience" and "the facts." "Reason" might end up in a deistic or even Christian affirmation, but "experience," or rather the lack of it, dictated the agnostic position. "Finding no halting position in Deism," John Stuart Mill said of his father, "he yielded to the conviction, that, concerning the origin of things nothing whatever can be known." The question of origins simply could not be answered "because we have no experience or authentic information from which to answer it." [17]

The wonder is, not that the agnostics were suspicious of the sort of knowledge claimed by "gnostics," but that they were content to abandon the search for it altogether. That they were content, however, is clear from what Comte taught in the very first "lesson" of his *Course on the Positive Philosophy:*

[16] Sir Leslie Stephen, *An Agnostic's Apology and Other Essays* (New York: G. P. Putnam's Sons, 1893), pp. 1-2.

[17] John Stuart Mill, *Autobiography*, chap. 2.

At last the human mind, recognizing the impossibility of obtaining absolute conceptions, abandons the search for the origin and goal of the universe and the inner causes of phenomena, to set itself the task merely of discovering, by reason and observation combined, the effective laws of things, that is to say, their invariable relations of succession and similarity.[18]

The explanation of the agnostic's contentment with "laws" rather than "causes" is probably to be found in his utilitarianism. Like Bentham, he was primarily interested in "useful" knowledge, and gnostic knowledge, even if it were ultimately obtainable, was a hindrance to man in his pursuit of experience useful to the human race.

Strictly speaking, of course, the agnostic did not deny God; he only said that man knew nothing about him. "My fundamental axiom of speculative philosophy," Huxley wrote to the Christian Charles Kingsley, "is that materialism and spiritualism are opposite poles of the same absurdity —the absurdity of imagining that we know anything about either spirit or matter." [19] Nevertheless, the new idea of nature which came to the fore in the nineteenth century persuaded a good many people, including some of the agnostics themselves, to press beyond the agnostic position and actually to negate religious interpretations of the world. This was the second time that modern science had confronted western man with a disturbing metaphysic. The first such metaphysic, the Newtonian, lent itself rather well to deistic, if not to strictly orthodox Christian, categories. The second, however, was not easily absorbed into any theistic system. The new idea of nature was most vividly summed up, as is well known, by Charles Darwin, not only

[18] Auguste Comte, *Cours de Philosophie Positive* (Paris, 1835-42), Vol. I, p. 4.

[19] Huxley to Kingsley, May 22, 1863, in Leonard Huxley, *Life and Letters of Thomas Henry Huxley* (New York: D. Appleton, 1901), Vol. I, p. 262.

in *The Origin of Species* (1859), "the most important book of the century," but also in its sequel *The Descent of Man* (1871). These two books, more than any others, provided the *casus belli* between science and religion during the latter part of the century. There is considerable irony in this, for Darwin himself tried hard to stick to the facts and to avoid metaphysical controversy. Yet the "facts" as he stated them raised all the age-old questions of relativism and the absolute, necessity and free will, and design versus chance.

It has been said, and correctly, that the new thing in Darwin was his hypothesis of natural selection, i.e., his explanation of the mechanism of evolution rather than the idea of evolution as such. By 1859, the idea of an evolution in nature from simple to complex forms was already a familiar story, thanks to the previous work of the geologist Sir Charles Lyell and biologists like Erasmus Darwin and Lamarck. But Darwin gave it its supreme expression and backed it up with impressive evidence, and as a result of his work, thinkers could no longer fail to see its profound implications for religion. In brief, the idea of evolution, principally as expounded by Darwin, persuaded people to think of everything in nature as the fruit of a gradual growth rather than an original creation. It was now difficult if not impossible for an educated man to conceive of a primitive revelation such as traditional Christianity taught, or even an original natural religion from which men had declined. In an evolving world, perfection obviously lay, not in the past, but in the future. What is more, religious ideas, like everything else, appeared not to be absolute, but on the contrary, to be forever fluctuating and changing into something different.

To make matters worse for the religious camp, Darwin's explanation of the evolutionary process appeared to banish intelligent design from the universe. Darwin himself wavered on the subject, often declaring to friends that he was in "an utterly hopeless muddle." His hypothesis of natural selection, however, was clear enough. According to this hypothesis, nature selects for survival those organisms which, by the accident of birth, are best fitted to get plenty of food and to reproduce; all others it drives to the wall. Darwin pictured nature as a great battleground, not unlike the world of contemporary economics, on which individuals competed for an insufficient food supply, and on which victory went to luck rather than to cunning. It was, moreover, a recklessly wasteful process which achieved its end in one case out of thousands; the general rule was destruction and failure. Nor was its "end" invariably so perfect as had been imagined. "Natural selection will not produce absolute perfection," said Darwin, citing the imperfections of the human eye and the example of the bee whose sting when once used inevitably causes the death of the insect by tearing out its viscera. According to the German scientist Hermann von Helmholtz, "whose judgment," said Darwin, "no one will dispute":

That which we have discovered in the way of inexactness and imperfection in the optical machine and in the image on the retina, is as nothing in comparison with the incongruities which we have just come across in the domain of the sensations. One might say that nature has taken delight in accumulating contradictions in order to remove all foundation from the theory of a pre-existing harmony between the external and internal worlds.[20]

If Darwin's hypothesis was correct, then mind was indeed "pitchforked" out of the universe, as Samuel Butler put it. To account for the phenomena of nature it was un-

[20] Charles Darwin, *The Origin of Species* (6th ed.; London, 1890), p. 163.

necessary to assume any metaphysical or religious factor at work. Blind chance (fortuitous hereditary variations) and mechanical selection by the environment would, so to speak, contrive a watch (though an imperfect watch) without the purposiveness of a watchmaker. In the famous preface to *Back to Methuselah*, written some years later, George Bernard Shaw skillfully reconstructed the atmosphere in which Darwin's star first appeared. Darwin's friends, he said, actually regarded the banishment of mind as "a glorious enlightenment and emancipation" from a moribund theology and Biblicism. "We were intellectually intoxicated with the idea that the world could make itself without design, purpose, skill, or intelligence: in short, without life." Reminiscing about his college days, Frederick Pollock similarly recalled a knot of Cambridge friends led by W. K. Clifford who "were carried away by a wave of Darwinian enthusiasm." "We seemed to ride triumphant on an ocean of new life and boundless possibilities. Natural Selection was to be the master-key of the universe; we expected it to solve all riddles and reconcile all contradictions. Among other things it was to give us a new system of ethics." [21] And true to that early inspiration Clifford later deduced a naturalistic, as distinguished from a religious, ethic from *The Descent of Man*. In several brilliant articles he accounted for ideas of right and wrong entirely in terms of tribal evolution; conscience had evolved because it was useful to the tribe in its struggle for existence against other tribes or against the environment.

The new science of anthropology which arose, not accidentally, in a great age of European travel and exploration, similarly told against religious premises. Oddly, for the reverse is probably the case today, the anthropologists were

[21] Frederick Pollock, Introduction to *Lectures and Essays by the Late William Kingdon Clifford* (London, 1879), Vol. I, p. 33.

on the whole less sceptical personally than the natural scientists or the propagandists of science. Perhaps this was because no theory quite so comprehensive as natural selection illuminated anthropological studies, perhaps also because they dealt with human *mores*, a subject more complex by far than Darwin's *Edentata*, pigeons, and cockroaches. Yet thoughtful readers could and did perceive the sceptical implications of such works as E. B. Tylor's *Primitive Culture* (1871), William Robertson Smith's *Religion of the Semites* (1889), and above all, Sir James Frazer's *Golden Bough*. Their naturalistic treatment of the origins of religion, their researches into savage superstitions, the resemblances they noted between the myths and rites of savage and civilized peoples raised serious questions about the uniqueness of Christianity or any other religion.

Frazer stands as the great symbol of this anthropological scepticism, not only because of his prodigious scholarship but also because of his inimitable style which aroused, as few scholarly works can, the interest of nonspecialists. *The Golden Bough: A Study in Magic and Religion*, his *magnum opus*, first appeared in two volumes in 1890, and later swelled to thirteen volumes in the third edition. In this and other works Frazer claimed to be treating the religions of the world "not dogmatically but historically"—that is to say, not as systems of truth or falsehood to be demonstrated or refuted, but as phenomena of consciousness to be studied like any other aspect of human nature. But by his brilliant exposition of the comparative method, and by his formulation of a law of the development of human thought, which resembled Auguste Comte's famous "law of the three intellectual stages," he unquestionably helped to undermine the foundations of dogma.

Never lacking for a vivid metaphor, Frazer compared the course of thought in history to a web woven of three different threads, black, red, and white, signifying respectively magic, religion, and science. The first part of the web looks like a chequer of black and white, mostly black; toward the middle it takes on a dark crimson stain which finally shades off into a lighter tint. Similarly, in history magic is displaced by religion which in turn gives way to science. All three, religion included, are represented as modes of explaining and controlling nature. In Frazer's view, magic and science are somewhat akin because both postulate an inflexible regularity in natural events, but the natural order assumed by magic is purely imaginary whereas the order of science is the true one based on observation. Magic was superseded by religion when man discovered the errors he was making about nature. Turning to religion he ceased to rely on his own intelligence and tried to achieve the same end by propitiating "certain invisible beings" behind the veil of nature. By and by this solution also failed as the keener minds descried a real order in nature, and consequently rejected the religious theory as "inadequate." That Frazer saw this development from magic to religion to science as a boon to mankind we know from his conclusion:

Here, at last, after groping about in the dark for countless ages, man has hit upon a clue to the labyrinth, a golden key that opens many locks in the treasury of nature. It is probably not too much to say that the hope of progress—moral and intellectual as well as material—in the future is bound up with the fortunes of science, and that every obstacle placed in the way of scientific discovery is a wrong to humanity.

Elsewhere in his *opus* Frazer had more sympathetic things to say about religion, but as an evolutionist he thought of it not as a system of absolutes, but as subject to change like everything else under the sun. "The old view that the principles of right and wrong are immutable and eternal is no longer tenable. The moral world is as little exempt as the physical world from the law of ceaseless change, of perpetual flux." [22]

Frazer, as we have said, also turned "the battery of the comparative method" against the venerable walls of belief. What this method meant he explained in his essay on his master and friend William Robertson Smith. It assumed, in the first place, that the religions of the world could be accounted for naturalistically, that they were "largely modified and determined" by their physical surroundings, material culture, contacts with neighboring peoples, and the like. It then examined these religions side by side and discovered, as Voltaire and others had done earlier but in an amateurish way, that there were fundamental resemblances between them. Smith pointed out, for instance, that the slaying of a divine victim and the partaking of his flesh and blood, in a word the Christian Atonement and Eucharist, was a conception by no means confined to Christianity but common to heathen and even savage religions. And what did this sort of resemblance signify? For Frazer it proved that many religious doctrines and practices were, if not necessarily false, at least based on primitive conceptions "which most civilized and educated men have long agreed in abandoning as mistaken." [23]

The three modes of sceptical thought thus far analyzed have, as we have said, a familiar ring about them. However, the three remaining modes—the psychological, economic, and historical—struck what were essentially new notes, notes that could scarcely have achieved real clarity before

[22] Sir James Frazer, *The Golden Bough* (3rd ed., London, 1911), Vol. III, p. vi.
[23] Sir James Frazer, *The Gorgon's Head and Other Literary Pieces* (London, 1927), p. 283.

the nineteenth century. They all explained religion, indeed more often than not explained it away, as a reflection of the human condition: man's psychological needs and wishes, man's social and economic milieu, man's cultural environment.

Ludwig Feuerbach's *The Essence of Christianity* (1841), which George Eliot translated into English and which created a sensation comparable to that aroused by *The Origin of Species*, was the first great exposition of the psychological critique of religion. Feuerbach belonged to that extraordinary group of intellectuals known as the Young Hegelians, who sat at the feet of the master but who later turned against him and undermined the philosophical and religious props of the old regime in Germany. His theory of Illusionism, which profoundly influenced Marx and foreshadowed Freud, can be best understood as a fusion of two contemporary intellectual forces, the romantic movement (which, however, Feuerbach often attacked) and empiricism. From romanticism he learned to look at the subjective side of the human psyche, at man's feelings and emotional needs, at the unconscious depths which produce dreams and fantasies. At the same time the empirical philosophy taught him to distrust what he could not see and verify by objective tests. As he explained it, his method, in contrast to Hegel's, called for "generalisations from the known manifestations of human nature," generating "thought from the object," not "the object from the thought." This method revealed to him "that what by an earlier religion was regarded as objective is now recognised as subjective," i.e., "religion is the dream of the human mind," "consciousness of God is self-consciousness," "the secret of theology is anthropology." By such aphorisms Feuerbach meant that man, out of his psychological need, created God in his own image, projected into God all his own attributes or rather the attributes that he most admired and wanted to have. Thus, the Greeks attributed great physical strength to their gods, while the ancient Germans, who admired the warrior-type above all others, made their supreme god Odin, the god of war. Similarly, if God were an object to the birds, he would surely have wings. Thus, Feuerbach reduced religion to unconscious self-projection; it was an illusion in the sense that there was no object corresponding to man's subjective yearnings. For Feuerbach the turning point in history came when men realized that what they had formerly regarded as objective was in fact subjective; "that is, what was formerly contemplated and worshipped as God is now perceived to be something *human.*" Feuerbach was acutely conscious of living in an age of science and technology which rendered religion in the old sense obsolete. He thought that the question of the existence or nonexistence of God belonged to the sixteenth and seventeenth centuries, but not to the nineteenth. Christianity, he wrote in the preface to the second edition of his book, has "in fact long vanished, not only from the reason but from the life of mankind," for it is "in flagrant contradiction with our fire and life assurance companies, our railroads and steam-carriages, our picture and sculpture galleries, our military and industrial schools, our theatres and scientific museums." [24]

Karl Marx's economic interpretation of religion was simply Feuerbach's psychological interpretation writ large. Though he bitterly criticized Feuerbach on a number of counts, Marx learned from him to resolve "the religious essence into the human." His quarrel with Feuerbach was that the latter abstracted this human essence into each single individual. "Feuerbach, consequently, does not see

[24] Ludwig Feuerbach, *The Essence of Christianity,* trans. George Eliot (London, 1854), Preface, chap. 1, and *passim.*

that the 'religious sentiment' is itself a social product, and that the abstract individual whom he analyzes belongs in reality to a particular form of society." [25] Hence, whereas Feuerbach reduced religion to anthropology, i.e., man's self-projection, the most famous of all the Young Hegelians reduced it to sociology, i.e., the wishes of a whole society or group, and ultimately to economics, since social wishes reflected the tensions of the class system which in turn grew out of current relations of economic production. Marx's reduction of religion to economics came at a time, it should be noted, when European intellectuals were becoming acutely conscious of the importance of economic factors in history. In the world of the Industrial Revolution it is scarcely surprising that materialists should have risen to challenge the idealistic interpretation of history as the product of the Hegelian "Idea" or "consciousness." "Wholly in contrast to German philosophy [i.e., Hegelian idealism], which comes down from heaven to earth, we here ascend from earth to heaven," Marx wrote in *The German Ideology* (1846). That is to say, what counted in history was not the coming of the Idea to self-consciousness but how men earned their living and divided into classes. Seen through these economic spectacles, religion appeared to be mere "superstructure" or "ideology." It was a superstructure which rested upon the real, the economic structure of society: "the religious world is but a reflex of the real world." It was ideology in the sense that men employed it, along with philosophy, jurisprudence, and art, to further or maintain the interests of their class: "the ruling ideas of each age have ever been the ideas of its ruling class." Marx also taught that as the economic foundations changed, so did "the whole immense superstructure of ideas," including

---

[25] Karl Marx, *Theses on Feuerbach* (1845), *passim*, especially Nos. IV, VI, and VII.

religious ideas. In other words, Marx treated religion as relative to a particular economic and social system. "Does it require deep intuition," he asked in the *Communist Manifesto*, "to comprehend that man's ideas, views, and conceptions, in one word, man's consciousness changes with every change in the conditions of his material existence, in his social relations and in his social life?" Believing that this was so, Marx's strategy was not to attack religion as such, but to concentrate on changing the underlying economic and social conditions which made religion possible. "Religion" would disappear when the capitalist regime and class system had been overthrown. This was by far the most devastating attack that had yet been made on religion. Marx did not question the sincerity of individual religious leaders or theologians, as Voltaire and Bentham had done. He did far worse; taking his cue from Feuerbach, he brushed religion aside as unreal and illusory in comparison to the "real" forces which influenced and moved men in history.

Marx's argument brings us to the final, and in many respects the most devastating of all the modes of nineteenth-century sceptical criticism, viz. the historical. *Historismus* (significantly, a nineteenth-century neologism) or "historicism" is implied in all of the above arguments except the utilitarian. It may fairly be said therefore that it was more pervasive than any of the others. It was what otherwise so different thinkers as Marx and Frazer, the evolutionists and the Higher Critics, had in common; in a word, it became a universal idiom. It was also relatively novel, distinguishing rather sharply the nineteenth-century sceptic from his forbears of the Enlightenment. Friedrich Meinecke hardly exaggerated, therefore, when he called the upthrust of *Historismus* "one of the greatest spiritual revolutions which western thought has experienced."

Historicism was the product of a number of converging intellectual forces: chiefly perhaps, though Meinecke carries it much farther back, the romantic movement with its emphasis on the individuality and plasticity of historical events, and the new scientific view that everything was in a state of flux. Precisely what historicism meant was admirably stated by Lord Morley, himself an eminent historian. It meant "the triumph of the principle of relativity in historic judgment," "the substitution of *becoming* for *being*, the relative for the absolute, dynamic movement for dogmatic immobility." It meant referring everything, men's ideas and beliefs included, to its origins, understanding it in terms of its historical milieu. Above all, it meant the posing of an entirely new set of questions. As a result of the vogue of "the historical method," Morley wrote in 1874:

Opinions are counted rather as phenomena to be explained, than as matters of truth and falsehood. Of usages, we are beginning first of all to think where they came from, and secondarily whether they are the most fitting and convenient that men could be got to accept. In the last century men asked of a belief or a story, Is it true? We now ask, How did men come to take it for true? [26]

The problem posed for religion by historicism became even more explicit with the great German historian Ernst Troeltsch (1865-1923) who in fact agonized over it and spent a large part of his life trying, unsuccessfully, to solve it. Troeltsch was trained as a Protestant theologian, was for twenty-one years professor of systematic theology at Heidelberg, and wrote a book entitled *The Absolute Validity of Christianity*. In a remarkably frank autobiographical passage, however, he tells us that the problem of historicism

[26] Morley, *On Compromise*, in *Works*, Vol. III, p. 14; *Recollections, ibid.*, Vol. I, p. 65.

vis-à-vis religion gave him trouble almost from the outset of his academic career. The problem arose for him, he said, from the clash between his historical education and his concern to reach an effective religious position which would give him a center of reference and a sense of meaning and purpose.

I soon discovered that the historical studies which had so largely formed me, and the theology and philosophy in which I was now immersed, stood in sharp opposition, indeed even in conflict, with one another. I was confronted, upon the one hand, with the perpetual flux of the historian's data, and the distrustful attitude of the historical critic towards conventional traditions. . . .[27]

How could he realize "the demand of the religious consciousness for certainty, for unity, and for peace" when history so obviously taught "the relativity and transitoriness of all things, even of the loftiest values of civilisation." On his own testimony Troeltsch became increasingly convinced that historical Christianity was "a purely historical, individual, relative phenomenon" which could only have arisen in the peculiar milieu of the classical world. "The inference from all that," he concluded, "is that a religion, in the several forms assumed by it, always depends upon the intellectual, social, and national conditions among which it exists." [28] Thus, in the end, though he never became a complete sceptic, Troeltsch was forced to climb down from his earlier view of "the absolute validity of Christianity."

[27] Ernst Troeltsch, *Christian Thought. Its History and Application*, trans. Baron F. von Hügel (London, 1923), p. 6. This passage is from the first of a series of lectures which Troeltsch had prepared for delivery at Oxford in 1923. These lectures outlined the theme which, if he had lived, he hoped to develop as the second volume of his *Der Historismus und seine Probleme*.

[28] *Ibid.*, p. 22.

By the last quarter of the century, historicism had become the *Weltanschauung*, not merely of a few perceptive individuals like Morley and Troeltsch, but of an entire culture. It had literally invaded all departments of thought, the sciences, literary and art criticism, and also, what is chiefly germane to our purpose, those fields which touched most directly on religion. The Irish historian William Edward Hartpole Lecky had already applied it to ethical concepts, in his *History of European Morals* (1869), a work which aimed, in its author's words, to study "the relative importance that in different ages has been attached to different virtues." "Changing circumstances produce changing types," said Lecky; "religions, considered as moral teachers, are realised and effective only when their moral teaching is in conformity with the teaching of their age." [29] Similarly, a host of Higher Critics had by then applied historical categories to the study of the Bible.

Because of its shaping influence the Higher Criticism deserves special mention. The mental development of men like Morley and Troeltsch is inconceivable without it. It taught scores of people to think of religion as in large part historical "myth." It got into novels, for example, Mrs. Gaskell's *North and South*, and, spectacularly, Mrs. Humphry Ward's *Robert Ellsmere*, a vastly popular book in which the hero, an Anglican clergyman, renounced clerical orders when the squire of his parish, a scholar and Higher Critic, convinced him that supernatural Christianity was incompatible with a historical study of early Christian testimony. The scandal created by the publication of *Essays and Reviews* in 1860 testifies to the fact that the Higher Criticism had infected the thought of the clergy in real life

[29] William Edward Hartpole Lecky, *A History of European Morals from Augustus to Charlemagne* (New York: D. Appleton, 1877), Vol. I, p. 157.

as well as literature. Two of the seven essays in this famous volume, both by clergymen, dealt specifically with the Higher Criticism and indubitably threw doubt on the doctrine of the Inspiration of the Bible.

The seminal thinker among the Higher Critics was the Young Hegelian David Friedrich Strauss whose *Life of Jesus* (1835-1836), also translated into English by George Eliot, cost him his teaching post at Tübingen and earned for him the sobriquet of "Modern Iscariot." Briefly, what Strauss did was to apply the historical method and the concept of myth, popularized contemporaneously by Jacob Grimm and others, to the New Testament. In so doing he exploded the older supernatural and rationalistic interpretations of the Bible which, however else they might differ, had been agreed upon the historicity of the events recorded in the synoptic Gospels. All religions, said Strauss, originated in myth, i.e., in beliefs arising from the experiences and hopes of a community, and early Christianity was no exception to the rule. The writers of the Gospels were weaned on the Old Testament or, in the case of John, Greek philosophy too, and when they came to write about Jesus, they naturally read into him the mythical properties of the Jewish messiah or the Greek logos. Thus, what was reported of Jesus was not, for the most part, historical fact but historical myth. The revolutionary thing about Strauss' criticism was that it interpreted Christianity as ideology, i.e., as the product of a particular historical and mental environment. It is easy to see how Marx, for instance, taking off from Strauss, could explain religion in terms of the economic environment, and why Troeltsch was puzzled by Christianity's claim to "absolute validity." No wonder Ernest Renan, France's Higher Critic and likewise the author of a life of Jesus, could declare that to write the

history of a religion it was necessary, first, to have believed
it (for otherwise the writer would never be able to understand how it had charmed people), but in the second place,
"to believe it no longer in an absolute manner, for absolute
faith is incompatible with sincere history." [30]

The philosopher Henry Sidgwick was therefore only
stating the simple truth when toward the close of the century he wrote that "a belief in the Historical Method is the
most widely and strongly entertained philosophical conviction at the present day." He was also correct in pointing
to historicism as one of the chief solvents of religious conviction in the nineteenth century. Like Troeltsch he de-
murred, or tried to demur, at the general conclusion; but he
understood only too well the philosophical and religious
implications of what Walter Pater was currently calling
the "nimbly-shifting Time-Spirit."

It seems to me that the historical study of human beliefs, in
some very important departments of thought—such as ethics,
politics and theology—does tend to be connected with a general scepticism as to the validity of the doctrines studied. . . .
[Scepticism] partly tends to result from the historical study,
because of the vast and bewildering variety of conflicting beliefs . . . which this study marshals before us. The student's
own most fundamental and most cherished convictions seem
forced, as it were, to step down from their secure pedestals,
and to take their places in the endless line that is marching past.
. . . Thus to the historian . . . the whole defiling train of
beliefs tends to become something from which he sits apart,
every portion of which has lost power to hold his own reason
in the grip of true conviction: for peace's sake, he accepts the
beliefs that are pressed on him by public opinion in his own

[30] Ernest Renan, *The Life of Jesus* (New York: Dutton—Everyman's
Library, 1927), p. 31. Renan's *Vie de Jésus* was first published in 1863.

age and country; but in his heart he believes in nothing but history.[31]

3.

If the nineteenth century was an Age of Doubt it was also, like the Enlightenment, an Age of Faith. It was an Age of Doubt in two respects. In the first place, as we have seen, it was rife with "honest doubt" of religion, and not merely Christianity, as traditionally conceived. Second, and more profoundly, it was full of perplexed men who, like Matthew Arnold, not only had religious doubts but were truly oppressed by the "multitudinousness," the "hopeless tangle" of modern civilization which made it difficult for a man to believe in anything with his whole heart and mind. John Stuart Mill noted this shaky state of mind among nine-teenth-century intellectuals in an entry in the diary which he kept briefly in 1854.

The inferiority of the present age is perhaps the consequence of its superiority. Scarcely any one, in the more educated classes, seems to have any opinions, or to place any real faith in those which he professes to have. . . . The multitude of thoughts only breeds increase of uncertainty. Those who should be the guides of the rest, see too many sides to every question. They hear so much said, or find that so much can be said, about everything, that they feel no assurance of the truth of anything.[32]

This, however, was only one end of the nineteenth-cen-tury sceptical spectrum. At the other end, the more lumi-

[31] Henry Sidgwick, "The Historical Method," *Mind*, Vol. XI (1886), pp. 213-14.
[32] John Stuart Mill, *Letters*, ed. Hugh S. R. Elliot (London, 1910), Vol. II, p. 359.

nous end, we might say, were the numerous men of faith, of whom Mill himself was one, who believed positively in something. As a recent historian of nineteenth-century English thought has said, Victorian scepticism "never involved a denial of the mind as a valid instrument of truth"; faith in the existence of ultimate truths and the capacity of the human mind to discover them was "the one intellectual certitude in Victorian England" [33] (and also on the continent). But this was by no means all. Most of the sceptics mentioned above, and many others too, thought that they were already in possession of certain truths, or at any rate certain methods, which were sufficient to pilot humanity to a brighter future. The impression given by Benthamites, Young Hegelians, and Positivists, even by an agnostic such as Sir Leslie Stephen, is one of robust faith rather than frustrated doubt. With a confidence bordering on arrogance they substituted new "gods" for the "God" they had assassinated, new ersatz-religions for the religions of their forefathers. Thus, the Great Substitution which had begun during the Enlightenment and the Revolution can be said to have continued with scarcely abated vigor into and through most of the nineteenth century.

In general, the new ersatz-religions represented versions of the humanistic faith of the Enlightenment, adapted, however, to new movements and events. Like Condorcet's faith, they were mostly all antimetaphysical and earth-bound. Essentially, what they worshipped or deified was Man—man's power, man's works in some shape or form—as, again, the Enlightenment had done. Man, said W. K. Clifford, "made all Gods and shall unmake them." "From the dim dawn of history and from the inmost depth of every soul, the face

---

[33] Walter E. Houghton, *The Victorian Frame of Mind 1830-1870* (New Haven: Yale University Press, 1957), pp. 13-14.

of our father Man looks out upon us with the fire of eternal youth in his eyes, and says, 'Before Jehovah was, I am!' " [34] At the same time, reflecting the new mass culture and the powerful new forces of mass nationalism and mass socialism, some of the new "gods" bore a collectivistic stamp which was largely absent in the Enlightenment. These "gods" of the masses showed a tendency to sacrifice man's individual dignity to man's collective power and thus, by a curious dialectic, to become actually antihumanistic.

Chief among the new family of "gods," to be discussed in the following order and wherever possible in terms of actual life histories, were Humanity, Society, Science, History, and Culture. To this list, if we pretended to complete coverage (which we do not), we should have to add a large number of more or less private faiths like Nietzsche's philosophy of power, and the new ethical "Brotherhood" which Mrs. Humphry Ward had her hero Robert Ellsmere establish in a working-class section of London. Moreover, it should be noted that the devotees often divided their allegiance between two or more of these faiths, just as the critics examined above (with whom they were, in fact, synonymous) frequently employed more than one type of sceptical argument.

Significantly, many nineteenth-century sceptics thought of themselves as genuinely religious men. Certainly Auguste Comte, the founder of Positivism and the "Religion of Humanity," did so. He left his mother's church to establish a new church based, as he expressed it, on objective facts rather than subjective illusions, on unselfish love of humanity ("altruism," a word which he himself coined) rather than selfish love of God. His motive in manufacturing his

[34] *Lectures and Essays by the Late William Kingdon Clifford*, Vol. II, p. 243.

new "religion" was twofold. In the first place, he appreciated, better than most in the days following the upheaval of
the Revolution and the Napoleonic wars, the need to replace the old religion with something positive. "To destroy
you must replace." He also understood, as many of his
sceptical contemporaries did not, that the replacement must
be something more than a new intellectual synthesis. He
kept talking about "the prosaic dullness of modern life."
To relieve this dullness, men, as he thought, needed a new
"religion" which would engage their feelings and imagination as well as satisfy their reason.

And so this Roman Catholic apostate, who aspired to be
to his century what St. Thomas Aquinas had been to the
Middle Ages, gave them a new "god." He called it the
"Great Being," but it no more resembled the Supreme Being
of the deists than the God of the Catholics or Protestants;
it was more like the "god" of Diderot's and Condorcet's cult
of Posterity. It was nothing more nor less than humanity
conceived in its collective and ideal aspect, and comprised
of past and future as well as present generations. "The Great
Being whom we worship is not immutable any more than it
is absolute. Its nature is relative; and, as such, is eminently
capable of growth. In a word, it is the most vital of all
living beings known to us. It extends and becomes more
complex by the continuous succession of generations."
Thus, its very existence, as well as its perfectibility, depended upon the actions of men. Comte considered the
moral effects of this "Religion of Humanity" to be vastly
superior to those of the old religions. Principally, it encouraged "social feeling" whereas Christianity, or so Comte
thought, had emphasized a selfish search for personal salvation. "To become incorporate with Humanity, to sym-
pathize with all her former phases, to foresee her destinies

in the future, and to do what lies in us to forward them; this is what it puts before us as the constant aim of life." [35] It also taught men to be self-reliant, to look to their own unremitting activity for the only "providence" possible.

Plainly, the "Religion of Humanity" signified the apotheosis of Man. Comte envisaged the establishment of an actual church with worship services, sacraments, catechisms, and festivals—the likeness to Roman Catholic ceremony is obvious—all celebrating "the greatness of man," and especially man's social life. The service of artists was to be enlisted to immortalize "the marvellous advance of man, from brutish appetite to pure unselfish sympathy." Eighty-one annual festivals would honor the "Great Being" and those "saints" in history—Archimedes, Charlemagne, Dante, Gutenberg, Columbus, Descartes, Bacon, and Newton among them—who had contributed to man's knowledge and the refinement of human living. *The Catechism of Positivism* contains not one word about sin or the fall of man; the emphasis was upon man's moral and intellectual capabilities and his progress in history.

It was in something like this "Religion of Humanity," broadly conceived, that probably the majority of nineteenth-century sceptics found their home. This is not to say that many of them wanted to join Comte's church, for Comte was suspect, to the liberals for his authoritarianism, to all but a few fanatical followers for his vagaries into a sort of "Catholicism minus Christianity." It means only that Comte, in his apotheosis of Humanity, dramatized an idea that was in the air and which proved to be most congenial to those humanists for whom supernatural religion had become unpalatable. Without benefit of Comte, Strauss and Feuerbach, for example, came up with their own version of

[35] Auguste Comte, *A General View of Positivism*, trans. J. H. Bridges (2nd ed.; London, 1880), pp. 246-47, 259.

a "Religion of Humanity," Strauss by allegorizing Jesus Christ the God-man as the human species, sinless, immortal, progressively realizing its ideal nature in history; Feuerbach by making Man the object and bond of universal love, the spur to human improvement. George Eliot owed something to Comte, more to Feuerbach, in her stern devotion to a "religion" of Duty: duty to man, her only real absolute once she had jettisoned the Christian God and Christian Immortality. How like Comte's or Feuerbach's Humanity was her "choir invisible"

> Of those immortal dead who live again
> In minds made better by their presence; live
> In pulses stirred to generosity,
> In deeds of daring rectitude, in scorn
> For miserable aims that end with self. . . .
> So to live is heaven:
> To make undying music in the world . . .[36]

John Stuart Mill, who would have none of Comte's political and intellectual authoritarianism, nevertheless also joined with Comte in his "Religion of Humanity." Reared in Benthamism, Mill gradually became disenchanted with the Benthamite ethic, with its basis in the principle of self-interest and the happiness of the individual. Ethical hedonism, he thought, could never be a substitute for ethical idealism. Hence, his conversion, one might almost call it, to the "Religion of Humanity," which emphasized altruism, and to which he frequently alluded, always with praise, in his writings. One such allusion, from his diary of 1854, not only directly refers to Comte, but shows how both he and Comte thought of it as a substitute for religion.

The best, indeed the only good thing (details excepted) in Comte's second treatise, is the thoroughness with which he has enforced and illustrated the possibility of making *le culte de*

[36] George Eliot, "O May I Join the Choir Invisible."

l'humanité perform the functions and supply the place for religion. If we suppose cultivated to the highest point the sentiments of fraternity with all our fellow-beings, past, present, and to come . . . ; universal moral education making the happiness and dignity of this collective body the central point to which all things are to trend and by which all are to be estimated, instead of the pleasure of an unseen and merely imaginary Power . . . : there is no worthy office of a religion which this system of cultivation does not seem adequate to fulfill.[37]

The "Religion of Humanity" never spread to the masses nor was it ever objectified in an institution unless it was Comte's *culte*. But as the century wore on, another god took shape which claimed the allegiance of millions and which threatened, in the end, to destroy Humanity. This god, of bloody mien, was severally known as Nation, State, Race, and Class, but its generic name was Society. "Society, from which we have everything," wrote Max Stirner in his anarchist manifesto *The Ego and Its Own* (1845), "is a new master, a new spook, a new supreme being, which takes us into its service and allegiance!" Stirner rightly observed that the nationalists and socialists of the nineteenth century were still "imprisoned in the religious principle" and zealously aspired after "a sacred society." To put it in other words, in an age when cosmic consciousness was evaporating, much of man's latent religious feeling was drained off into worship of society. For society, as Stirner also did not fail to note, whether conceived as the state or an association of workers, was rapidly becoming the dispenser of all good things, economic, cultural, and psychological. "People think that society *gives* what we need, and we are *under obligations* to it on that account, owe it everything." [38] Indeed, Comte himself worshipped at this shrine—his "Great Being"

[37] John Stuart Mill, *Letters*, Vol. II, pp. 362-63.
[38] Max Stirner, *The Ego and Its Own*, trans. S. T. Byington (New York: B. R. Tucker, 1907), p. 162.

was, in a sense, society personified—but there was just this difference, a vital difference, between his sociolatry and the sociolatry of which Stirner speaks: his "spook" comprised all humanity, whereas the new spooks divided humanity into warring factions, pitting nation against nation, and class against class.

Of all the forms that sociolatry assumed in the nineteenth century, nationalism was by far the most powerful. As Carlton Hayes has said, nationalism, which originated in its modern form during the French Revolution, became "the dominant religion of the nineteenth and twentieth centuries." Nietzsche, as a "good European," complained frequently and bitterly of the growth of nationalistic and racist thinking in his lifetime. But he did more than testify to the fact; he properly identified it as a quasi-religious phenomenon, a "new idol." "Yea, it [the nation-state] findeth you out too, ye conquerors of the old God!" spake Zarathustra. "Weary ye became of the conflict, and now your weariness serveth the new idol!" Nietzsche also saw that nationalism was spreading to the masses as well as the intellectuals. "Many too many are born: for the superfluous ones was the state devised! See just how it enticeth them to it, the many-too-many! How it swalloweth and cheweth and recheweth them!" [39] Nietzsche was alarmed, for in his view the old religious picture of man was finished and something even worse, cultural philistinism and chauvinism, threatened to take its place.

He had good reason to be alarmed, for he seemed to encounter the new idolatry wherever he looked, even in his own family circle and among intellectuals whom he had once admired. His own brother-in-law, for example, was a fanatical racist who founded a Teutonic colony in Para-

[39] Friedrich Nietzsche, *Thus Spake Zarathustra*, Part I, chap. 11, "The New Idol."

guay; his erstwhile friend, the musician Richard Wagner, whom he denounced as "*reichsdeutsch*," wrote pamphlets extolling German cultural superiority and attacking the Jews; and even old David Friedrich Strauss ended his days as an ardent nationalist who saw in the Hohenzollern monarchy a profound "mystery." If Nietzsche had taken the trouble to look beyond Germany, he would have observed the same idolatry in the other European nations, in France and Italy, among the Slavic peoples, even in England. This period from the Franco-Prussian War to the outbreak of World War I was, as every student of European history knows, the heyday of "integral nationalism" which put the nation above all other values.

Three examples, one German and two French, will illustrate the tendency of the integral nationalists—by no means all the nationalists even of this period, of course, were so extreme—to exalt the nation into a religious principle, or even to substitute nationalism for religion. Professor Heinrich von Treitschke thought of himself as a pious Christian, yet in his lectures on history and politics at Berlin in the eighties and nineties he taught the Germans "pious and earnest attachment to the state." Strictly speaking, neither Treitschke nor Hegel, who influenced him, considered the state to be the supreme value; it was rather the incarnation of the "Absolute Idea" or "the objectively revealed Will of God." It was a demigod through which the nation realized its highest potentialities, and the individual his "earthly immortality." To it, however, the individual owed his supreme devotion. "The high moral ideal of national honour," he preached, "is a factor handed down from one generation to another, enshrining something positively sacred, and compelling the individual to sacrifice himself to it." [40] Treit-

---

[40] Heinrich von Treitschke, *Politics,* trans. Blanche Dugdale and Torben de Bille (New York: Macmillan, 1916), Vol. I, p. 15.

schke called upon the nation to indoctrinate its youth in this myth of the state, and that the myth was widely taught in the schools may be inferred from directives issued by the Prussian ministry of education and popular textbooks of the time. What was wanted of history teachers was clearly stated by Carl Reim in his text on historical method—the religious imagery is unmistakeable:

To defend honor, liberty, and right; to offer up life, health and property on the altar of the Fatherland, these have always been the joy of German youths. . . . Our Fatherland is a holy land. Our ancestors preserved it with their blood. . . . More national consciousness, much more than we now possess! That is the end to which we history teachers must help our youth." [41]

This same lesson was being driven home in France, although with less emphasis on the state as such, by persons like Maurice Barrès and Charles Maurras. The life histories of these two men illustrate a not unusual cycle. Both were reared as Roman Catholics, Barrès in Lorraine, Maurras in Provence; they then experienced the conversion in reverse, upon reading, among other sceptical authors, Renan and Comte (especially Maurras, who wrote a book on Comte); but finally, living as they did in the feverish atmosphere of *revanche* against Germany which enveloped France after the defeat at Sedan, they underwent, as it were, a second conversion—Barrès specifically referred to it as such—to the "religion" of the *patrie*. What they finally came to believe in is summed up in Maurras' famous article on "Integral Nationalism," published in *Le Soleil* on March 2, 1900:

A nationalist believes that a good citizen subordinates his sentiments, his interests, and his systems to the good of the Patrie.

[41] Quoted in Walter Langsam, "Nationalism and History in the Prussian Elementary Schools under William II," in *Nationalism and Internationalism*, ed. E. M. Earle (New York: Columbia University Press, 1950), p. 251.

. . . Like the Roman of whom Bossuet spoke, the love of the Patrie surpasses everything for him. . . . French nationalism tends to excite among us a religion of the goddess France.[42]

Barrès' odyssey is highly significant. His first trilogy, significantly entitled *Le Culte du Moi* (completed in 1891), preached the primacy of the Ego. But already in the third novel of the series he had become aware of a wider ordering principle. He admits to his garden a beautiful young girl, Bérénice, who symbolizes his native country and his subconscious soul, and through her he experiences the sentiment of solidarity with his ancestors and attachment to the soil of France. He comes to have thereby a sense of harmony and security such as he had never had before. This feeling of expansion from a personal to a national egotism was buttressed in his next trilogy, entitled *National Energy*, by a theory of psychological determinism. What Frenchmen of his day needed, he said, was an emotional submission—comparable to Pascal's idea of a true conversion—to their determinism by their ancestors; they must dig their roots deep into national soil and thus rediscover themselves "in the family, in the race, in the nation." Maurras similarly migrated from negative scepticism to a positive nationalistic faith. In his book on Comte, which was more about himself than about Comte, the young Parisian student Jundzill encounters science and Positivism, and as a result abandons God, indeed feels a "rigorous need of being without God" since all theological and metaphysical interpretations of the world have become unendurable to him. However, Maurras soon discerned a need equally rigorous to discover an ordering principle by which to guide his life, and Maurras accordingly moved on, not to Comtism, but to what he called (it was he who coined the term) "integral nationalism."

[42] Quoted in William C. Buthman, *The Rise of Integral Nationalism in France* (New York: Columbia University Press, 1939), p. 183.

Paradoxically, both Maurras and Barrès retained the Catholic church as an integral part of their new cult, not because they believed its doctrine, but because it was an ancestral institution around which French nationalism could rally; they belonged to that peculiar breed known as "Catholic atheists."

Their countryman Ernest Renan worshipped at a different, but for many sceptics in the nineteenth century a much purer, shrine. He too became a French patriot, although his nationalism—articulated in a famous lecture on the meaning of nationality at the Sorbonne in 1882—was sane and liberal by comparison with the tribalism of Maurras and Barrès. But it was not to the Patrie that he turned when "historical criticism" convinced him that he could no longer be a Catholic. In his memoirs he describes the dark days immediately following his decision to leave the seminary: "with Christianity untrue, everything else appeared to me indifferent, frivolous, and undeserving of interest." Soon, however, he was hard at work on a book entitled *The Future of Science*, in which he summed up "the new faith" which for him had replaced shattered Christianity. "Science," he wrote—meaning by science the scientific method or the scientific way of knowing—"is a religion, science alone will henceforth make the creeds, science alone can solve for men the eternal problems, the solution of which his nature imperatively demands." [43]

This was the faith that has since come to be known as "scientism," or as Renan himself called it, "the religion of science." "Science," Samuel Butler caustically observed in his notebooks, "is being daily more and more personified and anthropomorphized into a god. By and by they will say that science took our nature upon him, and sent down his only begotten son, Charles Darwin, or Huxley, into the

[43] Ernest Renan, *The Future of Science* (Boston: Roberts Bros., 1891), p. 97.

world so that those who believe in him, etc." [44] Butler hardly exaggerated. Not only illustrous figures, including many of the scientists themselves, but lesser men, popularizers of science and third-rate intellectuals, had begun to talk about science with awe and to ascribe to it most of the healing powers formerly associated with religion. In Butler's time Huxley, who has been called, not inaptly, the "prophet of science," spoke the language of the pulpit and spread the new gospel among politicians, businessmen, and laymen in general. But long before Huxley, the founders of Positivism, Saint-Simon and Comte, had wanted to make scientists the new priests of western society. By the middle of the century, scientism was sufficiently widespread to be lampooned by the great French novelist Gustave Flaubert who was himself so badly bitten by it that he tried to endow his art with the exactness of the physical sciences. In *Madame Bovary*, for example, there is the unforgettable example of Homais, the druggist, who was forever talking about "keeping pace with science" and who insisted on giving a scientific explanation for everything.

What was the essence of this "religion of science"? In general, as the English scientist Karl Pearson so well put it, it meant "single-eyed devotion to truth," as differentiated from "myth" and "dogmatism." Yet, as Pearson knew perfectly well, there were differences of opinion among scientists as to the extent and kinds of truth to which it was thought the scientific method might attain. Hence, in his *Grammar of Science* (1892), which attempted to summarize scientific method and language, he properly distinguished between those who held that "we *shall* be ignorant," "mankind must *always* be ignorant," and those who said merely that "we *are* ignorant." To the first group belonged

[44] Samuel Butler, *Works,* ed. H. F. Jones (London, 1923-26), Vol. XX, p. 346.

the extreme agnostics, men like Huxley, the brothers Du-
bois-Reymond, and the later Renan, who thought that the
human mind was forever cut off from knowledge in certain
fields, and who therefore did not look to science to solve
the great metaphysical problems. The second group, which
comprised the majority of those addicted to scientism, argued to the contrary that present ignorance did not necessarily mean future ignorance. Pearson himself was of this
latter persuasion. As an evolutionist he was unwilling to
set limits to the human intellect. Who could gainsay that
some day it might unriddle basic enigmas of life and mind
in the same way that it had solved cosmical problems in
the seventeenth century and invented a cable for talking
across the Atlantic Ocean in the nineteenth? Science, said
Pearson, does much more than demand that it shall be left
in possession of what metaphysicians and theologians please
to call its "legitimate field." "It claims that the whole range
of phenomena, mental as well as physical—the entire universe—is its field. It asserts that the scientific method is the
sole gateway to the whole region of knowledge." [45] In an
earlier lecture Pearson had spoken with truly prophetic zeal
of the role that this second group, the "freethinkers" as he
called them, could play in furthering the cause of civilization. It was their "mission," first of all, to spread actually
acquired truth, not only among the lower classes, but also
among the educated, the average clergyman and churchgoing lawyer and businessman, who was still abysmally ignorant of the implications of modern science. Their mission,
however, would find "its holiest meaning" in the discovery
of new truth, i.e., new scientific laws.

It is in this aspect that the essentially *religious* character of freethought appears. It is not a stagnant religious system with a

[45] Karl Pearson, *The Grammar of Science* (London, 1900), p. 24.

crystallized and unchangeable creed, forced to reject all new truth which is not in keeping with its dogma, but one which actually demands new truth, whose sole end is the growth and spread of human knowledge and which must perforce adopt every great discovery as essentially a portion of itself. . . . It is no little future which I would paint for this new religious movement, yet it is perhaps the only one which has a future; all others are of the past. . . . The day I believe will come when its evangelists will spread through the country, be heard in every house, and be seen on every street preaching and teaching the only faith which is consonant with the reason, with the dignity of man.[46]

The title of Pearson's lecture—"The Ethic of Freethought"—indicates that he thought the "religion of science" supported an ethic superior in certain respects to the Christian ethic. Without much doubt, so did most of the "freethinkers" of the two groups he described. Science, they reiterated over and over again, inculcated intellectual honesty, suppressed credulity, and taught men to regard themselves less and society more—all virtues of which society had need. But the emphasis was on simple honesty. Theologians, Huxley wrote in an article for the *Nineteenth Century*, would do well to consider that "in the matter of intellectual veracity, science is already a long way ahead of the Churches; and that in this particular, it is exerting an educational influence on mankind of which the Churches have shown themselves utterly incapable." [47] In a famous figure at the conclusion of his article on "Religion and Morals" this "prophet of science" represented Theology and Philosophy as the ugly sisters, and Science as Cinderella who, he said, had learned in her heart of hearts the lesson

[46] Karl Pearson, *The Ethic of Freethought* (London, 1888), pp. 24-5.
[47] Thomas Henry Huxley, "An Episocopal Trilogy," *Essays upon Some Controverted Questions* (New York: D. Appleton, 1893), p. 243.

"that the foundation of morality is to have done, once and for all, with lying; to give up pretending to believe that for which there is no evidence, and repeating unintelligible propositions about things beyond the possibilities of knowledge." [48] Belief accepted on insufficient evidence, said W. K. Clifford in a paper on "The Ethics of Belief," is "sinful," for it encourages credulity, and "the credulous man is father to the liar and the cheat."

The Grammar of Science did not include in its classification still a third group of science worshippers, namely the "monists" and materialists who claimed that "we already know." Yet they too were a numerous crew in the nineteenth century, including, among others, the Saint-Simonians who substituted for the old religion a new creed appropriately labeled "Physicism" by their master, which affirmed the Newtonian law of gravitation as the sole cause of all physical and moral phenomena; the Comtists who thought that they were already in possession of the fundamental laws of social Statics and Dynamics and hence had the key to social engineering; and schools of German philosophers—the tendency was especially marked in Germany —who invaded the metaphysical realm and explained the universe in terms of the scientific laws of the conservation of energy and Darwinist evolution. Significantly, Strauss was one of these philosophers. In his last major utterance, a book entitled *The Old Faith and the New* (1872), Strauss affirmed a faith which he did not object to having called "pure unmitigated materialism." Are we still Christians? No, said Strauss, at least not those among us who have absorbed the Higher Criticism, for we can no longer accept the Bible as the Word of God nor can we even be sure of what Jesus actually said and did. Have we still a religion? It depends, of course, on what we mean by religion. If by

[48] *Ibid.*, p. 183.

religion we mean the old religion based on prayer and sacrifice, the religion centering in a personal deity, then we do not have a religion, for modern science has made that type of belief untenable. Strauss consigned religion so defined to the childhood of the race and thought that it had retreated in proportion as civilization had advanced. Religion more broadly conceived, however, is not extinct in us, for we retain "the sentiment of unconditioned dependence"—dependence on the "Cosmos" which in Strauss' description was a reasonable facsimile of the universe revealed by the latest nineteenth-century concepts of physics and biology. To account for the universe it was unnecessary any longer to postulate God, design, purpose; its origins, indeed the origin of life and the development of higher forms of life, could be explained on purely mechanical and materialistic principles. In other words, for Strauss science was the new revelation. He had now gone full circle from Christianity to Hegelian Idealism to, finally, a curious combination of national idealism and "unmitigated materialism."

Linking up with the "religion of science" and the "Religion of Humanity," and in fact resting squarely upon them, was still another "religion," namely, the Religion of History, the nineteenth-century word for which was "Progress." This was the Enlightenment idea of progress, but with a difference. The Enlightenment idea, it will be recalled, derived largely from the Lockean idea of the *tabula rasa*, and hence of environmentalism; progress therefore depended on man's success in changing the environment for the better, by means of a more rational education and more rational legislation. This idea continued to flourish in the nineteenth century, as is evident from the Mills' "doctrine of circumstances" and Comte's sociology, but it now often had joined to it the idea of "law" or necessity. More often than not, progress was now conceived as a world process, almost an iron law, similar to the great laws observable in the physical universe, realizing itself, to be sure, with the help of man and yet, in a sense, regardless and even in spite of man. "Progress," said Herbert Spencer, "is not an accident, but a necessity"; the modifications men have undergone "result from a law underlying the whole organic creation; and provided the human race continues, and the constitution of things remains the same, those modifications must end in completeness." [49] Undoubtedly, the chief impulse to this new development in the idea came from the cult of science which, as Karl Pearson said, pointed up in the discovery of "laws." It also owed something to the Hegelian dialectic, and in its later stages, something to the idea of evolution, not to speak of current political and economic developments.

This is not the place to describe the historical systems of Saint-Simon and Comte, Hegel and Marx, John Stuart Mill, Spencer, and Henry Thomas Buckle, all of whom discovered in history a "law" of progress. For our purposes the important thing to note is the quasi-religious imagery which they employed, the sense in which, for them (and also for many others) History served as a kind of substitute for God. For the young Troeltsch, history might be grounds for worry, posing fundamental problems of value. But for the optimists, an ever increasing band, history was a semidivine principle, full of apocalyptic promise. In the system of Marx and Engels—to take just one example— History behaved suspiciously like divine Providence. It moved inexorably toward its final goal, regardless of what men might choose to do, and despite Marx and Engels' occasional protestations that "men make their own history" and "history does nothing." The negation of the thesis by the antithesis, the victory of the proletariat over the bour-

[49] Herbert Spencer, *Social Statics* (London, 1851), p. 65.

geoisie in modern times, was written in the doom of history, and out of the dialectical opposition would inevitably come the final synthesis of the classless society. It takes no great perspicacity to see that Marx smuggled back into his supposedly "scientific socialism" a species of metaphysical and quasi-religious belief which he thought he had exorcized when he stood Hegel on his head. As a result of his deification of History, the Marxist could feel that the universe was on his side, and that morality and rationality meant doing what History required him to do in pursuit of the final end.

In a word, for the nineteenth-century believers in progress, history promised nothing less than an earthly Paradise in which, depending on the point of view, the human mind would become conscious of its capabilities, physical suffering would be meliorated if not eradicated, better institutions established, class tensions relieved. According to Karl Pearson, history (he called it "freethought") would also relieve "spiritual misery," "very prevalent nowadays, owing to the rapid collapse of so many concrete religious systems." [50] The freethinker Winwood Reade gathered up most of these strands of nineteenth-century utopism in the peroration of his *Martyrdom of Man* (1872), which might be called a history of mankind in the light of the bad effects of religion and the good effects of science.

The beautiful legend will come true; Ormuzd will vanquish Ahriman; Satan will be overcome. . . . Earth, which is now a purgatory, will be made a paradise, not by idle prayers and supplications, but by the efforts of man himself, and by means of mental achievements analogous to those which have raised him to his present state. . . . Hunger and starvation will then be unknown. . . . Governments will be conducted with the quietude and regularity of club committees. The interest which

[50] Pearson, *The Ethic of Freethought*, p. 21.

is now felt in politics will be transferred to science. . . . Poetry and the fine arts will take that place in the heart which religion now holds. . . . Not only will Man subdue the forces of evil that are without; he will also subdue those that are within. . . . A time will come when Science will transform [men's bodies] by means which we cannot conjecture. . . . Disease will be extirpated; the causes of decay will be removed; immortality will be invented. . . . Man then will be perfect; he will then be a creator; he will therefore be what the vulgar worship as a god.[51]

The great Swiss historian Jacob Burckhardt (1818-89) had a very different conception of history. For Burckhardt history was emphatically not a demiurge propelling man toward the promised land; on the other hand, it was the key that unlocked the door to still another nineteenth-century sanctuary—Culture. Faith in Culture was the resort of those who, unlike the sceptics described above, deplored the trend of recent history, but who, like them, had lost their belief in religion, or at any rate orthodox religion. As critics of modern civilization, they necessarily constituted a small group, almost an esoteric group, voices crying in the wilderness like the Christian monks of the declining Roman Empire, with whom Burckhardt himself compared them.

Burckhardt's early life paralleled the career of Ernest Renan. At the University of Basle to which his father, a Christian minister, sent him to study theology, he encountered the Higher Criticism and in consequence lost his Christianity. "Today, finally," he wrote to a friend, "I realized that he [Dewette, his professor of theology at Basle] regards the birth of Christ simply as a myth—and

[51] Winwood Reade, *The Martyrdom of Man* (London, 1872), pp. 512-15.

that I do too." [52] During the next ten years he had an even more unsettling experience. Returning to Basle after studying in Germany, he encountered the new revolutionary movement in Switzerland. As an old-style liberal he was appalled at what he observed both inside and outside Switzerland: the spectacle of the masses revolting against authority, with no respect for tradition or duty, the middle classes in pursuit of mammon and reducing art to commercialism, the growth of fanatical nationalism and militarism. Europe, Burckhardt thought, was lapsing into universal barbarism. What could save Europe? Like Matthew Arnold, Burckhardt thought that if anything could save it, it would be Culture, and thenceforth as teacher and scholar he devoted himself to spreading the gospel of "the culture of Old Europe." By culture Burckhardt meant something different from religion (although, unlike many sceptics, he believed that religion had had a civilizing mission in history, as also did Arnold). Culture differed from religion in that it had no metaphysical pretensions. It was simply, as he defined it in one of his lectures, "the sum of all that has *spontaneously* arisen for the advancement of material life and as an expression of spiritual and moral life—all social intercourse, technologies, arts, literatures and sciences." [53] History alone could reveal this cultural treasure. In this sense *"Historia vitae magistra"* (history is the guide of life), for while it pretended to no knowledge of beginnings and ends, or even of universals, it recorded man's culture, i.e., his attempts to seize upon the true, the good, the beautiful; "the best which has been thought and said in the world," as Arnold put it.

[52] Burckhardt to Johannes Riggenbach, August 28, 1838, in *The Letters of Jacob Burckhardt*, ed. Alexander Dru (New York: Pantheon Books, 1955), p. 36.

[53] Jacob Burckhardt, in *Force and Freedom*, ed. J. H. Nichols (New York: Pantheon Books, 1943), p. 107.

Without this knowledge of their spiritual heritage men become barbarians; with it as guide Europe might yet be saved.

The nineteenth-century school of aesthetics known as "art-for-art's sake" shared this worship of Culture, although in a much more specialized sense. According to Walter Pater, who was the most conspicuous representative of the school in England, "the desire of beauty, the love of art for its own sake," afforded man his best chance of living pleasantly and fully. While still a student at Oxford, Pater had revolted against his religious upbringing. Influenced by modern science he had become convinced that the human mind could not have metaphysical knowledge, that the only real or secure thing in man's experience, poised as he was between two hypothetical eternities, was a series of sharp but fleeting impressions. The wise man would therefore seek to experience these impressions to the utmost, but not to theorize about them. "Not the fruit of experience, but experience itself, is the end," Pater wrote in his famous conclusion to his studies on the Renaissance, and clearly, for Pater, the experience made possible by "culture" (education in the arts) was best calculated to enable man to burn with a "hard, gemlike flame." That Pater at one time proposed his "New Cyrenaicism" as a modern substitute for religion seems abundantly clear from his novel *Marius the Epicurean* (of course, *Marius* also shows that by 1885 Pater had himself moved beyond the "Cyrenaic" position). Living in the sceptical world of Marcus Aurelius, young Marius mused that the Cyrenaic manner of life

might come even to seem a kind of religion—an inward, visionary, mystic piety, or religion, by virtue of its effort to live days "lovely and pleasant" in themselves, here and now, and with an all-sufficiency of well-being in the immediate sense of the object contemplated, independently of any faith, or hope that might be entertained as to their ulterior tendency.[54]

4.

For many nineteenth-century sceptics the "death of God" was an acutely chilling experience to live through. Many of those mentioned above, and others besides, tell us how when they first lost their religious faith the bottom fell out of their world and they felt alone in a mysterious universe. In a particularly graphic passage George Romanes, for example—Romanes was one of those scientists who renounced an early intention to take holy orders—describes how with the "negation of God" the universe had lost its soul of loveliness for him. He could not agree, he said, that the "new faith" constituted a desirable substitute for "the waning splendour of 'the old.' " "When at times I think, as think at times I must," he wrote in the conclusion to his *Candid Examination of Theism* (1878), "of the appalling contrast between the hallowed glory of that creed which once was mine, and the lonely mystery of existence as now I find it,—at such times I shall ever feel it impossible to avoid the sharpest pang of which my nature is susceptible." [55]

Renan had a similar experience, not once but twice, first when he left the seminary and again late in life. He never wavered in his faith in science, but at the last he appears to have relinquished his hope that it would reveal the truth to man. The experience was saddening to him, if not precisely chilling. He thought it possible that the ruin of idealistic beliefs would follow hard on the ruin of supernatural be-

[54] Walter Pater, *Works* (London, 1900-1901), Vol. II, p. 152.
[55] Physicus (George Romanes), *A Candid Examination of Theism* (Boston: Houghton, Osgood, 1878), p. 114.

liefs, "and that the real abasement of the morality of humanity will date from the day it has seen the reality of things." This statement was amazingly like Nietzsche's current prediction of the collapse of European morality once the report of God's death had reached and been apprehended by the western peoples. "Candidly speaking," said Renan in the new preface he wrote for *The Future of Science* (finally published in 1890), "I fail to see how, without the ancient dreams, the foundations of a happy and noble life are to be relaid." Renan could only console himself with the thought that, after all, science protected man against error, and there was an advantage "in being certain of not being duped." [56] George Eliot thought that morality might stand even when belief in God and immortality had evaporated, but she was not very happy about it. Basil Willey has rightly observed of the great English novelist that she was by temperament a religious person whom the climate of scepticism had cut off from traditional objects of veneration and traditional religious formulations. Her ordeal permanently saddened her, for in her case the "religion" of humanity to which she turned failed to provide an adequate psychological substitute for the religion in which she had been reared.

For most sceptics, however, the experience seems to have been only momentarily chilling. Thus, Clifford's experience was probably more typical than George Eliot's. The Cambridge mathematician felt no sense of bereavement once he discovered the "creed of science" (before he died he had sketched the contents for a book bearing that title). He too had seen "the spring sun shine out of an empty heaven, to light up a soulless earth" and had felt "with utter loneliness that the Great Companion is dead." But soon he was recording in his notebook his exhilaration—significantly,

[56] Renan, *The Future of Science*, p. xix.

he used religious language to describe it—at perceiving the new creation of nature revealed by science, and he shouted for joy. "It may well be," he wrote, "that the new world also shall die. Doubtless there shall by and by be laws as far transcending those we know as they do the simplest observation. The new incarnation may need a second passion; but evermore beyond it is the Easter glory." [57]

On the whole, the nineteenth-century sceptics were well satisfied with their substitute gods. These gods—Humanity, Society, Science, History, even to some extent Culture—promised "the Easter glory," a future scarcely less roseate than Condorcet's "Tenth Epoch." Walter Mehring said of his father, the nineteenth-century socialist, that he was convinced that at the stroke of midnight on the New Year's Eve that marked the transition from the nineteenth to the twentieth century, a new and more glorious era would come into being. The senior Mehring, heir of the Enlightenment and the nineteenth-century doctrine of progress, and a materialist who "insisted on absolute abstinence from theological spirits," put his faith in "the god of technological improvement." "World fraternity and the individual's right of self-determination would be won by the machine—*deus ex machina.*" [58] Clearly, this new machine-God of Mehring and the others was Man himself—"Him who made all Gods and shall unmake them," as Clifford had said. Few foresaw, like Nietzsche's madman, the "Age of Longing" to come when man would also despair of Man and the gods he had made.

[57] *Lectures and Essays by the Late William Kingdon Clifford*, Vol. I, pp. 36-37; Vol. II, p. 247.

[58] Walter Mehring, *The Lost Library. The Autobiography of a Culture* (Indianapolis: Bobbs-Merrill, 1951), p. 30.

CHAPTER IV

"The Age of Longing"

1.

The future historian who sits down to write the intellectual history of twentieth-century Europe will be well advised to undertake, as a preliminary task, a careful study of the writings of Arthur Koestler. For Koestler has made it his main business as a writer, in essays and novels and in his autobiography, to dissect the European mind, especially in its more satanic aspects, between the World Wars—not simply as a reporter, moreover, but as one who has participated in the world he describes, who knows it from the inside as the result of personal experience. Born in 1905 in Budapest, he knew something of the old intellectual world which preceded the march of Fascism and Communism. "I was born at the moment when the sun was setting on the Age of Reason," he writes in his autobiography. Elsewhere he describes his early life in a "typical Continental middle-middle-class family," the collapse of this "middle-class idyl" during World War I and the Austrian inflation of the early twenties, and his decision soon thereafter to join the Communist Party because, as he says, he was ripe for it and lived in "a disintegrating society thirsting for faith." [1] Sub-

[1] Arthur Koestler, in *The God that Failed*, ed. Richard Crossman (New York: Harper and Brothers, 1949), pp. 17-19; *Arrow in the Blue* (New York: Macmillan, 1952).

sequently, he left the Party to fight totalitarianism wherever he found it, first in Spain during the Civil War where he was imprisoned by the Fascists and sentenced to death, and later in Paris and England where he operated as both an antifascist and anticommunist refugee. Out of this wealth of firsthand experience has come his most mature work on the European mind of the twentieth century. In his brilliant essay *The Yogi and the Commissar* (1945) he sketched with nervous strokes the disastrous effects which he thought mechanistic and materialistic thinking has had upon western ethics and politics. A trilogy of novels enlarged upon this and other themes suggested in the essay. *Darkness at Noon* (1941), his greatest novel, and *Arrival and Departure* (1943) studied, respectively, the Communist mind and aspects of the mental outlooks of Fascism and psychoanalysis. The third, *The Age of Longing* (1951), which gives this chapter its title, turned to the mind of the free world, pitilessly laying bare its poverty of faith as contrasted with the faith of the world on the other side of the Iron Curtain. More than any of Koestler's works, *The Age of Longing* focuses attention on the dilemma of the modern sceptic. It is, therefore, at bottom a book about religion and scepticism.

Its setting is Paris at mid-century, its *dramatis personae* an extraordinary group of intellectuals drawn from all parts of the western world. Chief among these are Julien Delattre, a French poet who is said to have enjoyed a vogue in the thirties and who so often seems to speak for the author; Hydie, convent-bred, the daughter of an American colonel; M. Anatole, representative of the dying aristocracy; Commanche, an official of the French government; a Catholic priest, Father Millet; and two Russians, Leontiev, renegade literary star of the "Free Commonwealth," and Fyodor Nikitin, cultural attaché of the "Free Commonwealth" in France. What all these people have in common—with the significant exception of the priest and the Communist—is a longing for faith, faith in a meaningful world. "We are the dispossessed," says Delattre, "—the dispossessed of faith; the physically or spiritually homeless." Hydie observes of herself that she has "no core, no faith, no fixed values." Kneeling down on the priedieu which she had carried about with her ever since leaving the convent, she cries out in a loud and agonized voice, "LET ME BELIEVE IN SOME-THING." [2] It is this longing for faith that draws her, temporarily, to Nikitin as to a magnet, for he at least believes in something, even if it is only a Utopia measured in terms of kilowatt hours, bushels, and tons. Like Nietzsche, Koestler hints that the state of mind he is describing grips the cast of thousands as well as the principal actors of the drama. Commanche specifically says so. "Each time a god dies there is trouble in History," and the last time a god had died was on July 14, 1789, the day of the storming of the Bastille. Since then—for as it has turned out, the three-word slogan of the Revolution was not a satisfactory substitute for the Holy Trinity—the people have been deprived of their only real asset: "the knowledge, or the illusion, which-ever you like, of having an immortal soul. Their faith is dead, their kingdom is dead, only the longing remains." Looking into the faces of the workmen lining the boule-vard for M. Anatole's funeral, Hydie corroborates Com-manche's judgment that "they were all sick with longing." [3]

Koestler's book actually describes a new species of *homo sapiens*, or rather a new species of sceptic, substantially dif-ferent from the eighteenth- and nineteenth-century species we have studied. The essential thing about the new sceptic is that he combines scepticism with "longing." The scep-

[2] Arthur Koestler, *The Age of Longing* (New York: Macmillan, 1951), pp. 28, 32.
[3] *Ibid.*, pp. 317, 361.

ticism is still there. Delattre is as outspoken in his opposition
to the old religion as any rationalist of the two preceding
centuries: "What you ask of me," he says to Father Millet,
"is the unconditional surrender of my critical faculties"; "I
won't have any of your patent medicine." [4] Significantly,
however, the scepticism of Delattre and his companions
extends to the new gods as well as the old. Delattre, indeed,
reserves his heavy fire, not for the Christian God, who for
him is dead and buried, but for the gods which have been
manufactured since the Year I. The most menacing of these
gods is "the new Baal" Society, which, he thinks, dictates
an ethic of pure expediency. But he also shudders at History according to Karl Marx, which promises a new Middle
Ages, and at Science, or rather modern technology, which
when put into the hands of social idolaters threatens universal extinction. The only element of the old humanitarian
humanistic faith left over in Delattre's philosophy is the
determination to fight to preserve human dignity. Delattre,
who here talks somewhat like a French existentialist, pro-
poses an "active humanism" even while maintaining a contemplative scepticism. This, to be sure, is something. But it
is rather like the last gasp of a drowning man who knows
that however nobly he may conduct himself at the end, he
will nonetheless go down and so will all the other ship-
wrecked people around him. Commanche says to Hydie
that when the test comes, i.e., when the new "Neanderthal"
makes his move against Europe, he and his friends will
know how to make their exits "with a flourish." "But if you
ask me why I insist so much on the flourish, I will tell you
in confidence that it will merely serve to cover our bewilderment. For you can only die simply and quietly if you
know what you are dying for." [5]

[4] *Ibid.*, p. 352.
[5] *Ibid.*, p. 318.

According to Delattre, the only real hope for the individual and for Europe is the emergence of "a new transcendental faith" which will re-establish man's relations with the universe and thus give him something to live and die for other than mere expediency. He therefore longs for such a faith, as the ancient Jew thirsted for God in a dry and weary land where no water is. His nostalgia is not like that sense of bereavement previously noted in nineteenth-century sceptics like George Romanes and George Eliot. It is compounded, not so much of a sense of the loss of an old home, as of longing for a new home—a new cosmic loyalty "with a doctrine acceptable to twentieth century man." But as yet he has not got it, and indeed he does not know how to go about getting it, for he understands perfectly well that religions are not invented in the laboratory, that one has to "wait" for them to materialize.

Thus, with Koestler's cast of characters we move into a new phase of the sceptical tradition which differs in important respects from the phases which preceded it. This is assuming, of course, that Koestler reads the sceptical mind of the twentieth century correctly, but that he has done so I think there can be very little doubt. On this reading the twentieth century, at least thus far, is not a new age of religious faith, as some people have maintained. It too is an age of scepticism, but its scepticism is of a new and different type. To repeat, its hallmark—obviously, the generalization does not apply to every individual or group—is a combination of scepticism and longing. As a general rule nineteenth-century sceptics did not long for a faith, at least not for sustained periods, for they already had one; certainly not many of them longed for "a new transcendental faith." Koestler's Delattre, however, does, and it is this "longing" that makes him unique.

2.

Older types of scepticism, of course, have continued to exist, and even to flourish, side by side with the new. They are conspicuous, for example, in "diamat" (the dialectical materialism of the Marxists) as expounded by Lenin in his *Materialism and Empirio-Criticism*, in the newer forms of positivism and "scientism" (a twentieth-century neologism, and now in wide use), in the cultural relativism of the anthropologists and historians, among Freudians and "new humanists." Putting "diamat" aside, this traditional scepticism is liable to go unnoticed only because its arguments, by now traditional arguments, have become quietly held assumptions. There is no longer any need to argue and exhort, as in the days of Strauss and Darwin, for God is so obviously a "dead hypothesis." From the standpoint of this older scepticism the "warfare" between scepticism and religion is over, with the palm of victory palpably gone to the former.

Nevertheless, warfare has been resumed on several occasions, in something like the charged atmosphere of the nineteenth century. Two such occasions form an important part of the chronicle of twentieth-century scepticism and therefore require special comment. The first is the "warfare between psychiatry and religion," which has been more or less continuous since the publication of Sigmund Freud's *Totem and Taboo* (1907) and *The Future of an Illusion* (1926). The second, which has created rather less stir, is the counterattack launched more recently by a group of intellectuals, self-styled "new humanists," against the contemporary "new turn toward religion."

More than any other single individual, Sigmund Freud is responsible for the prolongation of the old warfare into the new century. The fact that in a "psychological age" the most influential of all psychologists chose to throw his full weight behind religious scepticism guaranteed that the old warfare between biology and religion should blaze into a new warfare between psychoanalysis and religion. Actually, Freud's antireligious arguments were not new, at least in their main drift, but they seemed to be new because they bore the trademark of the exciting new science of psychoanalysis. In fact, they were a blend of traditional rationalistic, positivistic, and Feuerbachian arguments. In *The Future of an Illusion,* his chief pronouncement on the subject, Freud represented religion, à la Feuerbach, as essentially wish-fulfillment. Religion, he said, originated in man's feeling of helplessness and need for protection, at a time in history when his rational intelligence was not yet fully developed. Man invented the gods, i.e., he "wished" them into existence, in order to allay his anxieties in the face of life's dangers, including the crushing superiority of nature— hence the doctrine of Providence; and in order to insure long-range if not short-range justice—hence the doctrine of immortality. Man invested his gods with the qualities of his human father toward whom he has an ambivalent attitude of love and fear. These gods, like the father remembered from childhood, make everything turn out to man's advantage; they console him in his tragic situation and they give him answers to his curiosity. Hence, for Freud religion was, first of all, a "neurosis," since it involved, or at least so he thought, not only wish-projection into a father image but also a veritable obsession with guilt and the expiation of guilt by means of penance and sacrificial rites. It was also an "illusion" because Freud could find no evidence for belief in the gods as objective entities. Indeed, the presumption was against their authenticity because they derived from our ignorant ancestors ("the comparative method of research," he wrote, "has revealed the fatal resemblance between religious ideas revered by us and the mental productions of primitive ages and peoples");[6] also because their existence was postulated in untrustworthy documents—shades of the Higher Criticism—and because, above all, they corresponded so neatly to man's wishes. Like so many nineteenth-century sceptics, Freud pointed out that religious belief was not open to the same kind of testing and proof as other beliefs which we are asked to accept, e.g., the belief that the earth is shaped like a globe, which can be checked by actual circumnavigation. In any case, why resort to a supernatural explanation when we have a perfectly good natural one? Why postulate an objective God when we can account for God as a projection of unconscious wishes? Clearly, Freud exemplifies the reductive type of thinking which had become so fashionable in the nineteenth century; like Feuerbach and Marx, he found it possible to reduce everything religious to something else in the natural order. He also thought that religion sanctified bad institutions and stultified the critical intelligence.

Because it does all these things, religion does not deserve to have a future. It keeps men from growing up. Contrary to what most people think, it does not even make men happier or more moral. Unlike his erstwhile pupil and colleague Carl Jung, Freud even denied the therapeutic efficacy of religion, either for the mass or the individual. He denied the dependence of human culture on religion. As he saw it, getting rid of religion would enable man to face up to reality, to liberate the scientific intelligence, and, by withdrawing the expectation of life in another world, to concentrate on making life tolerable in this world. He had

[6] Sigmund Freud, *The Future of an Illusion,* trans. W. D. Robson-Scott (Horace Liveright and the Institute of Psycho-Analysis, 1928), pp. 67-8.

only contempt for such compromises as the contemporary philosophy of "as if" (as expounded, for example, in Hans Vaihinger's book *Die Philosophie des Als Ob*, which was published in 1911) which, while acknowledging that religious beliefs were "fictions," advocated behaving "as if" they were true because of their great importance for the maintenance of society. He would not even compromise to the extent of retaining the word while transposing its traditional meaning in the manner of John Dewey and some of the new humanists. He insisted on calling a spade a spade: "religion," he said, "consists of certain dogmas, assertions about facts and conditions of external (or internal) reality, which tell one something that one has not oneself discovered and which claim that one should give them credence." [7] In the future, he said, let us proceed empirically and see what will happen by bringing up our children without benefit of religious education. We have never given this sort of education a chance, and we might be pleasantly surprised by its results.

Largely as the result of Freud, the psychological argument has taken on a special prominence in twentieth-century sceptical thinking. It is, of course, not possible to measure exactly its impact, but that it has been considerable no one can doubt. Two examples, one of a professional psychologist and one of a "layman," will suffice to illustrate the nature if not the extent of the influence. By no means all professional psychologists have taken Freud's side in the contemporary "warfare between psychiatry and religion," as will be noted in the next chapter. Many, however, have done so, and one of these is J. C. Flügel, well known expounder of Freudianism in England and Fellow of the British Psychological Society. Professor Flügel's *Man, Morals and Society* (1945) is especially noteworthy in that it

[7] *Ibid.*, p. 43.

not only closely follows Freud's sceptical argument but seeks to substitute for traditional religion a new "religion of humanity" which is strongly reminiscent of Auguste Comte. It is in any case an excellent example of what Professor Joad calls, in *Decadence*, the "Psychologizing of Morals and Conscience" in contemporary thought. Flügel begins by admitting that psychoanalysis cannot "disprove" religion, any more than can the biological and physical sciences. On the other hand, it "has in truth done much to undermine religion." We are justifiably sceptical of an idea like God which corresponds so closely to human wishes and to the father image of childhood. Flügel also concedes that, at its best, religion produces an elevation of spirit. But here again he questions whether what we call "religious" experience differs qualitatively from "experiences that would not usually be termed religious," e.g., the high devotion to their respective tasks of the scientist, artist, or social reformer. He thinks Christianity displays some characteristics of moral progress, but he severely criticizes it for its otherworldliness and hence its indifference to larger social problems.[8] This last criticism explains his personal preference for a "religion of humanity." "The religious emotions," he writes, "must be largely or entirely secularized and be put in the service of humanity. The religion of humanity is surely the religion of the nearer future." [9]

Flügel does not appear to realize how old this "religion of the nearer future" really is. For God he substitutes what another psychologist, Raymond B. Cattell, called the "Group Mind" or "Theopsyche," and which Comte and others had called, long before Cattell, simply "Humanity" or "Society." The "Theopsyche" plays a role similar to that

[8] J. C. Flügel, *Man, Morals and Society* (New York: International Universities Press, 1945), chap. 17, "The Problem of Religion."
[9] *Ibid.*, p. 275.

of God: it provides an outlet for man's emotional needs, creates his ideals and goals, calls for his sacrifice, and rewards his services by perpetuating his name. Flügel obviously prefers the "Theopsyche" to God because it requires no assumptions about the metaphysical or the supernatural for which there is no scientific evidence. He recognizes that in the final analysis the Group must seem inadequate in comparison with an Almighty Being. But he concludes his critique of religion in a manner that would have pleased Freud, and indeed almost any sceptic in the main line from the nineteenth century.

And here the final ineluctable renunciation must be made. Men must abandon the last shred of that longed-for but illusory "omnipotence" to which, even after the relinquishing of magic, they sought to cling through their relation with a divine ruler of the universe. . . . But this very sense of loneliness and isolation may well serve to bring them closer together than would otherwise be possible; and they have the consolation of knowing that in the human heart and brain they possess instruments which, faulty though they may be, have brought them far along the path of evolution, and, if wisely used, may bring them almost infinitely farther. . . . Within this sphere of influence (which is so rapidly expanding) man himself is far from being impotent and, as Freud reminds us in the last passage of his earlier book on religion, science at least has no appearance of being an illusion.[10]

The second example is taken, perhaps somewhat surprisingly, from the life history of the Oxford don C. S. Lewis, who is best known today as an apologist for Christianity. Before he returned to Christianity, however, Lewis went through a long sceptical phase in which he encountered, among other contemporary intellectual forces, "the new psychology." In his recent autobiography he tells how

[10] *Ibid.*, p. 280.

during his school days, under the influence first of Victorian rationalism and later of the new psychology, he lost his belief in the Christian God, whom he came to loathe as the "transcendental Interferer." From one of his school masters, "a 'Rationalist' of the old, high and dry nineteenth-century type," who was "great on *The Golden Bough* and Schopenhauer," he learned to believe in nothing but "atoms and evolution." Then at Oxford, soon after World War I, he was introduced to the new psychology which taught him and others, he says, to have done, once and for all, with childish romantic delusions about life and to behave "with the greatest good sense." In a passage reminiscent of what Frederick Pollock and George Bernard Shaw had once written about Darwin he says that

The new Psychology was at that time sweeping through us all. We did not swallow it whole (few people then did) but we were all influenced. What we were most concerned about was "Fantasy" or "wishful thinking." . . . Now what, I asked myself, were all my delectable mountains and western gardens [i.e., his romantic dreams] but sheer Fantasies? [11]

Lewis, of course, did not rest with this experience but found his way back, via Idealism and Theism, to a Christian position. But exposure to "the new psychology" undoubtedly helped to confirm many another "layman" in a permanently sceptical position.

Matching the militancy of "the new psychology" but provoked by a different cause is another species of contemporary scepticism which has sometimes been called "the new humanism." As used here, the term refers to those intellectuals, chiefly British and American, who during the past twenty years have reacted rather violently to the "reli-

[11] C. S. Lewis, *Surprised by Joy* (New York: Harcourt, Brace and Company, 1955), p. 203.

gious revival" as epitomized by such converts as C. S. Lewis himself, and who in opposition to that revival have felt impelled to reaffirm a traditional sceptical-humanist position. This new humanism is not an organized movement with a body of doctrine like Freudianism; it is simply a rallying point for a number of men, both young and old, who are angry and alarmed by what the English novelist E. M. Forster labels "the present rise of obscurantism amongst intellectuals." What it shows is that in the contemporary climate there is still plenty of scepticism, old style, which can be aroused to action when the occasion seems to demand it.

Recent discussions in two journals, one American and one British, show the new humanists answering the call to arms. It will be recalled from the Introduction that in 1950 the editors of *The Partisan Review* invited a number of writers to a symposium on "Religion and the Intellectuals." They were asked to evaluate, and if possible to explain, "the new turn toward religion among intellectuals" in the last decade, which the editors assumed to be a movement of considerable magnitude. As noted above (see p. 9) many of the contributors, those who can be identified as "new humanists," rejected the movement out of hand as a "failure of nerve" and a surrender to obscurantism. The following are typical statements: "religious converts surrender their critical rights"; "acceptance of religious myths violates the knowledge it has taken so many generations to gather together"; "supernatural religion is a source of violent conflict among men and destroys human values." "Failure of nerve," however, was the chief battle cry, conspicuously in the statement by the philosopher Sidney Hook, where it is the core of the argument. The phrase was not new with Professor Hook. He had used it in another article, published seven years earlier by the same journal, in making a comparison between ancient and contemporary western civilization. Our age, he had said, unfortunately exhibits many of the signs that were characteristic of the epoch which saw the rise of the mystery religions and Christianity: on the one hand, belief in man's depravity and despair of patient inquiry, and on the other, a frenzied search for values and a cry for religious revelation: in a word, "failure of nerve." Returning to the charge in the later article, he denounced the "God-seeking intellectuals" of today who, he said, were looking, not primarily for truth, but for justification and comfort in a time of social crisis. Relating the religious renaissance to "the more inclusive movement of irrationalism in modern thought," he deplored the credulity of the religious converts and their short-circuiting of reason by emphasis on feeling or intense experience as the source of truth. Most of the recent religious converts, he pointed out, were men in literary and political life who had never earned the intellectual right to either religious belief or disbelief, and who had chosen belief simply because they were bewildered by the shock of recent events. "As a set of *cognitive* beliefs," he concluded, "religion is a speculative hypothesis of an extremely low order of probability." [12]

Similarly aroused were the Cambridge humanists who contributed articles for the February, 1955, number of *The Twentieth Century*.[13] In the opening letter to the editor, which amounts to a humanist manifesto, E. M. Forster declared that "since the second world war" he had been worried about "certain tendencies in Cambridge and elsewhere." "I find that people much younger than myself—men and women in their thirties, undergraduates too—are

[12] *The Partisan Review*, Vol. XVII, No. 3 (March, 1950), p. 230. Cf. *ibid.*, Vol. X, No. 1 (Jan.-Feb., 1943).

[13] This entire issue was edited in Cambridge University. Its aim was to show Cambridge "looking at the world to-day," and it was the first of a series describing trends of thought in contemporary England.

getting worried in the same way, and that is why I now address this letter to THE TWENTIETH CENTURY for I understand that our common anxieties are to be voiced here." Forster's anxieties centered in "the present rise of obscurantism amongst intellectuals," as manifested in the rise of religious authoritarianism and "the arbitrary theory of Original Sin," which, to his mind, negated "Humanism." [14] Subsequent essays denounced "the new animism," exemplified by the frequent reference among the *avant-garde* to such persons as Simone Weil, Jung, and Kierkegaard, and the "recrudescent Age of Faith," as shown in the "migration to churches," "the evangelical appeal," and "prayer meetings over university teas." According to a Cambridge undergraduate, "We have lost part of the manly backbone of Victorian England." [15] In an essay entitled simply "People," the literary scholar Noel Annan called attention to the powerful influence on "the present postwar generation" of Herbert Butterfield's *Christianity and History* which, he said, "corresponded to the disillusioned mood of the post-war generation, yet offered them reassurance." But Annan himself will have none of it, or at least not most of it, for what he describes as "humanist" reasons. "Not only does modern humanism treat belief in dogmatic religion merely as one way of regarding life; it suggests that its postulates are likely to produce ruinously wrong judgements about human nature and behaviour"—"ruinously wrong" in that dogmatic religion "postulates a single ideal towards which the whole of humanity must strive" and which therefore does not take into account the necessary tentativeness of human judgment.[16]

[14] *The Twentieth Century*, Vol. CLVII, No. 936 (February, 1955), pp. 99-101.
[15] *Ibid.*, p. 122.
[16] *Ibid.*, pp. 128, 136.

It is not easy to say exactly what the "new humanism" stands for, since the emphasis varies considerably from one individual to another. In Mr. Annan, for example, the emphasis is on intellectual "humility" or agnosticism (*Que scais-je?*), doubtless in revulsion against the threat of a new religious orthodoxy, whereas in a "scientific humanist" like the biologist Julian Huxley, it is much more positive. In spite of our legitimate doubts about God and a transcendental order, Huxley has said, we can still believe in man's power and dignity. "Scientific Humanism," he declared in a wartime radio address, "can provide a real and lively basis for faith in the business of living, and also a spur to effort by reminding man that he is now the sole trustee for any further progress to be made by life." [17] The difference between Annan and Huxley, however, is more apparent than real. Clearly, both represent strands of that humanistic strain which descends from the Enlightenment and which still has sufficient vigor to assert itself when it senses a new "rise of obscurantism."

A recent statement by the octogenarian philosopher Bertrand Russell summarizes the essentials of the new humanist position and at the same time shows that it is not new at all, but quite traditional. Significantly, this statement was elicited by an American editor who thought that a book of Russell's essays on religion would be worth publishing at a time "when we are witnessing a campaign for the revival of religion."

There has been a rumor in recent years [Russell said in his Foreword, dated 1956] to the effect that I have become less opposed to religious orthodoxy than I formerly was. This rumor is totally without foundation. I think all the great reli-

[17] *Humanism. Three B. B. C. Talks by Dr. Julian Huxley, Prof. Gilbert Murray, and Dr. J. H. Oldham* (London, 1944), p. 6. See also Julian Huxley, *Religion without Revelation* (London, 1927).

gions of the world . . . both untrue and harmful. . . . Scholastics invented what professed to be logical arguments proving the existence of God, . . . but the logic to which these traditional arguments appealed is of an antiquated Aristotelian sort which is now rejected by practically all logicians except such as are Catholics. There is one of these arguments which is not purely logical. I mean the argument from design. This argument, however, was destroyed by Darwin. . . .

The harm that is done by a religion is of two sorts. . . . As regards the kind of belief: it is thought virtuous to have Faith—that is to say, to have a conviction which cannot be shaken by contrary evidence. . . . The consequence is that the minds of the young are stunted and are filled with fanatical hostility. . . .

I should wish to see a world in which education aimed at mental freedom rather than at imprisoning the minds of the young in a rigid armor of dogma calculated to protect them through life against the shafts of impartial evidence. The world needs open hearts and open minds, and it is not through rigid systems, whether old or new, that these can be derived.[18]

3.

Side by side with this older scepticism, however, has developed the new type of scepticism epitomized by the inhabitants of Koestler's universe. To repeat, what distinguishes the latter from the former is a mood compounded of an agonizing sense of loss and hence of "longing." Not only has God died, but so have the new gods to which so many eighteenth- and nineteenth-century sceptics were able to shift their faith. With what result? One alternative is nihilism which is the road to death. Another is the undertaking of a long and painful journey in search of some new

[18] Bertrand Russell, *Why I Am Not a Christian,* ed. Paul Edwards (New York: Simon and Schuster, 1957), pp. v-vii.

god, faith, or life; or in some few instances, actually return to the old God. This mood was by no means unknown before the second decade of the twentieth century, but it has become increasingly catching, indeed widespread, between then and now.

In this section we shall deal with the evidence for this new type of "longing" scepticism, deferring to the next section discussion of the reasons for it. The evidence upon which we shall draw is of three kinds: the diagnoses of the contemporary "crisis" of civilization by relatively objective observers; the life histories and "confessions" of the sceptics themselves; and creative literature, chiefly poetry and the novel. Obviously, the literature is vast, and we can but take a sample of it. But one thing that seems reasonably clear, even from the sample, is that the new sceptics are recruited from practically all the intellectual disciplines. The creative writers, however, would appear to constitute the majority, possibly because they have pondered longest and deepest the condition of man in the twentieth century.

The diagnoses of civilization need not detain us long, for we have already considered them at some length in an earlier chapter (see pp. 12 ff.). What is wrong with "modern man"? Among such diagnosticians as Karl Jaspers and Carl Jung, Nicolas Berdyaev and Paul Tillich—the list could be multiplied endlessly—the key word is "anxiety." And why is he anxious? Not simply because he is sceptical, but because he is now aware, as never before, of the implications of his scepticism. "The modern mind," says Jaspers in his *Man in the Modern Age,* "has become *aware* of the loss of the sense of a divine presence in the world." In consequence, it feels an "unprecedented vacancy of existence," even a "dread of life" which has increased to such a pitch "that the sufferer may feel himself to be nothing more than a lost point in empty space, inasmuch as all human relation-

ships appear to have no more than a temporary validity."
In a passage on existentialism, Tillich similarly observes that
"twentieth-century man has lost a meaningful world and
a self which lives in meanings out of a spiritual center." But
the new thing is that he is now "*aware* of what he has lost
or is continuously losing." He experiences his loss as "despair," and in the case of the existentialist reacts with the
"courage of despair." [19] In other words, in the view of these
observers, the peculiarity of the contemporary sceptic consists, not so much in his loss of a spiritual center as such, as
in his awareness of the loss which makes his life seem
essentially meaningless. He longs for meaning because he
feels lonely and "anxious" in his scepticism, and this "anxiety," so they say, accounts for the flight of so many
modern people to the totalitarian systems. As Nicolas
Berdyaev put it in 1950, shortly before he died:

There is a craving for belief in modern man. . . . Faced with
the futility of his own existence the modern European finds
himself stranded high and dry. The trouble is not, of course,
political in the narrow sense. It concerns what are known as
the bourgeois values of life. These values have created an
appalling vacuum in the mind and heart of modern man. The
vacuum is still there and, as it appears, historical Christianity,
no less than politicians, fails to fill it.[20]

Carl Jung makes precisely the same diagnosis of "modern
man." To the extent that Jung's clinical observations stand
up, additional evidence comes therefore from psychology
itself. Mention was made on an earlier page of Jung's hypothesis of "modern man in search of a soul," but it is worth

[19] Karl Jaspers, *Man in the Modern Age* (*Die Geistige Situation der
Gegenwart*), trans. Eden and Cedar Paul (New York: Henry Holt,
1933), pp. 20-21, 64-65; Paul Tillich, *The Courage To Be* (New Haven:
Yale University Press, 1952), pp. 139-40. Italics mine.
[20] Nicolas Berdyaev, *Dream and Reality* (London, 1950), p. 326.

repeating here, if very briefly. In a lecture entitled "Psychotherapists or the Clergy" Jung compared the modern sceptic to a Bolshevist who has thrown over traditional opinions and wants to experiment with new ideas. The comparison, however, was not especially apt, for the Bolshevist, like comrade Nikitin in *The Age of Longing,* had a new faith to put in the place of the old, whereas Jung's sceptic has no such faith. Like the "dispossessed" in Koestler's book, he is a patient who in this case comes to the doctor for help. Of the hundreds of people, mostly Protestant, "all of them educated persons," whom he had treated for over a generation, "there has not been one," says Jung, "whose problem in the last resort was not that of finding a religious outlook on life. It is safe to say that every one of them fell ill because he had lost that which the living religions of every age have given to their followers." "They could find no meaning in life or were torturing themselves with questions which neither present-day philosophy nor religion could answer." [21] Here in Jung is the same image of the "anxious," "longing" sceptic which Jaspers and the other diagnosticians present: the man who is not happy, who is even neurotic, in his scepticism, and who consults the psychiatrist precisely because he is "in search of a soul."

Life histories and personal confessions provide firsthand evidence of the new type of scepticism observed by the diagnosticians. The confessional literature relating to the subject is abundant, and again we shall have to be satisfied with a sample. An exhaustive survey would necessarily include a close study of the extraordinary phenomenon of suicide in recent times, to which Ignazio Silone and Albert Camus, among others, have called attention. Suicide, or the

[21] Carl Jung, *Modern Man in Search of a Soul,* trans. W. S. Dell and Cary F. Baynes (New York: Harcourt, Brace and Company, 1933), pp. 254, 266-67.

contemplation of it, is a facet of the nihilistic climate in which so many intellectuals of the past two generations have lived, and the religious problem would seem to be, at least in part, at the bottom of it. But twentieth-century nihilism still awaits its historian, and the few examples chosen here are not so extreme, though perhaps for that reason more representative. These examples do not arrange themselves neatly into distinct types though it is possible to distinguish between them on the basis of the hope, or lack of hope, with which they look forward to some sort of solution of their problem.

Peter Moen is an example of a sceptic for whom there is no exit. Peter Moen, by profession an actuary in a life insurance company and something of a mathematician, became head of all the clandestine newspapers in Norway during World War II. In 1944, he was arrested by the Gestapo and imprisoned. While in an Oslo prison he kept a diary which was miraculously preserved, and which is an epitome of the new sceptical travail. "I do not believe, but I pray for faith," he wrote soon after being thrust into solitary confinement. And for the next three months he wrestled with his soul, now praying to the Lutheran God of his youth, now finding intellectual reasons for not doing so. He longs to believe, but at the same time he does not wish to delude himself, even in his extreme need. Perhaps religious belief is only "wishful thinking," he tells himself. Perhaps it is all "subjective," the idea of God an "illusion," a "cosmic projection of the framework of the Oedipus complex." He carries on a running dialogue with himself: a "blasphemous and sceptical voice," his "intellectual self," argues with his heart. He determines to deaden his ability to think and to find salvation in instinct and inner experience; but his intellect imposes a veto, and he has a clear sensation of standing before a "closed door." In the end his experiment fails, as he notes in a moving valedictory, written shortly after he was released from solitary confinement:

With a sad sigh I must state that the experiment gave a negative result. I found no anchor-ground for faith or conviction of anything divine speaking to me or in me. I found the *wish* for its existence but this wish is quite explicable from the point of self-preservation and egotism. I can only find that my altogether honest attempt led me back to my standpoint of twenty years: No truth is found outside man. *Everything* originates with man himself and that includes all thoughts and feelings concerning 'God'.[22]

"But," he wrote the very next day, "—the situation is further 'ironical'—a vague 'longing' counteracts the intellect's rejection of religion."

Not quite as ambivalent, but nearly so, is the personal position described by Bronislaw Malinowski as "tragic agnosticism." Speaking in a British symposium on "science and religion" the great anthropologist commenced by stating that he was an agnostic, that he could not accept any positive religion nor positively believe in any sort of Providence, that he had no conviction of personal immortality. "Science," he said, was responsible for his agnosticism, for science develops the critical sense and demands evidence, thus spoiling us for the acceptance of secondhand truth through sacred tradition or scriptures. The comparative study of religions, in which he himself had done much research, also showed that the cravings of the soul are often satisfied by "obvious fictions" which nevertheless work well, and that religious ideas are instruments created for a special need. There, however, his resemblance to a nineteenth-century agnostic like Sir Leslie Stephen ends. For Malinowski, unlike Stephen, is not happy with his agnos-

[22] *Peter Moen's Diary*, trans. Bjorn Keofoed (New York: Creative Age Press, 1951), p. 81.

ticism. Science accounted for his attitude, yes, but, he added, "therefore I do not love science, though I have to remain its loyal servant." He confessed to a need of God which, however, he could not satisfy. "The typical rationalist says: 'I don't know and I don't care.' The tragic agnostic would rejoin: 'I cannot know, but I feel a deep and passionate need for faith, of evidence, and of revelation.'" To him personally and to many others "nothing really matters" except the answer to the burning questions of immortality and the meaning of suffering. "The doubt of these two questions lives in us and affects all our thoughts and feelings. Modern agnosticism is a tragic and shattering state of mind."[23]

Another example of this "tragic agnosticism" is Spain's universal man, Miguel de Unamuno, who, however, came to the position, not from science, but from literature and philosophy. In his masterpiece *The Tragic Sense of Life* (1913), Unamuno reveals himself as a religious exile long before he became, in fact, a political exile (later in life he was twice removed from the Rectorship of the University of Salamanca, first for attacking the dictatorship of Primo de Rivera, and afterwards the Fascists). On his own statement he could be at home neither with the Roman Catholic solution of the religious problem nor with the rationalist dissolution. The former, he thought, did violence to the adult reason, by demanding dogmatically that it believe too much, while the latter nullified the longing of the human heart, ending up in absolute relativism. And so, he tells us, he was plunged into "the depths of the abyss." In an intensely personal passage of his chapter by that title he describes "the tragic sense of life" which is, "though more

[23] Bronislaw Malinowski in *Science and Religion. A Symposium* (New York: Charles Scribner's Sons, 1931), pp. 77-8. This volume consists of a series of talks delivered over the B. B. C. in 1930.

or less hidden, the very foundation of the consciousness of civilized individuals and peoples today—that is to say, of those individuals and those peoples who do not suffer from stupidity of intellect or stupidity of feeling." For such people "nothing is sure. Everything is elusive and in the air. . . . Absolute certainty and absolute doubt are both alike forbidden to us. We hover in a vague mean between these two extremes, as between being and nothingness. . . ." [24] To be sure, Unamuno expressed confidence that out of this warfare, this dialectic between the head and the heart, a new faith could arise, but it would be a faith, like the faith of the eternal exemplar Don Quixote, "based upon incertitude, upon doubt." "Lord, I believe [i.e., my heart longs to believe]; help thou mine unbelief [i.e., my intellectual scepticism]."

Ex-Communists like Koestler exemplify a somewhat different experience in that they found in Communism a temporary answer to their "longing," only to discover in the end that it too was a false god. No one has described better than Koestler the spiritual vacuum in which the European bourgeoisie lived after World War I. The bourgeois society of the twenties, the society in which he himself grew up, was "scourged by inflation, depression, unemployment and the absence of a faith to live for." In this situation there took place "a mass migration of the sons and daughters of the European bourgeoisie trying to escape from the collapsing world of their parents." Some migrated to the Right, others to the Left, while the remainder "lived on pointlessly." [25] Koestler was one of those who chose Communism. At first it seemed to him to be a rational deci-

[24] Miguel de Unamuno, *The Tragic Sense of Life in Men and in Peoples,* trans. J. E. Crawford Flitch (New York: Dover Publications, 1954), p. 117, 125.

[25] Koestler, *Arrow in the Blue,* pp. 270-80.

sion: Western capitalism represented the past, the Five-Year Plan the future; Russia was building a new Utopia in steel and concrete. In retrospect, however, the true explanation appeared to him to be psychological or religious. "I became converted because I was ripe for it and lived in a disintegrating society thirsting for faith."

To say that one had "seen the light" is a poor description of the mental rapture which only the convert knows. . . . The new light seems to pour from all directions across the skull; the whole universe falls into pattern like the stray pieces of a jigsaw puzzle assembled by magic at one stroke. There is now an answer to every question, doubts and conflicts are a matter of the tortured past—a past already remote, when one had lived in dismal ignorance in the tasteless, colorless world of those who *don't know.*[26]

As is well known, Koestler's new god failed, and he has confessed a number of times since to falling back into the anguished world of the "don't know." Nevertheless, he would appear to have more hope than the "tragic agnostics," certainly more than Peter Moen, of some sort of ultimate solution to the "faith" problem. Even while "shivering in the darkness" he has admitted to longing and hoping for the emergence of "a new type of faith" which will somehow satisfy "the great sober thirst of man's spirit." We shall return to this theme in a later section.

C. E. M. Joad and Aldous Huxley are examples of sceptics who eventually found a permanent answer in religion, Joad in Christianity, Huxley in the "perennial philosophy" of mysticism. However, before arriving at their haven they too experienced all the agonies of the new scepticism. Joad in fact never quite got rid of them, as he tells us in *The Recovery of Belief.* Having told why he now considered

---

[26] Koestler, in *The God That Failed,* p. 23.

"the religious hypothesis" to be more satisfactory than any other, he confessed to "moments of disbelief, days of doubt and periods of absolute indifference." His newly found "assurance" after years of militant agnosticism "never hardens to the point of absolute conviction. I could wish that it did." The questioning intellect simply would not keep quiet. "Constantly, continually, it perceives fresh grounds for doubt and poses new, unanswerable questions." [27] This "plight of the intellectual," as Joad calls it, is probably quite common among contemporary sceptics turned religious. It afflicted even a religious mystic like the young Frenchwoman Simone Weil, who described herself as an "outsider" and as living, since her birth, "at the intersection of Christianity and everything that is not Christianity."

Aldous Huxley has never set down in a connected narrative his experiences as he migrated from scepticism to mysticism. However, that he personally knew the state of mind we are here describing can be inferred from scattered autobiographical remarks in *Ends and Means* (1937) and from a novel like *Eyeless in Gaza* (1936). Clearly, his scepticism, while he still had it, was of a quite different type from that of his famous grandfather or his brother Julian. In the former essay, in which he first sketched fully his new religious outlook, he told how, after World War I, he and many of his contemporaries tried to live by "the philosophy of meaninglessness" and how they became dissatisfied with it and longed for another. In *Eyeless in Gaza* he had his hero keep a diary in which doubtless he recorded some of his own travail. At any rate, Anthony Beavis, described as a sociologist, tells how he was reared not to believe in God, but how he took to reading the mystics mostly it would seem because he had begun to doubt the dogma of environ-

[27] Joad, *The Recovery of Belief: A Restatement of Christian Philosophy*, pp. 20-22.

mental progress preached by contemporary sociology, and to long for "progress from within as well as from without." For a long time he floundered, Hamlet-like. He had a distinct sensation of lacking even a personality which he could call his own, of succumbing, as he put it, to the demands of "a scepticism that has ceased to believe even in its own personality"—shades of Luigi Pirandello! He was afraid of making a fool of himself; it occurred to him that perhaps his new urge to find a guiding principle for his life was nothing but "the headaches, the hiccoughs of yesterday's religion." Finally, he decided that "to be shaken out of negativity," an unendurable state, he must take action, any kind of action. So he went to Mexico to join the revolutionaries and happily encountered there a Quaker doctor who showed him how to find spiritual peace. But before migrating to a recognizably religious position Huxley's hero knew all the anxiety and longing that bedevilled sceptics like Unamuno, Peter Moen, and Koestler.

Huxley's novel, like *The Age of Longing*, is a prime example of the last class of evidence to be considered here, namely, creative literature. Twentieth-century literature of both the first and second generations is full of the sceptical travail; indeed, this travail is one of its major themes, almost, it might be said, its chief preoccupation. We need not go into the problem here of the extent to which the poem or play, the novel or prose allegory reproduces the personal view of the author. Sometimes it clearly does, as in the case of Franz Kafka's *The Castle*. Sometimes it does not, as in the case of T. S. Eliot's *The Waste Land* or *Ash-Wednesday* in which the author is moving, or has already moved, beyond the position he describes. Sometimes, as with Albert Camus' *The Stranger*, the author outlines a view with which he has only partial sympathy, as we know from his other writings. For our purposes all we need to know is that the author is describing a state of mind with which he is familiar and which he thinks is sufficiently important to objectivize. Presumably he would not write about it if it did not fascinate him and also impress him as a real, perhaps even a universal, problem of his times. And the creative writers are seldom wrong in this latter respect, though they may exaggerate. Their writings, therefore, are the richest and most convincing evidence we have of the new type of scepticism.

Significantly, death presents itself as the starting point to many of these writers. Is there a life after death? Does life have any meaning if death is man's fate? Is there any good reason why man should not commit suicide? "There is but one truly serious philosophical problem, and that is suicide": this is the opening gambit of Camus' *Myth of Sisyphus*, which is a long, and utterly serious, disquisition on death and suicide. Why should this be "the fundamental question of philosophy" for Camus, as for so many others? The same reasons are always given. The first and primary reason is the death of God which, however, is not cause for exultation, as it was with Nietzsche, but reason for despair. A second and scarcely less important reason is disenchantment with all the substitute gods, including, very often, man himself. Ignazio Silone provides a vivid example of this sort of disenchantment in *Bread and Wine*. In a visit to Rome the hero of the novel looks up an old friend who had been a Communist and whom he hopes to win back to "the movement." However, he finds Uliva in an acute state of despair, having abandoned hope in "revolution," whether of the Communist or Fascist variety. "Every revolution, every single one, without any exception whatever," he observes bitterly, "started as a movement for liberation and finished as a tyranny." It goes without saying that Uliva does not believe in God; now, however, he is saying that experience has also robbed him of his belief in "progress." The only alternative for an intelligent man therefore is "non-life, the destruction of life, death, beautiful death," and Uliva later commits suicide.[28] Unlike Uliva, Silone and Camus say "no" to suicide, but they share with him his disenchantment, not only with God, but also with the new gods which history has thrown up in modern times.

Chiefly for these reasons the creative literature of the past two generations presents a shatteringly pathetic picture of man. Man is seen as obsessed with death, to a degree unknown in Victorian literature. He is "lonely," a "stranger," an "outsider" inhabiting an "absurd" universe. He lives in a state of "tragic ambiguity," shut in by "absurd walls." He feels "hollow" and "alienated"; he is subject to "anguish" and "despair." But his chief characteristic, which includes all the rest, is "homelessness," to which the philosopher Martin Buber has so often alluded. In *What Is Man?* (1938) Buber observed the "special human homelessness and solitude" of twentieth-century man, and went on to say that man becomes a real problem to himself in such times

when as it were the original contract between the universe and man is dissolved and man finds himself a stranger and solitary in the world. The end of an image of the universe, that is, the end of a *security* in the universe, is soon followed by a fresh questioning from man who has become insecure, and homeless, and hence problematic to himself.[29]

This homelessness, and the search for a home or painful recollection of a lost home, is a recurring figure among the creative writers. Another of the same order is thirst; still

[28] Ignazio Silone, *Bread and Wine,* trans. G. David and E. Mosbacher (New York: Harper and Brothers, 1937), pp. 175-77.

[29] Martin Buber, *What is Man?,* in *Between Man and Man,* trans. R. G. Smith (London, 1947), p. 132.

another, sickness. In one of Alberto Moravia's early novels, for instance, the young hero, who is anguished because he has no notion of where he is going, longs for a lost paradise "where everything—gestures, words, feelings—would have a direct connection with the reality in which they had originated." [30] Similarly, W. H. Auden's quartet of sceptics in *The Age of Anxiety* go in search of "The Quiet Kingdom" because they have "a feeling . . . of having lost their bearings, of a restless urge to find water." Significantly, however, they turn back at the edge of the desert which they know they must cross in order "to find water," preferring, in the end, confusion to commitment. And the same figure appears prominently in T. S. Eliot's early work, in *The Hollow Men* ("This is the dead land/ This is cactus land"), and conspicuously in *The Waste Land*, that great allegory of the modern world whose inhabitants are so parched (i.e., sceptical, who "can connect Nothing/ with nothing") that they can be aroused only with difficulty to search for water, and who when they finally do see water mistake it for a mirage. More recently, in *The Cocktail Party*, Eliot has pursued the same theme with the figure of sickness. Edward and Lavinia Chamberlayne and Celia Coplestone, who may be regarded as sceptics, are sick from their scepticism and consult a psychiatrist. Edward Chamberlayne has ceased even to believe in his own personality; he suffers from the "death of the spirit." Celia Coplestone is acutely aware of being alone and of not wanting to be alone, of going into the forest to find a treasure "which was not there/ And perhaps is not anywhere." As Eliot will have it in this particular play, however, the sceptics are cured of their scepticism and ultimately find "communion" in their several ways.

[30] Alberto Moravia, *The Time of Indifference*, trans. Angus Davidson (New York: Farrar, Straus, and Young, 1953), p. 237.

Roughly speaking, these sceptics of twentieth-century literature divide themselves into two categories which might be called the negative and the negative-positive. The negative sceptics are those who, like Peter Moen, long for a home in vain, whereas the others, while also quite negative, have some hope of finding a home somewhere and sometime. The young Englishman Colin Wilson describes both these types in his long and rambling, but frequently penetrating, essay *The Outsider* (1956). Of the negative sceptic, or outsider *in extremis*, he writes:

This is one of the Outsider's worst dilemmas: to feel the whole being groaning for some emotional satisfaction, some solid reality to touch, and to feel the reasoning faculty standing apart, jeering at the possibility of satisfaction and discouraging its approach. What should such an Outsider do? Should he deliberately repress his reasoning faculty, accept a faith and hope that his reason will be reconciled to it one day? Accept *Credo ut intelligam?* No. The Outsider cannot countenance such an idea.[31]

Koestler's Commanche, Auden's Malin in *The Age of Anxiety*, Eliot's Gerontion, Estragon and Vladimir in Samuel Beckett's *Waiting for Godot*, all more or less fit this description. Gerontion, for example, is described as "an old man in a dry month . . . waiting for rain." He has rationalized all his ghosts away. Late in life he accepts the need for belief, but he pathetically finds that he has lost forever the faculty of believing passionately. The theme of the poem is obviously the pathology of disbelief in the contemporary world. In the play by the Irishman Samuel Beckett, which was first produced in Paris in 1952-1953, the main characters do nothing but wait hopelessly for Godot (God) "on this bitch of an earth." "Nothing to

[31] Colin Wilson, *The Outsider* (Boston: Houghton Mifflin Company, 1956), pp. 199-200.

be done," they say over and over again. "I feel lonely," says Vladimir, yet he and his friend continue to wait, hoping against all hope. "I'm curious to hear what he [Godot] has to offer. Then we'll take it or leave it." But they never have the choice, for Godot never comes, and they remain alone "in the midst of nothingness," contemplating suicide.

But the supreme example of this negative scepticism is the work of Franz Kafka (1883-1924) whom a German critic aptly characterized as "the servant of a God not believed in." Like his hero "K" in *The Castle*, Kafka yearned for God, yearned to have God give him an identity, and to have spirit permeate the material world. Also like "K," however, he could never quite get through to God. Indeed, he frequently doubted God's very existence; and insofar as he could conceive of God at all, it was as an infinitely remote being who cared nothing about mere earthlings and who permitted his officials and servants to tyrannize over them. All of Kafka's doubts rise to the surface in a posthumously published short story entitled *The Great Wall of China*. The story, which is obviously an allegory about God and man, deals with the relationship between peasants living in the far south of China and the imperial court located in the north at Peking. The peasants are always trying to get information about the reigning Emperor, from pilgrims and sailors, from near or distant villages—but, says the narrator, "one hears a great many things, true, but can gather nothing definite." There are a number of reasons why they cannot do so. The first is epistemological: the subject of God is incommensurable with the human mind. The Great Wall of China was built in piecemeal fashion rather than as a whole because the human mind simply cannot comprehend the whole, nor even what the decrees of the high command in Peking are about. Similarly, in *The Castle* the villagers down below simply cannot comprehend the figure of the castle official named Klamm, nor even agree among themselves as to how he looks: Klamm's appearance fluctuates according to "the mood of the observer." That is to say, any metaphysical idea is subjective, relative to the degree of excitement and "the countless gradations of hope and despair" possible to human beings. Kafka's explanation, however, is also historical. The Chinese peasants live too far away, temporally as well as spatially, to have any tidings of the Emperor. In other words, the sceptical tradition has made it next to impossible for men to comprehend "the Word." There was once a time, says the narrator in *Investigations of a Dog*, when "the Word" was on the tip of everybody's tongue and anyone might hit upon it. But "today one may pluck out one's very heart and not find it. Our generation is lost. . . ." The metaphysical dog goes on to explain:

When our first fathers strayed they had doubtless scarcely any notion that their aberration was to be an endless one, they could still literally see the cross-roads, it seemed an easy matter to turn back whenever they pleased. . . . They did not know what we can now guess at, contemplating the course of history: that change begins in the soul before it appears in ordinary existence, and that . . . they were by no means so near their starting-point as they thought.[32]

With the consequence that today people are characterized by "a certain feebleness of faith and imaginative power" which prevents them from grasping the empire at Peking "in all its palpable living reality." And with the consequence too that in the schools a great deal is taught about past dynasties with their dates of succession, but nothing about the living ruler about whom there is universal con-

---

[32] *Selected Short Stories of Franz Kafka*, trans. Willa and Edwin Muir (New York: Random House—Modern Library, 1952), p. 233.

fusion, even among the scholars. "If from such appearances any one should draw the conclusion that in reality we have no Emperor, he would not be far from the truth." Clearly, for Kafka's peasants and dogs, as for Eliot's Gerontion, the idea of God had become a largely historical conception, buried deep in the remote past and inaccessible to modern man, at least on the passional level.

The scepticism depicted in *Ash-Wednesday* (1930), however, strikes a more positive note than *Gerontion* (1920), as does that of the later Malraux and recent works by Simone de Beauvoir and Albert Camus. In *Ash-Wednesday*, for example, the sceptic has begun an ascent up the stairway, i.e., has begun to have a new sense of direction, a new vision of the regeneration which depends upon the fruit of Mary (both Eliot and Auden, of course, have ended up in the Christian faith). Yet in these negative-positive works the negative still lies just beneath the surface: the sceptics in *Ash-Wednesday* are described as "those who wait in darkness," who "cannot pray" but "will not go away" (i.e., who have no faith but who long for a faith), who "are terrified and cannot surrender." Moreover, in works like those by the French triumvirate, the positive note often sounds more like bravado and defiance, more like a desperate stratagem than a real solution to the sceptical problem.

This is conspicuously so in Camus' *The Myth of Sisyphus* (1942) which epitomizes negative-positive scepticism in contemporary literature as Kafka's *The Great Wall of China* and *The Castle* epitomize the more purely negative position. Written during France's darkest hour, Camus' "myth" nevertheless tries to wring something positive out of an "absurd" situation and an "absurd" world. Kafka's anti-heroes always concede defeat in the end; they long for God but can never find him and consequently fall into a hopeless scepticism which denies even the possibility of achieving a measure of justice in this world. But Sisyphus, the "absurd hero," raises rocks even while he negates the gods. Like the members of the French Resistance he refuses to resign himself to "the certainty of a crushing fate"; he finds it possible to build and create in a universe without a master; he even exults in his freedom. He has managed, against great odds, to combine a sceptical metaphysic with an ethic of positive action. Independently of Camus, André Malraux had arrived at much the same position. Malraux has never deviated from the view that modern times have witnessed "the end of the absolute." But whereas his early works emphasized *weltschmerz*, man's essential loneliness in an absurd and meaningless universe, his war novel, *Les Noyers de l'Altenburg*, and especially his recent work on the psychology of art, stress man's creativeness. The history of art, if not the history of politics, shows conclusively, he now thinks, man's refusal to accept chaos, his courageous determination to impose his own order on the chaos he is condemned to live in. Both Camus and Malraux take a recognizably humanistic position. Both are sceptics, but not completely negative sceptics like Kafka.

Nevertheless, their type of scepticism obviously more nearly approximates that of Kafka than that of Comte, Mill, or George Eliot. The myth of Sisyphus is, after all, a "tragic" myth—Camus himself has so labeled it—and it is of the essence of Sisyphus' tragedy to long for clarity where there is none, to feel nostalgia for a home irretrievably lost. No one has described more vividly than Camus what it means to be shut in by "absurd walls." Man is doomed to ignorance about the universe because he cannot know anything beyond the senses. The evidence such as it is reveals only an "absurd world," hopelessly fragmented and chaotic, apparently ruled by chance. Yet it is human nature to wish that this were not so: "I can negate every-thing of that part of me that lives on vague nostalgias, except this desire for unity, this longing to solve, this need for clarity and cohesion." [33] What can he do in this di-lemma? He cannot take the leap into religious faith recom-mended by Kierkegaard, for instance, for that would be to abandon reason, and he rightly prizes his intellectual integ-rity. Unless he is to commit suicide, his only recourse then—or so it seems to him—is to defy the universe, to rebel against it, to build in spite of it. "That revolt is the certainty of a crushing fate, without the resignation that ought to accompany it." [34] The result is a life of tension in which joy alternates with profound melancholy. At times—Camus confesses it—Sisyphus succumbs to the rock which he is condemned ceaselessly to roll to the top of the mountain only to see it roll down again; to put it in Chris-tian terms, he has his nights of Gethsemane when his grief seems too heavy to bear. But at other times he has the joy of knowing that at least he can keep the rock rolling and that "there is no fate that cannot be surmounted by scorn." In subsequent books by Camus the note of affirmation increases and his Sisyphus evolves into a sort of Prometheus who, by learning compassion and pity, can not only rebel but actually achieve a measure of justice in this recalcitrant world. Yet the note of anguished scepticism lingers, for even with this new vision of limited power it is not easy to live without belief in God or historical progress. "Those who find no rest in God or in history are condemned to live for those who, like themselves, cannot live; in fact, for the humiliated." Still that same note of being "condemned," though now the emphasis is more on life than death.

[33] Albert Camus, *The Myth of Sisyphus and Other Essays*, trans. Justin O'Brien (New York: Alfred Knopf, 1955), p. 51.
[34] *Ibid.*, p. 54.

The words which reverberate for us at the confines of this long adventure of rebellion are not formulae for optimism, for which we have no possible use in the extremities of our unhappiness, but words of courage and intelligence. . . . We are at the extremity now. However, at the end of this tunnel of darkness, there is inevitably a light, which we already divine and for which we only have to fight to ensure its coming. All of us, among the ruins, are preparing a renaissance beyond the limits of nihilism. But few of us know it.[35]

4.

The explanation of the new scepticism is implicit in what has been said above, but we must now try to make it explicit. What needs to be accounted for, of course, is the new factor in the sceptical equation, the "longing" or, as it might more appropriately be called in some cases, the disillusionment. The old scepticism continues, has indeed now hardened into a tradition which amounts to a mental and psychological block. The new sceptic, however, as we have seen in case after case, is not reconciled to his scepticism. Like Julien Delattre in *The Age of Longing*, he feels dispossessed and homeless; hence he longs for a faith. How has this state of mind come about?

It has come about, it seems clear, for both internal and external reasons acting conjointly. By "internal" I mean man's metaphysical thirst which, judging by history, cannot be quenched for long by philosophies of agnosticism and naturalism. This thirst is written in the historical record of the past seventy-five years. It is already noticeable in the late nineteenth century, in the symbolist movement in literature, in the revival of metaphysical speculation at Ox-

[35] Albert Camus, *The Rebel*, trans. Anthony Bower (New York: Alfred Knopf, 1954), pp. 270-72.

ford and elsewhere, and in the new philosophy of Henri Bergson. *Marius the Epicurean,* published in 1885, exemplifies these early stirrings, and foreshadows what we may call the coming internal revolution. Walter Pater, when we encountered him last (see pp. 183-84), had abandoned the religion of his youth and become, under the influence of nineteenth-century empiricism, a sceptic and preacher of a new "religion" of art. Like his hero Marius, however, he afterwards experienced a change of heart. In his sceptical or "Cyrenaic" phase, Marius' thoughts, wrote Pater, "did but follow the line taken by the majority of educated persons" in an age (the age of Marcus Aurelius) "completely disabused of the metaphysical ambition to pass beyond 'the flaming ramparts of the world.'" Marius (Pater) later discovered, however, that this unmetaphysical Cyrenaicism gave but a partial and limited "apprehension of the truth of one aspect of experience." He then began to thirst for a metaphysic which would give him a view of the whole of reality, not only that aspect of it which impressed itself upon his senses, but also that which possibly lay "just hidden behind the veil of a mechanical and material order." [36] Although he subsequently went back to church, Pater never regarded his Platonic or Christian vision—the vision that Marius had while riding alone in the Sabine hills—as anything but a "working hypothesis." That is to say, he remained a sceptic to the last, but with his scepticism he now coupled, as he expressed it in another essay, a "wistful yearning towards home." [37] It is this combination of doubt and metaphysical longing (although in his case without acute anguish) that makes Pater a prototype of the new type of scepticism.

For something like what happened to Marius-Pater has

[36] Walter Pater, *Marius the Epicurean,* Part III, especially chaps. 16 and 17.
[37] Pater, *Works,* Vol. VIII, p. 180.

since happened to a great many twentieth-century sceptics. The metaphysical thirst is unmistakable in writers like Unamuno, Kafka, Koestler, and Camus. They are always raising, without being able to resolve, the old metaphysical questions, particularly the problem of death and what Koestler calls the "Man-Universe," as distinguished from the "Man-Society," connection. I think they would agree with the sentiment expressed in a letter written by Pater to Mrs. Humphry Ward in the same year that *Marius* was published. "The question," he wrote, "whether those facts ["the supposed facts on which Christianity rests"] were real will, I think, always continue to be what I should call one of the *natural* questions of the human mind." [38]

We may doubt, however, whether this internal longing would have assumed major proportions without the concomitant shock of external events. So long as the world seemed to be getting better, so long as faith in man and history held firm, there was no overpowering need to come to grips with "the natural questions of the human mind." It was therefore the mounting social crisis of the twentieth century that galvanized the need on a large scale. The impact of the two great wars, the decline of the bourgeoisie, the inhumanity of the Fascists and Nazis, disillusionment with the new Russian Utopia had the effect of producing in the minds of many (although not, of course, all) sceptics, a two-pronged scepticism. The old scepticism about God continued more or less unabated. But alongside it there now grew up a second scepticism directed at those new "gods" which had been so widely substituted for the old God since the eighteenth century. It was to this second scepticism that Dean Inge of St. Paul's referred when he spoke of "the fall of the idols"; the poet Auden and the philosopher Emman-

[38] Quoted in A. C. Benson, *Walter Pater* (New York: Macmillan, 1906), p. 200.

uel Mounier, when they called attention, respectively, to "the epoch of the Third Great Disappointment" and the "mass collapse of the two great religions of modern man, Christianity and rationalism."

Where, a century ago [Mounier declared in a lecture delivered at the opening session of UNESCO at the Sorbonne in 1946] among a hundred men you could count a majority professing Christian doctrines, and certainly a large number of the others having a more or less blind faith in the infallibility of reason and science, nowadays you would doubtless find some ten per cent of Christian believers, and I do not think that the proportion of convinced rationalists can be much higher.[39]

Professor Mounier's statistics may not be exact, but statements such as his, which are legion,[40] testify to a growing disillusionment about human nature itself and the tools and methods which men use to achieve progress. The catastrophic events of the twentieth century have seriously shaken modern man's conviction, the conviction so well expressed by Walter Mehring's father at the stroke of midnight on New Year's Eve, 1900, that he is in control of his destiny. Quite clearly, Humanity, Science, Society, and History do not command the same quasi-religious awe that they did in the days of Comte, Marx, and Karl Pearson—with the consequence that a great many sceptics have been left high and dry, without a faith, yet longing for a faith.

World War I was the first major jolt to the faith in progress hatched during the Enlightenment. Jung recognized this when he observed, in his essay on "The Spiritual Problem of Modern Man," that the War had contributed materi-

[39] Emmanuel Mounier, in *Reflections on Our Age* (New York: Columbia University Press, 1949), p. 28.

[40] For a number of similar statements see my article "Twentieth-Century Version of the Apocalypse," *Journal of World History*, Vol. I, No. 3 (Jan., 1954), pp. 623-40.

ally to "the shattering of our faith in ourselves and our own worth" and to modern man's loss of faith in the possibility of the rational organization of the world and his dream of the millennium. Pitirim Sorokin, the Harvard sociologist who served as a member of Kerensky's cabinet in the early stages of the Russian Revolution, similarly recognized it in a revealing confession which deserves to be quoted at length because it embodies a common experience and penetrates to the heart of the problem. His major work, Sorokin wrote in the preface to *Social and Cultural Dynamics*, grew out of his effort to understand something of what had been happening in the new bewildering world around him.

I am not ashamed to confess that the World War and most of what took place after it were bewildering to one who, in conformity with the dominant currents of social thought of the earlier twentieth century, had believed in progress, revolution, socialism, democracy, scientific positivism, and many other "isms" of the same sort. . . . I expected the progress of peace but not of war; the bloodless reconstruction of society but not bloody revolutions; humanitarianism in nobler guise but not mass murders; an even finer form of democracy but not autocratic dictatorships; the advance of science but not of propaganda and authoritarian *dicta* in lieu of truth; the many-scale improvement of man but not his relapse into barbarism. The war was the first blow to these conceptions. The grim realities of the Russian Revolution provided the second.[41]

For others the political and social events of the thirties were the eye opener. It was because of politics, specifically the advent of the Nazis, says Professor Joad in his book on *God and Evil* (1943), that he ceased to worship at the shrine of progress. The spectacle of "cruelty, savagery, oppression, violence, egotism, aggrandisement, and lust for power" in

[41] Pitirim Sorokin, *Social and Cultural Dynamics* (New York: American Book Co., 1937-1941), Vol. I, p. ix.

the contemporary world convinced him of "the obtrusiveness of evil" throughout history. Evil, he thought, was not to be got rid of so easily, by act of Parliament so to speak, as George Bernard Shaw, Herbert Spencer, and other progressivists had imagined; it is "endemic in the heart of man," an idea which Joad found "almost intolerably distressing." [42] About the same time, Aldous Huxley and Auden also became disillusioned with the "idiotic dream" of the "social-reform conception of progress," and for not dissimilar reasons. Huxley, for example, was much impressed, as Joad was impressed, by the lust for power manifested in contemporary Fascism, and by the fact that "reforms (good so far as they go) may deliver men from one set of evils only to lead them into evils of another kind." [43] Koestler's and Silone's disillusionment stemmed from their confrontation with the inhumanity of the Communist revolution, as in a way also did Simone Weil's. Partly as a result of her experience in the Spanish Civil War, to which she was originally drawn as a committed radical, Simone Weil concluded that "the revolution is the opiate of the people" and that the social myth as such was "a trap of traps . . . an *ersatz* divinity" which produced mayhem and murder. [44]

Camus etches this double loss of faith with extraordinary clarity in *The Rebel*. The great question that dominated the nineteenth century, he says, was "How to live without grace" (i.e., without God), and the answer, at least for many, was "By justice." "To the people who despaired of the Kingdom of Heaven, they promised the kingdom of men." The preaching of this second kingdom increased in

[42] Cyril E. M. Joad, *God and Evil* (New York: Harper and Brothers, 1943), pp. 14-17, 103-104.

[43] Aldous Huxley, *Ends and Means* (London, 1938), p. 18.

[44] Quoted by Leslie Fiedler, in Introduction to Simone Weil's *Waiting for God* (New York: G. P. Putnam's Sons, 1951), p. 21.

fervor up to the end of the century, but it has since sub-
sided. "The kingdom has retreated into the distance, gigantic
wars have ravaged the oldest of countries of Europe, the
blood of rebels has bespattered walls, and total justice has
approached not a step nearer." Hence, the question that
tortures the twentieth century is not only "How to live
without grace," but "How to live without grace and without justice." [45] As we have seen, Camus' own answer to this
peculiarly twentieth-century question is "rebellion" which
in his conception of it has a positive as well as negative aspect. He rebels against both metaphysics and history but
"on behalf of life" or in compassion for his fellow man.
This rebellion, unlike "revolution," does not claim that it
can achieve anything like total justice, but it can mitigate
the suffering of individuals threatened by a heartless God
and soulless history. For many other contemporary sceptics,
however, there simply is no answer, not even so modest an
answer as this—at least not yet. Like Koestler's Delattre
they live in a state of "longing," without faith in God or
man, not knowing what to expect, yet waiting and hoping
that somehow a new "god" may be born.

[45] Camus, *The Rebel*, p. 195.

CHAPTER V

A "Layman's Religion"

1.

In a recent essay Arthur Koestler, returning to a theme which has engrossed him for over a decade, writes of a possible "spontaneous emergence of a new type of faith which satisfies the 'great sober thirst' of man's spirit." [1] How, when, or even whether this will occur he does not say categorically. It is, he says, only a "guess and hope" on his part. It is a very strong "hope" because he thinks that without some sort of spiritual mutation to accompany the technological revolution, western civilization could well go the way of the dinosaur. It is a "guess" because he professes to see unmistakable signs that, to switch to another of his metaphors, the pendulum is swinging back to a more religious point of view. Already in *The Yogi and the Commissar* he had observed that "since the early 'thirties we are all travelling, more or less consciously, more or less willingly, towards the ultra-violet end," [2] i.e., toward the "Yogi" end of an imaginary spectrum which emphasizes the "Man-Universe connection" and "Change from Within,"

[1] Arthur Koestler, *The Trail of the Dinosaur and Other Essays* (New York: Macmillan, 1955), p. 250-51.

[2] Arthur Koestler, *The Yogi and the Commissar* (New York: Macmillan, 1946), p. 7.

and away from the infrared end of "Commissar-science" whose focus is on the "Man-Society connection" and "Change from Without." Although Koestler's "guess" is not a prediction, he is convinced of one thing: if there is to be a spiritual reawakening, it will be like nothing that we have ever seen before. At this point in his argument the pendulum metaphor breaks down. There can be no question of a swingback to the traditional churches which are "venerable anachronisms," which ask us to split our brains into halves and speak the language of a past epoch. What will be required—at least for most thinking people—is the birth of new gods, the emergence of a "new religion," a "new type of faith" which, as Delattre remarks to Hydie in *The Age of Longing*, will demand "a cosmic loyalty with a doctrine acceptable to twentieth century man." "Is it really too much to ask and hope," Koestler says again in *The Trail of the Dinosaur*, "for a religion whose content is perennial but not archaic, which provides ethical guidance, teaches the lost art of contemplation, and restores contact with the supernatural without requiring reason to abdicate?" [3]

The merit of Koestler's discussion lies more in his questions than answers. He raises important questions—historical as well as metaphysical questions, questions which are being raised not only by him but by his whole generation, and which might be rephrased as follows. What of the future, religiously speaking? In the next decades, what if anything will come of that "longing" for a spiritual home, depicted in the previous chapter? Will it develop into a genuine religious revival? Or will it be overwhelmed by a great new surge of secularism? If the "longing" persists and finds an object, what can the object conceivably be? Will it be traditional in form, or will it take some new shape, different in important respects from all previous historical shapes?

[8] Koestler, *The Trail of the Dinosaur*, p. 251.

Will it perhaps be a "Layman's Religion," as distinguished from the religion taught by clergymen? To restate the last question in the terms used in this book, is it possible that a significant segment of the educated western community may even now be entering still another stage of the sceptical tradition, the chief characteristic of which is some sort of creative combination of scepticism and religion?

To these questions there can be, of course, no definitive answer, least of all by the historian who knows, or who at least ought to know, better than to play the prophet. There is simply no telling what will happen in the future, for mutations in religion as in biology result from combinations— in this case combinations of experience and circumstance— which cannot be fully known in advance. That is to say, there is an element of freedom in any historical situation which does not lend itself easily if at all to scientific prediction or prophecy. However, if the historian cannot predict, he can make an educated guess, though always with the understanding that his guess may turn out to be partially or even wholly wrong. He can do this because he has in his possession two related pieces of knowledge—to him they seem like commonplaces—which throw at least some dim light forward on the near future. The first is that well-established traditions have staying power. Traditions like the sceptical tradition are not built in a day, nor without good reason, and in the course of their history the "facts" upon which they supposedly rest come to be accepted almost as assumptions. Hence, no historian in his right mind expects them to be easily or quickly dislodged. On the contrary, his expectation is that they will continue to be an important, even a decisive, influence in the solving of new problems. At the same time he knows that even the most durable traditions may crack, or at least be significantly modified, under the impact of events different from those that birthed and supported them. Hence, he will be on the alert to detect in certain contemporary events and trends the seeds of a possible new development. In short, he will expect convolutions but not revolutions in a tradition, at any rate not revolutions which force return to a *status quo ante*.

It is therefore not as a would-be prophet but merely as a historian that we shall address ourselves in the following pages to the aforementioned questions. First, we shall attempt a sounding of the contemporary European "mind" in order to assess the chances for and against Koestler's "guess and hope" for a significant religious mutation. Then, if we find that the chances are not overwhelmingly against, we can hazard our own guess as to the lineaments of the religion which such a mutation might produce or perhaps has already begun to produce.

2.

At first blush the odds would seem to be heavily weighted against any such "mutation." As noted in Chapter IV, there remains in the West today a hard core of unreconstructed sceptics, by no means a vanishing breed, who labor manfully and not ineffectively to combat the "failure of nerve" which they descry particularly among the literary people (see p. 199). In addition to these sceptics there is the "secularist man" identified by Helmut Thielicke and Karl Heim: the man who has ceased to ask the great religious questions, for whom these questions simply have no relevance to life as he knows it, who sees in life nothing but a brutal struggle for existence.

But today [Karl Heim wrote in 1949] there is growing up to an ever-increasing degree a generation of people who are separated from any kind of Church by a far deeper gulf than were the "atheists" and "anti-clericals" of earlier times. The genuine "men of the world"—and we came up against them in barrack rooms and officers' messes far more often in the second than in the first world war—can be recognized precisely by the fact that the fundamental questions . . . are no longer mentioned at all by these true secularists.[4]

Even among those who feel the need and long for a religious faith there is considerable and often complete scepticism. Koestler's Delattre knows perfectly well that "longing" for a faith which will restore psychic metabolism, and the possession of such a faith are two different things. "Faith," Barbara Ward says rightly, "will not be restored in the West because people believe it to be useful. It will return only when they find that it is true." [5] But that is precisely what Delattre and his kind do not find, as we have seen. Nor are Church people themselves free of the sceptical problem, as may be gathered, not only from the statistics of part-time churchgoing, but also from bitter controversies within the theological sanctum, like, for instance, the controversy over the theology of Rudolf Bultmann in postwar Germany. Whether or not Bultmann (of whom more later) reduces Christianity to psychological experience, as some of his opponents have claimed, he is certainly sceptical of its "mythology," which he says flatly is "finished."

This scepticism, which does not stop even at the church door, is attributable to two main causes. The first is, of course, the cumulative weight of the sceptical tradition whose history we have been tracing in this book. The second is contemporary life itself, or rather certain conditions of modern living which are decidedly not conducive to religious life and which help to perpetuate a sceptical or at least secular outlook. This second point is not easy to prove,

---

[4] Heim, *Christian Faith and Natural Science*, p. 16.
[5] Ward, *Faith and Freedom*, p. 265.

but no discussion of the contemporary religious situation would be complete without taking it into account.

The principal results of the sceptical tradition may be summarized briefly as follows. In general, after several centuries of rapid growth it has succeeded in creating an intellectual climate in which it is not easy for religion to flourish. More concretely, it has encouraged habits of thinking which are subtly adverse to religion, habits which have become ingrained by repetition of the written and spoken word and eventually, to some extent, by the school systems. Chief among these is the habit of analytical or reductive thinking, of which we have seen so many examples in previous pages. In brief, this type of thinking explains phenomena mechanically, which means (1) to explain them wholly within a naturalistic framework, and (2) without reference therefore to a supernature or to "final causes"; in other words, to reduce them to mechanical causes rather than transcendental purposes. To explain things in this way first became general among natural scientists who understandably wished to get precise information about physical nature with a view to understanding its mechanism, and thus to controlling and using it for human purposes. Carried to its extreme this mode had the effect of reading purpose out of nature, of reducing nature to a mathematical machine or an evolutionary process devoid of design. However, its full effects were not felt until it spread from the study of physical nature to the study of man. As natural science gained prestige it became increasingly common to think of man, too, as a sort of machine. Scientific orthodoxy made it almost a foregone conclusion that man as well as nature should be understood more and more as the product of wholly natural forces, biological, environmental, and psychological. The temptation, which was by no means always resisted, was to think of man—his consciousness, his conscience, his ideals, his religion—as nothing but these forces. His standards of right and wrong, for instance, could they not be best explained as the mores of the tribe intent upon survival? Man's earliest religious rites, what were they but a primitive attempt to control nature before anything was known about natural laws? Even his more sophisticated religious ideas, what were they at bottom but wishful thinking, or alternatively an opiate for killing the pain of a miserable existence on earth and for keeping certain classes of people in subjection? Some people obviously carried this reductive thinking much farther than others, but the point is that it became more or less habitual—habitual to try to explain religious phenomena in terms of naturalistic or physical categories.

Other scarcely less ingrained habits of thinking are the comparative and the historical which, as we have seen, came into their glory in the nineteenth century. Comparative thinking, developed chiefly by modern anthropology, means to compare the ideas and mores of different cultural areas of the world. Its chief effect has been to erode the claims of particular religions to uniqueness and superiority, and to interpret them in terms of the social needs of the "tribe." Historicism puts the stamp of time on them. Under the searching light of historical analysis a sacred document, dogma, or institution is seen to be the product of a particular time and place or "myth," and further to be subject to change like everything else in the temporal world. Obviously, such thinking makes it difficult to conceive of religious absolutes or of an ideal religious order good for all time.

The reverse side of the coin is the decline of metaphysical thinking, i.e., thinking beyond observable phenomena of the physical or "natural" world. Ever since the time of

Francis Bacon the Western intellectual world, or important segments thereof, has evinced a healthy suspicion of metaphysics. This suspicion germinated in the revolt against medieval scholasticism and in the desire for a kind of knowledge that would be "useful" to man. It was nourished during the wars of religion when innumerable and conflicting claims were made to special "revelations," and it flowered in the positivistic and agnostic movements of the nineteenth century. John Locke's metaphor of the sailor's line was its great symbol; the human mind, like the sailor's line, cannot and should not try to plumb "all the depths of the ocean," but should stick to the main business of man, which is conduct. As it has seeped down into the popular consciousness this antimetaphysical bias has come to mean something like this: human knowledge is limited to the space-time order; if there is an order of being other than the space-time order we cannot know it; in any case such knowledge is useless, especially seeing that natural occurrences can be explained perfectly well without reference to it. The importance of this attitude for religion is patent. It cuts man off from any meaningful order beyond that in which he normally lives or which he can create for himself. It precludes any correspondence between the mundane and what may possibly be beyond the mundane or ordinary sphere of existence.

It is important to understand, however, that contemporary scepticism is by no means merely the product of an intellectual tradition, powerful as that tradition is and will doubtless continue to be. Despite what was said at the conclusion of the previous chapter, scepticism (or at least secularism) threatens to increase rather than to diminish because of certain features of contemporary life. Although these features are conspicuous enough they often go unnoticed in discussions of the religious problem. "The threat to the religious attitude," says Erich Fromm, "lies not in science but in the predominant practices of daily life." [6] In making this statement Fromm had particularly in mind what he calls the "marketing orientation" of modern man, man's idea of himself as a commodity for sale in the market, his worship of the idol of success. However, there are other "practices" which constitute an even graver threat, as is made clear in three recent books by continental Roman Catholic thinkers. The titles of these books are almost self-explanatory: *The World of Silence* (1948) by Max Picard, Swiss philosopher and erstwhile doctor of medicine; *Leisure the Basis of Culture* (1947) by the German Dominican Josef Pieper; and *The Decline of Wisdom* (1955) by the French existentialist philosopher Gabriel Marcel. All three make the same point, though in different words. They all center on the technological revolution of modern times and the implicit threat posed by that revolution to what Pieper calls the religious "sense of wonder."

None of these men is an obscurantist. Marcel, for example, in an essay entitled "The Limitations of Industrial Civilization," recognizes the positive value of technical progress, welcomes it in fact not only for liberating man from a dull routine but also for giving him power over a lower order of reality, viz., inanimate nature, which is "meant" to be controlled by him. Some of its effects, however, are not so salutary. It exposes man to enormous temptation—the temptation and abuse of power. Still more important, it discredits reflection. The man who has mastered one or more techniques, says Marcel, tends to distrust whatever is alien to these techniques. "He will usually be most unwilling to accept the idea that a meta-technical activity [such as reflection] may have value." "And in fact, everything goes to show that in a civilisation of this sort the importance

[6] Erich Fromm, *Psychoanalysis and Religion* (New Haven: Yale University Press, 1950), p. 100.

of reflection will be minimised if not denied." [7] Consequently, there is less opportunity for "wisdom" to manifest
itself today than heretofore, for wisdom depends on reflection. And by wisdom Marcel means, of course, a religious
view of life—what he calls in one place "cosmocentrism"
or man's attempt to be integrated in a universal order, as
opposed to "practical anthropomorphism" whose purpose is
to transform the world by bringing it into subjection to the
human will. Marcel might have pressed his argument still
further by calling attention to the incredible rate of change
which is an ineluctable function of the technological revolution. In the modern world of flux, it is obviously hard to
fix attention on, or to abide long in, an absolute. At any
rate, his point is that despite the disillusionment with "progress" following two world wars, the technological revolution goes on, and along with it all its latent threats to religious reflection.

Appropriately, Marcel wrote the preface to Max Picard's
remarkable book on silence. According to Picard, the technological revolution also begets noise, and noise is the enemy
of "being." "Being and silence belong together." But the
world today is full of noise, noise "has infiltrated into everything." "The machine is noise turned into iron and steel."
"Radio has occupied the whole space of silence," "aero-
planes scour the sky for the silence encamped behind the
clouds," "the great cities are like enormous reservoirs of
noise." "The mechanized language of the dictator is a part
of the general verbal noise." The result is that in the present age man is but a "space for the noise to fill." Silence "no
longer exists as a *world*, but only in fragments, as the remains of a world." This is ominous, for it is only in the
world of silence that the spirit can grow. Silence, though it

[7] Gabriel Marcel, *The Decline of Wisdom* (New York: Philosophical
Library, 1955), p. 11.

is "useless" as seen by the world of profit and utility, restores men to wholeness, makes them see the ontic in things.[8]

Picard stresses noise, Pieper work. The current age is not only too noisy, it is too busy for religion to flourish. Religion requires "leisure"—not leisure in the sense of idleness or vacationing, but leisure in a sense scarcely understood any more, leisure as Aristotle and St. Thomas Aquinas understood it, as a contemplative attitude in which the mind lays aside the "work" of discursive thought and holds itself receptive to an immaterial and invisible reality. To put it another way, true leisure aims to see life as a whole and not to be completely absorbed in one's particular and limited function. But the modern world allows very little leisure of this sort. The modern world is consumed by "total labor," overvalues the sphere of work, very nearly makes work into a cult or "religion." In such a world the pressures are enormous on men to bend all their efforts to immediately utilitarian ends, leaving simply no time for the leisure upon which "contemplation" depends.[9]

Reflection, silence, leisure—three words signifying essentially the same thing, the *sine qua non* of significant religious life. What chance is there for a religious mutation in a world geared to the very opposite, which perhaps can scarcely understand what Marcel, Picard, and Pieper are talking about, a profoundly secular world which is, moreover, the heir of a powerful sceptical tradition?

3.

However, as Koestler and others have observed, there are unmistakable signs pointing in the opposite direction; ten-

[8] Max Picard, *The World of Silence*, trans. Stanley Goodman (Chicago: Henry Regnery, 1952), pp. 77, 181, 187, 198, 211-12.

[9] Josef Pieper, *Leisure the Basis of Culture*, trans. Alexander Dru (New York: Pantheon Books, 1952), *passim*.

dencies in thinking which clearly counteract, at least to
some extent, the aforementioned sceptical habits; new intellectual developments which provide a climate somewhat
more favorable to religious hypothesizing and religious experiencing. "We have entered a historical epoch," says Basil
Willey, "which is at once unfavourable to religion and fa-
vourable to it"—unfavorable in that the "secular drift" has
proceeded to "unheard-of lengths," but favorable in that
the social effects of secularism and scepticism are now so
readily apparent. "This realisation has produced in some
minds (though not on any general scale) a counter-drift
towards religion." [10]

Willey is right in his observation that this "counter-
drift" has not been at all general. But what perhaps has been
general is a new receptiveness to religious questioning
among intellectuals, and there are several good reasons why
this should be so. The first is the shock of events described
at the end of the last chapter. "Reality has changed," says
Tillich, "and the interpretation of reality has changed with
it." [11] The "reality" to which he refers is, of course, the almost continuous chain of historical catastrophes which has
disillusioned more than one man about "progress" and
opened more than one man's eyes to the evil endemic in man.
Of course, the loss of a secular faith does not of itself induce
religious receptiveness, or at least it does not do so often.
At best it generates in the heart a vague longing which is
thwarted, more often than not, by long established sceptical
habits of thinking. Real willingness to reopen the religious
question depends, therefore, on something more intellectually positive, something that can remove at least some of the
mental blocks set up by the sceptical tradition and that ac-

[10] Willey, *Christianity Past and Present*, p. 7.
[11] Paul Tillich, in *Partisan Review*, Vol. XVII, No. 3 (March, 1950), p.
254.

cordingly convinces the mind that a religious outlook is not necessarily "contrary to reason"—even though in certain respects it may be "above reason." To the extent, then, that there has been a new religious receptiveness among the past two generations, we may be sure that it has been generated, not only by political and social events, but also by trends in thought which are partly or wholly independent of these events and which in some cases actually predate them.

Where, exactly, does one see signs of a new receptiveness to religion—signs, that is, more definite than the "longing" detected in the last chapter? Willey cites the reinvigoration of Christian theology itself, which he rightly observes has recovered some of its primitive militancy and given up that appeasement of the natural and historical sciences which had been more or less its hallmark since the Enlightenment. It may be doubted, however, whether the new theologies (neo-thomism, Karl Barth's "theology of crisis," neo-ortho-doxy) have had any great impact on the lay sceptical world which is predisposed in so many ways not to listen to them. More conspicuous signs, at least as regards this latter world, are certain observable movements in other areas of thought: the revolt against mechanistic thinking in the natural sciences and the philosophy of science; the growth concurrently, since the meteoric rise of the French philosopher Henri Bergson, of a concept of knowledge a great deal broader than that inculcated by nineteenth-century positivism or agnosticism; the tardy but nevertheless emphatic recognition by some prominent depth psychologists of the need to enlarge their conception of the human psyche to include its "search for meaning"; the misgivings expressed by some historians about the moral relativism implied by historicism, and the revival of interest in the role played by religion in history; the new metaphysical concern in creative literature, particularly the preoccupation of leading writers with the themes of timeless myth and time itself. None of these signs points indubitably to a "counter-drift toward religion," but taken together they do argue a changed mental climate in which religious questions are being mulled over and considered with a new seriousness. A few examples should make this fairly evident.

The natural sciences and the philosophy of science are a preserve which the layman hesitates to enter for fear of making the most elementary blunders. However, it takes no special training or perspicacity to see that in recent years the shooting war between science and religion has come to an end, not because science has won the field, as some have maintained, but because science has changed its outlook. This is primarily the result of the revolution in physics, "the twin-revolution in the realms of the infinitely large and the infinitely small." At least two important conclusions for religion have been drawn from quantum and relativity physics. The first, which is the more widely accepted, is that science has serious limits as a way of knowing, and the second is that the facts of science as we now know them may to some extent actually support an idealistic or religious view of reality.

The scientific popularizer J. W. N. Sullivan was undoubtedly right when he wrote in 1933, in a book significantly entitled *The Limitations of Science*, that "Science has become self-conscious and comparatively humble. We are no longer taught that the scientific method of approach is the only valid method of acquiring knowledge about reality." [12] This humility, which contrasted with the often arrogant pronouncements of nineteenth-century scientism, was born of science's new uncertainty about the "reality" it was investigating. The old absolutes of classical physics

[12] J. W. N. Sullivan, *The Limitations of Science* (New York: Viking, 1933), p. 220.

(space, time, matter, and causality) having collapsed, science could now be certain only about the mathematical structure, but not about the inner nature of the physical world. Nor, it appeared, was it likely to become more certain, owing to the "uncertainty" or "indeterminacy" which Werner Heisenberg detected in the behavior of individual electrons. Thus, science contemplated a mystery, and some scientists became pessimistic about science's ability ever to penetrate it or to transcend the human reference point in its search for "reality." This recognition by science itself of its own limitations, limitations of both method and knowledge, opened the door to speculation about other possible modes of knowledge including the religious. As Sullivan remarked in his book:

The fact that science is confined to a knowledge of structure is obviously of great "humanistic" importance. For it means that the problem of the nature of reality is not prejudged. We are no longer required to believe that our response to beauty, or the mystic's sense of communion with God, have no objective counterpart. It is perfectly possible that they are, what they have so often been taken to be, clues to the nature of reality.[13]

This is certainly not the view of all or even a majority of modern scientists, but it would not be hard to show that sentiments not dissimilar to this have been expressed frequently by scientific leaders during the past three or four decades. For instance, the chief architects of quantum and relativity physics, Max Planck and Albert Einstein, have done so, though in language that sounds more like Cartesian dualism. Einstein said more than once that the old conflict between science and religion was based on a misapprehension, for they clearly belonged to different and equally legitimate realms of endeavor. Science, he said, is concerned

[13] *Ibid.*, p. 226.

with knowledge of "what *is*," i.e., "truth" about the world of nature. Apparently he did not share the epistemological pessimism of some of his colleagues. Religion, on the other hand, is concerned with "what *should be*," i.e., human goals and values. "If one conceives of religion and science according to these definitions then a conflict between them appears impossible. For science can only ascertain what *is*, but not what *should be*, and outside of its domain value judgments of all kinds remain necessary." [14] The position taken by Sir Arthur Eddington and Heisenberg is more up to date in the sense that it is more squarely based on considerations raised by the new physics. Because they deal with abstractions, the English physicist said in his Gifford lectures, "the entities of physics can from their very nature form only a partial aspect of the reality." "The symbolic nature of the entities of physics is generally recognised; and the scheme of physics is now formulated in such a way as to make it almost self-evident that it is a partial aspect of something wider." [15] In similar vein Heisenberg, author of the Principle of Uncertainty, has said that "existing scientific concepts cover always only a very limited part of reality." In order to understand "reality" it is necessary, he thinks, to consult the concepts, not only of scientific language, but also of what he calls "natural language." Natural language is language which, though imprecise, has "immediate connection with reality" and can give expression to such concepts as the human soul, life, and God.

We know that any understanding must be based finally upon the natural language because it is only there that we can be certain to touch reality, and hence we must be skeptical about

[14] Albert Einstein, *Out of My Later Years* (New York: Philosophical Library, 1950), p. 25.
[15] A. S. Eddington, *The Nature of the Physical World* (New York: Macmillan, 1928), pp. 323, 331-32.

any skepticism with regard to this natural language and its essential concepts. Therefore, we may use these concepts as they have been used at all times. In this way modern physics has perhaps opened the door to a wider outlook on the relation between the human mind and reality.[16]

At this point it is convenient to interrupt the narrative in order to observe that recognition of forms of cognition other than scientific cognition is by no means limited to a few scientists, that in fact it has become quite widespread in twentieth-century thinking. Of course, there has always been such recognition, but, as Heisenberg points out, the nineteenth-century cult of science created a bias in favor of the scientific over the "natural language." But during the past fifty years the "natural language" has been steadily gaining in prestige, to some extent within the stronghold of science itself, as we have seen, but also among philosophers, psychologists, historians, even some social scientists, and, of course, creative writers. Note the wide circulation and, on the whole, sympathetic use of such terms as "intuition," "empathic knowledge," "intimate," "infra-rational," and "mythical" thought, *"verstand"* and *"einfühlung."* Insofar as it is possible to reduce these terms to a common denominator, it would seem to consist in the cognizing subject's "ceasing to be an 'observing outsider' in regard to the object," [17] in his somehow getting inside the object and becoming identified with it. This "third way of cognition," as the sociologist Pitirim Sorokin calls it, has obvious affinities with religious mysticism. It does not rule out ordinary "logico-sensory" methods of studying phenomena, but it

[16] Werner Heisenberg, *Physics and Philosophy* (New York: Harper and Brothers, 1958), pp. 201-202.

[17] Pitirim Sorokin, *Social Philosophies in an Age of Crisis* (Boston: Beacon Press, 1950), p. 308. Sorokin says that he shares this point of view with Bergson, Berdyaev, Spengler, and some other twentieth-century thinkers.

denies that such methods can catch all, including some of the most profound, aspects of reality.

The most celebrated, and one of the earliest, exponents of this type of intuitional thinking in the twentieth century is Henri Bergson who, in his *Introduction to Metaphysics* (1903) and in later works, drew a sharp distinction between what he called "analytical" and "intuitional" knowledge. The former, which is produced by the mind or intellect, can give only a limited knowledge, knowledge of the relative and material. The analytical intellect moves all around its object, observing it, describing it mathematically, without, however, being able to grasp its inner "life." In order to comprehend this "life" one has to place oneself within the object, by means of "intuition" or intellectual sympathy. "No doubt," Bergson wrote in *Creative Evolution*, "this philosophy will never obtain a knowledge of its object comparable to that which science has of its own. . . . But, in default of knowledge properly so called, reserved to pure intelligence, intuition may enable us to grasp what it is that intelligence fails to give us, and indicate the means of supplementing it." [18] Echoes of the Bergsonian type of epistemology can be heard in such thinkers as widely removed from each other in other respects as the physicist Eddington, who distinguished between "Symbolic" and "Intimate" knowledge; the sociologist Sorokin, to whom we have already referred; the psychoanalyst Karl Stern, who describes an "integral" or "empathic" cognition which is intrinsically different from scientific cognition; the historian Oswald Spengler who postulated two different methods of cognition, the "naturalistic" and the "historical," which perceive, respectively, the world-as-nature from the outside and the world-as-history from the inside (through the "method of

[18] Henri Bergson, *Creative Evolution*, trans. Arthur Mitchell (New York: Random House, 1944), p. 195.

living into the object as opposed to dissecting it," and which imparts its knowledge by analogy, picture, and symbol); and another historian, Arnold Toynbee, who, in the auto-biographical epilogue to his *Study of History*, acknowledges his debt to Plato for teaching him to use his "imagination" as well as his "intellect" in order to reconnoiter regions of the "Spiritual Universe" which cannot be weighed and measured, which are "beyond the Reason's range." [19] The novelist and essayist Thomas Mann expounds a similar philosophy in his essay on Schopenhauer. Our normal conceptions which are created out of the phenomenal world do not give us "truth," says Mann. "The subject-matter of our thinking, and indeed the judgments we build up on it, are inadequate as a means of grasping the essence of things in themselves, the true essence of the world and of life." To grasp this essence we need to fall back on "the intuitive," "our most intimate self—something quite different and much earlier in time than the intellect." [20] The dangers of this kind of thinking need hardly be pointed out in the twentieth century. It can so easily degenerate into a vast "unreason" which depreciates ordinary rational and scientific modes of knowing. If used sparingly and cautiously, however, it can serve to reopen the gates to metaphysical and religious awareness without at the same time endangering the scientific enterprise. And in the twentieth-century mental climate this has been precisely the function of a thinker like Bergson who in one of his last works, *The Two Sources of Morality and Religion*, related "intuition" to the mystic's vision.

Coming back now to the philosophy of science, we noted

[19] Arnold Toynbee, "Acknowledgements and Thanks," *A Study of History* (Oxford, 1951-1954), Vol. X, p. 228.

[20] Thomas Mann, *Essays of Three Decades*, trans. H. T. Lowe-Porter (New York: Alfred Knopf, 1947), pp. 372-73.

above that a second conclusion has sometimes been drawn from the new scientific revolution. While some thinkers have stressed the negative side, namely the "limitations of science" as a way of knowing, others have insisted positively that the new science supports a religious interpretation of the universe. This second conclusion is not nearly so generally accepted as the first; in fact, Eddington and others expressly warned against it on the ground that scientific theories lack finality and are liable to be swept away by "the next scientific revolution." Yet there is considerable truth nevertheless in R. G. Collingwood's observation that modern scientific leaders "talk about God in a way that would have scandalized most scientists of fifty years ago." [21] They do this, according to Collingwood, because the new physics has taught them to think of "matter" in a new way, as energy or activity, in contrast to the inert "stuff" of classical physics, and hence as more like "mind" and "life"; also to think of the great universe as probably finite and hence dependent for its existence on something other than itself. One of the first popular exponents of this general point of view was the German scientist, Bernhard Bavink, who went up and down Germany in the early thirties lecturing on "the new view of the world which appears to arise out of the revolution in modern physics." Bavink's lectures are reminiscent of Thomas Henry Huxley's popular lectures to English audiences in the nineteenth century. But unlike Huxley, Bavink told his audiences that "this new knowledge is now on our side," i.e., on the side of religion. The new turn in scientific thought, he said, had pronounced "the death sentence of materialism" at the very time that materialism was setting out from Russia to conquer the world by force, and he looked to the time,

[21] R. G. Collingwood, *The Idea of Nature* (Oxford, 1945), p. 156.

soon to come, when the warfare between science and religion would be a matter of only historical interest.[22] In the same year that Bavink's *Science and God* was published, J. W. N. Sullivan furnished evidence that a number of scientific leaders shared this view. Interviews with Max Planck, Erwin Schrödinger, Eddington, and Sir James Jeans elicited the all but unanimous opinion that "consciousness" and possibly "life" too could not have been produced accidentally nor by the action of purely natural causes. In a typical statement Jeans said to Mr. Sullivan:

I incline to the idealistic theory that consciousness is fundamental, and that the material universe is derivative from consciousness, not consciousness from the material universe. If this is so, then it would appear to follow that there is a general scheme. My inclination towards idealism is the outcome largely of modern scientific theories. . . . In general the universe seems to me to be nearer to a great thought than to a great machine.[23]

Jeans's statement exemplifies what L. P. Jacks, in his Hibbert Lectures of 1933, called "the revolt against mechanism." The revolt began, not in the social sciences or psychology where "mechanical mindedness" still largely prevailed, but in philosophy with Bergson, in the physical sciences with Eddington and Jeans, and in the biological sciences with Hans Driesch (from whom the Roman Catholic philosopher Jacques Maritain learned so much) and John Scott Haldane. Doubtless, "mechanical mindedness" has by no means disappeared even in these sciences, but in the twentieth-century philosophy of science there has been a

[22] Bernhard Bavink, *Science and God*, trans. H. S. Hatfield (New York: Reynal and Hitchcock, 1934), pp. 167-70.
[23] J. W. N. Sullivan, *Contemporary Mind: Some Modern Answers* (London, 1934), p. 132.

noticeable trend away from a mechanical toward something like a teleological explanation of things. This trend is what prompted Collingwood to say, apropos of Alfred North Whitehead's philosophy, that the cycle of cosmological thought in the modern world "recapitulates the cycle running from Thales to Aristotle"; i.e., after an experiment in materialism it had returned to the main tradition of European thought represented by Plato and Aristotle.[24] Several examples will illustrate the tendency. By 1925, one year after he had migrated from England to Harvard, Whitehead had begun to expound his "philosophy of organism" which he claimed to have learned from modern science with its new theory of matter. Nature, he said in *Science and the Modern World*, palpably resembles an organism more than a machine in the sense that it consists not only of its parts or components but also of the pattern in which these are arranged. However, this pattern is not static but evolutionary, constantly striving toward new forms. In *Process and Reality* (1929), Whitehead further described nature as "process" which has "aim," a nisus toward the production of certain forms which not only are immanent in the world but which also transcend it in the manner of Plato's Ideas. And God, for Whitehead, provides this aim, is the infinite "lure" toward which all reality directs itself. The American botanist Edmund Sinnott expounds a not dissimilar "philosophy of goals" or "telism" in his *Biology of the Spirit* (1955). Like Driesch, whose general line he follows, Sinnott has reacted against "tough-minded mechanism" and "biological agnosticism." The scientific orthodoxy of the nineteenth century, he observes, ruled out prevision or design in nature. Clearly, however, a plant or animal "grows in an orderly fashion to a precise bodily form

[24] Collingwood, *The Idea of Nature*, p. 170; see also p. 155.

characteristic of the particular species to which it belongs, as toward a precise 'goal.' " [25] This sort of evidence leads him to conclude that all life including human life exhibits "goal-seeking" or "purpose" which defies a purely mechanistic explanation.

By now the revolt against mechanism has also spread to psychology. When Professor Joad wrote his *Guide to Modern Thought* in 1933, he could say with some justification that while the natural sciences were leaning somewhat toward teleological and even religious explanations, psychology (as exemplified by behaviorism and psychoanalysis) was moving in the other direction. And indeed, as we noted in the previous chapter, the warfare between religion and psychiatry still goes on today. Karl Stern calls Freudianism the "third revolution" which, like Darwinism and Marxism, takes mechanism as a premise and reduces religion to the natural order. However, even before the publication of Joad's book a reaction had begun to set in against this point of view. "Although it began as part of the protest against religion," says a student of recent movements in psychology, "the net result of modern psychology has been to reaffirm man's experience of himself as a spiritual being." [26] Although this statement may be too sweeping, it embodies an evident truth, namely that religion has received increasingly sympathetic treatment by some of Freud's former colleagues and by a younger generation of depth psychologists. Carl Jung is, of course, the central figure in this "transformation."

As early as 1916 Jung, erstwhile protégé and colleague of Sigmund Freud, expressed serious misgivings about the

[25] Edmund W. Sinnott, *The Biology of the Spirit* (New York: Viking, 1955), p. 15.

[26] Ira Progoff, *The Death and Rebirth of Psychology* (New York: Julian Press, 1956), p. 3.

"analytical" and "causal" method of the master. The essence of this method was to explain the human soul, including its neuroses, entirely in terms of past happenings, chiefly sex patterns and family conflicts occurring in infancy. However, as Jung pointed out in two ground-breaking prefaces to his *Collected Papers on Analytical Psychology*, psychic life cannot be reduced to the tension and relaxation of the genital glands, any more than a locomotive's function can be explained simply by identifying the kinds of steel of which it is made and the mines and ironworks from which the steel came. "Causality is only one principle, and psychology essentially cannot be exhausted by causal methods only, because the mind lives by aims as well." Hence, to the method of the Vienna School, which he regarded as overly mechanistic and smacking of the materialism of an outmoded science, Jung opposed the "heresy" of his own Zurich School which contended that the human mind was characterized not only by "causae" but also by "fines" (aims). "What is plainly directed towards a goal," he said, "cannot be given an exclusively causalistic explanation, otherwise we should be led to the conclusion expressed in Moleschott's famous enunciation: 'Man *is*, what he eats'." [27] This point of view has been reiterated many times, not only by Jung, but also by two other former disciples of Freud, Alfred Adler and Otto Rank, and by Karl Stern. In one of his last books Rank coined a phrase, "beyond psychology" (significantly, this is also the title of the last chapter of Stern's *The Third Revolution*), which is reminiscent of the phrase, "the limitations of science," so often employed by twentieth-century philosophers of science. "Beyond psychology" means that just as "science" cannot give full cognition of the universe, so "analysis" does not begin

[27] Carl Jung, *Collected Papers on Analytical Psychology* (New York: Moffat Yard, 1917), p. x.

to reveal all the depths of the human psyche. Freudian analysis, said Rank, "only acts backward." It thinks it has explained the ego when it has reduced it to id and superego (heredity and environment), and that it can effect therapy by explaining the irrational element in human life in rational —and mechanistic—terms. Man, however, is much more than the method of "mechanistic causality" can ever reveal. Man's deepest nature "lies beyond any psychology, individual or collective." "Man is born beyond psychology and he dies beyond it but he can *live* beyond it only through vital experience of his own—in religious terms, through revelation, conversion or re-birth." [28]

Obviously, some leading depth psychologists have been groping toward a teleological or religious conception of human nature, thus paralleling the attempt of some philosophers of science to delineate the universe on similar lines. As is well known, Jung broke with Freud on the subject of the nature of man. The more he thought about man the more he conceived him to be fundamentally *homo religiosus.* The soul, he declared in a characteristic recent statement, "cannot be 'nothing but,' " i.e., reduced to something known. "On the contrary it has the dignity of an entity endowed with, and conscious of, a relationship to Deity." "The soul is *naturaliter religiosa,* i.e., possesses a religious function." [29] Earlier, in *Psychology and Religion* (1938), Jung had asserted that religious experience was "indisputable."

No matter what the world thinks about religious experience, the one who has it possesses the great treasure of a thing that

[28] Otto Rank, *Beyond Psychology* (Camden: Haddon Craftsmen, 1941), p. 16.

[29] Carl Jung, "Introduction to the Religious and Psychological Problems of Alchemy," in *Psychology and Alchemy,* trans. R. F. C. Hull (New York: Pantheon Books, 1953), pp. 10-11, 13.

has provided him with a source of life, meaning and beauty and that has given a new splendor to the world and mankind. He has pistis and peace. Where is the criterium by which you would say that such a life is not legitimate, that such experience is not valid and that such pistis is mere illusion? [30]

Jung came to this view through his discovery that the "unconscious" contained not only personal and repressed material such as Freud supposed, but also deeper and more creative levels which suggested contact with greater-than-individual, perhaps cosmic forces in life. He called this the "collective unconscious" because it was often projected in religious dreams, myths, and symbols which seemed to be collectively held by all men. Thus, in the end Jung came round to a sort of teleological conception of human nature, somewhat reminiscent of Whitehead's "process" and Sinnott's "goal-seeking," according to which the human species exhibits purposiveness, its peculiar purpose being to discover and to become identified with the proto-image of the religious "Self" which is latent in the collective unconscious.

Otto Rank, who also broke with Freud, came up with a not dissimilar conception of man's nature. According to Rank, "the natural self of man" cannot be reduced to blind instinctual drives nor to the rational control of these drives. "Mankind's civilization," he wrote in *Beyond Psychology*, "has emerged from the perpetual operation of a third principle, which combines the rational and irrational elements in a world-view based on the conception of the supernatural." By this "third principle," for him the most fundamental principle of human nature, Rank meant man's "will to immortality" which, though partly attributable simply to the individual's effort to perpetuate himself in the face of death, represented basically man's reaching out to larger

[30] Carl Jung, *Psychology and Religion* (New Haven: Yale University Press, 1938), p. 113.

realities, to what Rank sometimes calls rather vaguely "the supernatural." Rank thought that the "will to immortality" was perpetually exhibited in history, by civilized as well as so-called primitive man, by various forms of immortality belief which, of course, differed according to different cultural situations. Like Jung, Rank traced this will back to a collective pattern or "prototype" of the human psyche. "What we really have in common with our remote ancestors," he said, "is a *spiritual,* not a primitive self," [31] and modern man's scepticism about this basic fact of his nature explains many of his current psychological difficulties. An interesting example of the seeping down of this conception into the popular consciousness is contained in a lecture delivered before a combined meeting of the Jung Institute and Psychological Club of Zurich in 1954 by the South African free-lance writer Laurens Van der Post. Though the lecture was ostensibly about Africa (it was later incorporated in a book entitled *The Dark Eye in Africa*) it was actually about the nature of man and the inadequacy of certain modern conceptions of it. Colonel Van der Post, obviously influenced by Jungian concepts, pictured man as, at bottom, one who has a "natural sense of religion," who senses the timeless and mysterious in things, who feels a side of life which lies outside the range of conscious awareness. This "natural man" in us is revealed by, among other things, the great myths of the world—for example, the myth of the Great Trek in Africa—which men produce spontaneously and which incite to a spiritual journey. Unfortunately, in recent centuries "natural man" has been heavily overlaid by "thinking man," with the result that the religious aspect of life has been neglected, and western civilization has become lopsidedly rational and scientific. The lecturer, however, thought that the two halves of human nature might again

[31] Rank, *Beyond Psychology*, pp. 62-3.

become a whole, and he cited as evidence of this possibility the new attitudes of modern physics and depth psychology.[32]

No such "transformation" has occurred in historical thinking; yet there are signs in this realm, too, of a "search for meaning," of a resurgence of interest in the relationship between metaphysics and history. These signs, as the Cambridge historian Herbert Butterfield has observed, are the result of seeing history in a new way in a catastrophic period of history. It is not entirely accidental therefore that since World War II a number of professional historians have issued manifestoes against relativistic historicism which parallel in a striking way the revolt against mechanism in science and psychology. These "manifestoes" make two points. The first is that historicism, the conception which emphasizes the particularity and variety of the human spirit in history (see pp. 156 ff.), leads to a relativism which makes belief in absolutes difficult or impossible, thus leaving men without standards and without the possibility of judging any historical movement except in the light of particular circumstances. Hence, the English medievalist Geoffrey Barraclough, in his essay on "The Historian in a Changing World," is constrained to say that "historicism, as a key to present living, is inadequate." "Who, to-day, would dare to claim that historicism provides an ultimate view of reality, an adequate philosophy either for thinking or for living?" Barraclough also rejects—and this is the second point—the historical dogma that the "interpretation [of history] has to wait on scholarship." If we seek "meaning" in history— and we must—we will not find it in the facts, partly because there is never a time when we have all the facts, and partly, and more importantly, because meaning never simply rises

[32] Laurens Van der Post, *The Dark Eye in Africa* (New York: Morrow, 1955), *passim.*

out of the facts. On the contrary, meaning comes from outside history, from the values which we bring to the study of history.

We must seek for history an end outside itself—as it had, for example, when it was viewed as a manifestation of the working of God's providence. This statement is not intended to imply a return to a theological view of history (which, whether desirable or not, I regard as impracticable to-day); but it does mean that its study should have a constructive purpose and a criterion of judgment, outside and beyond the historical process.[33]

Independently of Barraclough, some other historians have arrived at similar conclusions: Herbert Butterfield, for instance, who in *Christianity and History* (1950) argues "the case against academic history" which limits itself to the "how" rather than the "why" of history, i.e., to the mechanism of historical processes, falsely assuming all the while that history is a self-explanatory system; Arnold Toynbee, who in the tenth volume of *A Study of History* castigates modern historians for pursuing their fact-finding activities undisturbed by any search for meaning or "law" in history, in a word, for their "antinomian unfaith"; and sundry German revisionists of modern German history who score the sort of "naïve historical realism" that thinks it can make sense out of history without seeing it from the perspective of a value system or ideology. All of these historians agree with Barraclough that if there is meaning in history it comes from outside the historical process itself. "Revision of a historical picture [specifically, revision of the German conception which viewed history from the standpoint of the nation-state]," writes the Swiss historian Walther Hofer, "means differentiating anew between true and false values

[33] Geoffrey Barraclough, *History in a Changing World* (Oxford, 1955), p. 29.

in history by means of a value system already transformed or still to be transformed." [34] Toward the end of his life Friedrich Meinecke was similarly struggling with meaning, questioning whether historicism, of which he had written a history in 1936, had not inflicted serious wounds on the world. Perhaps, he now thought, the relativistic viewpoint inculcated by historicism was one of the factors that had made Hitler's triumph possible. Perhaps in order to find reassurance in history it was necessary to look beyond history, possibly to a metaphysical world such as Goethe described.

This incipient revolt against historicism, this straining for "meaning," does not, of course, necessarily lead to a religious or teleological interpretation of history. Indeed, as the above quotation shows, Barraclough expressly rejects such an interpretation, and Meinecke was never very sure about his metaphysics. In a few conspicuous cases, however, it does and has. For understandable reasons some of the aforementioned German historians, for example, have tended to reinterpret history as a struggle for the realization of universal religious and humanist values. "In political history," declared Professor Alfred von Martin, of Munich, in an essay entitled "Toward a New Picture of History" (1946), "the values of religion and culture must resume their leading role." Professor Butterfield sees history as a drama involving conflict between good and evil and in which, as he puts it, "God plays a role" and the planes of time and eternity intersect. But the supreme example of this type of thinking is, of course, Arnold Toynbee who in recent years has resurrected something like the Augustinian conception of history. Attacks on Toynbee by the professional historians (*A Study of History* has been labeled

---

[34] See *German History. Some New German Views*, ed. Hans Kohn (Boston: Beacon Press, 1954), p. 191.

"metaphysics," "theodicy," "prophecy," "unhistorical")
should not blind us to his importance as a symptom of the
changing attitudes we are describing in this section. Toynbee, unlike most academic historians, has been widely
read and discussed. And the message that he has brought to
his readers in the last four volumes of his *magnum opus* is
that history has spiritual meaning and purpose. Specifically,
he now holds that in history, civilizations exist, not as ends
in themselves, but as preludes to the birthing of "the higher
religions." Thus, Toynbee has stood on its head his earlier
thesis that churches are to be regarded as the chrysalises out
of which the great civilizations emerge. In his new perspective the earliest civilizations produced the rudiments of the
higher religions, and later civilizations produced the full-
fledged religions of this species. Toynbee now thinks that
the *raison* of "Modern Western Civilization," with its con-
quest of space, may be to provide the meeting ground, and
hence the meeting of minds, of these religions on a world-
wide scale. Whatever one thinks of Toynbee's interpretation one has to admit that he has called attention in a vivid
way to the importance of religion in the historical process.
In this respect at least Toynbee has been as important to
historical thinking in the twentieth century as Karl Marx
was in the nineteenth. Marx called attention, quite rightly,
to the enormous importance of economics and technology
in history. Toynbee has done the same for religion.

After an experiment in disillusionment, twentieth-century literature has also begun to show signs of a "New Seriousness." Joad completely missed these signs when in 1948
he accused the "literary culture of our time" of "decadence," the chief signs of which, according to him, were
subjectivism, i.e., inordinate preoccupation with the self
and its experiences, concentration on the psychologically
abnormal and the primitive, nihilism, scepticism. That scep-

ticism has been and still is rife in contemporary literature no one can possibly doubt. However, what Joad failed to note, absorbed as he was with the debunking period of the twenties, was precisely the "New Seriousness" among writers which began in the late twenties and which has continued ever since. By the "New Seriousness" is not meant primarily the accent on social responsibility usually identified with the thirties, important as that movement was, but rather the search for metaphysical meaning after a period in which, as Joad rightly says, it was widely assumed that the human mind could not know objects other than its own mental states. To be sure, not many writers have found the "meaning" they seek, at least not what could be called religious meaning. As we have seen, a great many have remained in that arrested state of "longing" which Koestler described so well in *The Age of Longing*. Nevertheless, they are now asking metaphysical questions, an interrogation which opens out to the "religious" even if it does not necessarily reach it or settle in it. In 1926 (in his first major work, *La Tentation de l'Occident*) André Malraux was raising those questions about death and man's fate which have continued to plague him through a lifetime. And others —Thomas Mann, T. S. Eliot, Aldous Huxley, W. H. Auden, Koestler, to name only a few of the best known— have done likewise, through the Great Depression and World War II down to the present time. What is the meaning of death and how can man find a defence against it? How can man become whole again and break out of his solitude? Is there more to life than experience of the "absurd," and if so, what is it? What is time, and is it possible to have an experience of timelessness, beyond and outside measurable time, possibly in myth or art—or religion?

Of all these questions none, clearly, has occupied contemporary writers more than the question of time. Why should this be so, and what, precisely, has been said about time in recent years? Strictly speaking, of course, the interrogation is not new. Indeed, according to Oswald Spengler, interest in time ("the World-as-History") is one of the peculiar characteristics of Western culture as a whole, from the earliest times to the present. Nevertheless, the "time-obsession of the twentieth century" would appear to be new, as we might infer from the spate of books on the subject: philosophical treatises such as Samuel Alexander's *Space, Time, and Deity;* essays like Wyndham Lewis' long essay on *Time and Western Man;* novels, for example, Marcel Proust's *A La Recherche du Temps Perdu* and Aldous Huxley's *Time Must Have a Stop;* poems, for example, W. H. Auden's *For the Time Being;* and an impressive number of books commenting on the books.[35] There are good reasons for this "time-obsession." It is partly, no doubt, a response to the new scientific conception of time which is a whole story in itself. Essentially, however, it signifies, as has been suggested, a search for meaning, thus paralleling a similar search by philosophers of science, psychologists, and historians. To state it in other words, it signifies a revolt against what Wyndham Lewis called the "Time-mind" which experiences the world as flux and which sees everything *sub specie temporis.* The "Time-mind" is the product, at least in large part, of the incredibly rapid social and technological changes of the past hundred years, which have had the intellectual effect of taking away from a great many men their sense of belonging to a permanent order and of their continuity with the past. Hence, the search,

[35] For example, A. A. Mendilow, *Time and the Novel* (London, 1952), and Hans Meyerhoff, *Time in Literature* (Berkeley: University of California Press, 1955); also two recent French works by Jean Pouillon (*Temps et Roman,* Paris, 1946) and Georges Poulet (*Études sur Le Temps Humain,* Paris, 1950).

almost the frantic search, of modern writers for an experience of timelessness.

Some have sought timelessness within a wholly secular context—the French novelist Marcel Proust, for example, who spent a lifetime trying to remember things past, and by remembering them to set them free from chronological time, i.e., from the time when they happened; and his compatriot André Malraux who, after spending the better part of a lifetime writing about the ephemeral and frustrating world of time, has discovered (see his recent work on the psychology and history of art) a kind of "Absolute" in man's artistic creativity which defies history and destiny and gives continuity and universality to civilization. Others, however, have experienced timelessness in a more recognizably religious mode, and of these there would seem to be at least two types. First, there are those who, like Thomas Mann, have discovered timelessness in the great myths of mankind, and second, those who, like Aldous Huxley, have reverted more obviously to the Platonic and mystical tradition which views the temporal world as but an imperfect copy of eternity beyond nature, and which therefore takes a more negative attitude toward time. In his *Joseph* novels Mann—to take the first type first—dug deep into "the well of the past," into the "time-coulisse" of ancient Israel, and dredged up the great timeless myths which in his view repeat themselves in history and in which men in all times participate whether they know it or not. The profound influence on Mann of depth psychology, particularly in this instance Jung's theory of the collective unconscious, is patent. But in Mann, as in Jung, the myth, which is seen as the expression of certain nonrational experiences that mankind has in common, takes on a religious dimension—as it does not, for instance, in Albert Camus, who has been similarly preoccupied with the myths of Sisyphus and Prometheus. Mann spelled out this religious dimension in so many words in his famous address on "Freud and the Future" (1936), which was not so much about Freud as about himself. There he tells us how at a certain stage in his career as novelist he took the step in his subject matter "from the bourgeois and individual to the mythical and typical." He became aware, he said, of "the timeless schema, the pious formula into which life flows when it reproduces its traits out of the unconscious."

What is gained is an insight into the higher truth depicted in the actual; a smiling knowledge of the eternal, the ever-being and authentic; a knowledge of the schema in which and according to which the supposed individual lives, unaware, in his naïve belief in himself as unique in space and time, of the extent to which his life is but formula and repetition and his path marked out for him by those who trod it before him. . . . His dignity and security lie all unconsciously in the fact that with him something timeless has once more emerged into the light and become present; it is a mythical value added to the otherwise poor and valueless single character.[36]

And farther along Mann remarked that life in the myth "becomes a religious act" when it celebrates the past in the present, as in the feast of Christmas.

T. S. Eliot, W. H. Auden, and Aldous Huxley are examples of the second type of response. The emphasis in this type is not so much on the embodiment of the timeless in time through the myth (though this note is by no means wholly absent among them) as on the destruction of time through the contemplation of the eternal. Evidently, these writers moved on from that state of "longing" scepticism described in Chapter IV and of which they were so acutely aware at a certain stage in their career. Whereas in his early

[36] Mann, *Essays of Three Decades*, pp. 422-23.

poetry Eliot, for example, emphasized the dessicated and sceptical world of the "wasteland," he later focused on the way out of that land, into timelessness. But he did so in a more negative way than Mann, for doubtless, in Eliot, the temporal world has always remained a wasteland which must be transcended if man is to find reality. *Four Quartets*, in which time is the dominant theme, reveals his new emphasis. "Time past and time future," he wrote in *Burnt Norton*, "Allow but a little consciousness./ To be conscious is not to be in time"—in other words, so long as men are bound by the time dimension all they can know is the illusion of flux. But it is possible to find a consciousness outside of time: "I cannot say where" except that it is in the silence, "at the still point of the turning world." Auden likewise came to conceive of time—chronological time, "the formal logic of the clock"—pessimistically. Auden's case is particularly striking because there had been a time when Auden, unlike Eliot, had believed in progress, i.e., in the possibility of turning the wasteland into an earthly paradise. But beginning in 1939, largely it would seem as a result of the impact of catastrophic world events upon him and the influence of two religious thinkers, Søren Kierkegaard and Reinhold Niebuhr, he concluded that "in Time we sin" (*New Year Letter 1941*) and that men cannot find salvation "in an ordre logique." He also balanced that outlook, however, with a newly found religious conviction that man can reach "The Good Place," and hence learn to love, by an intuition of timeless "Being" as opposed to "Becoming," by the realization "that we/ In fact, live in eternity" if we only knew it.

"Potential evil is *in* time," wrote Aldous Huxley who also set out on a "Pilgrim's Progress" beginning in the twenties. "Potential evil is *in* time; potential good isn't," says Huxley's mouthpiece in *After Many a Summer Dies the Swan*

(1939); "actual good is outside time." "True religion concerns itself with the givenness of the timeless," says another mouthpiece in the novel significantly entitled *Time Must Have a Stop* (1944); "an idolatrous religion is one in which time is substituted for eternity." And Mr. Propter, Bruno, and all the other late Huxleyan mouthpieces put their faith in a mystic "experience beyond time, of union with the divine Ground," which, as Huxley continually points out, is singularly difficult of achievement in the modern sceptical climate, but which can be induced with the proper sort of attitude and preparation. Thus, Huxley, like Auden, came to believe not only in the possibility but also in the supreme importance of inner religious progress—achieved by the annihilation of ordinary time—as contrasted to the outer progress preached by countless modern "idolatries."

These are only a few examples of the search for religious meaning among contemporary writers which while hardly general is yet symptomatic of a heightened interest in religion during the past two generations.

4.

One last question remains to be considered. That is the question posed at the beginning of the chapter. Assuming a mental climate increasingly favorable to the religious enterprise (as the evidence adduced in the last section, and indeed the previous chapter, might lead us to do); assuming a climate in which there is an agony of "longing," and at the same time a vigorous searching for "meaning" by a not inconsiderable number of persons in all realms of thought; assuming, we might almost say, a powerful new "will to believe" among the sceptics: what will come out of this ferment? What form or forms will it eventually take? Obviously, no categorical answer is possible. Yet perhaps some sort of general and tentative answer is possible if we rephrase the question more narrowly. What forms has it already, in fact, begun to take, and what forms *can* it conceivably take in view of the conditioning sceptical tradition? To phrase the question in this way is to bring it back somewhat within the purview of the observable evidence. Nevertheless, it should be clearly understood that in attempting to answer even this more limited question the intention is not to plead a special cause, but only to analyze a historical situation as the author sees it. We shall be concerned, then, not primarily with what ought to be, but only with what is or what can be, realizing, moreover, that even the question of "what can be" is not entirely amenable to historical analysis.

One possibility is a return to traditional forms of religious belief which had been thought to be outmoded, but which with the decline of the modern secular faiths and in the light of new circumstances have taken on new significance. And in fact there has been something of a return, particularly in clerical circles, since World War I, centering in what has been called "the theological renaissance." This theological renaissance has taken, to be sure, not one form but many, and some of the forms—the theologies of Rudolf Bultmann and Paul Tillich, for instance—are palpably less return-minded than others. Taken as a whole, however, the movement has certain common characteristics, or at least tendencies. The chief characteristic, carried to the extreme in the "neo-orthodoxy" of the Swiss theologian Karl Barth, is the rejection ("*diastasis*" or "cutting") of theological "modernism" or "liberalism" with its emphasis on divine immanence, optimism, and progress, and its attempt to fit Christianity into categories acceptable to modern scientific and historical criticism—the sort of theology expounded, for instance, by R. J. Campbell, minister

of the City Temple, London, in his *New Theology* of
1907 which was not "new" at all but rather a culminating
document of a century of similar expositions. In opposition
to this modernism—significantly, Campbell himself later
helped to lead the opposition, as did Barth; and significantly, for both men, the change of heart came during the
middle of World War I—the new theologies brought back
traditional words and concepts: biblical words such as
revelation, sin, redemption, atonement, faith, last things.
Where, for example, the accent in modernism was on God's
immanence, in the new theologies it was on his transcendence and absolute sovereignty. Likewise, in the latter it was
man's sinfulness and not his perfectability that received
emphasis. The tendency, especially marked in neo-ortho-
doxy, was toward a radical dualism, with the Creator
depicted as "Wholly Other," "above," "yonder," and the
creature as "beneath" and "here." In this view, man is saved,
not by his own efforts, as the liberal Campbell had thought,
but solely on God's initiative, as St. Augustine and the great
"orthodox" theologians of the Reformation had taught.
The chasm between God and man could be bridged only
by Jesus Christ the Savior, which is to say by direct supernatural intervention. The revival of Christology is striking,
not only in Barth, whose "Christomonism" is famous, but
also in Barth's German contemporary, Karl Heim; in the
Swedish theologian Gustaf Aulen, for whom Jesus broke
the power of Satan; and in Donald Baillie of St. Andrews
in whose Jesus, God dwells and seeks out his lost sheep.
The authority for these asseverations is primarily "revelation" rather than reason, revelation being conceived severally as the "Word of God" in the Bible (Barth), as man's
confrontation with God in an "I-Thou" relationship in
which man is shaken and remade by God (Barth's compatriot Emil Brunner), and as faith in the person of Jesus

Christ which precedes and illuminates reason (as in Archbishop William Temple's Gifford Lectures on *Nature, Man, and God*). All these theologies require some sort of "leap of faith," to use the Kierkegaardian expression which has been so much in vogue. In this respect Temple, not nearly so unsympathetic to natural theology as Barth, was closer in spirit to the latter than perhaps he suspected. For both men, for the extreme orthodox and the moderate orthodox, as they might be called, and for the new theologies in general, faith is primary for an understanding of theological mysteries.

Now few people would deny, I think, that these new theologies contain profound insights or that they have caught in their formulae much of the travail of twentieth-century man, his tragic sense of life, his "crisis." Nor can it be denied that they have had at least a limited appeal for laymen as well as clergymen. The question remains, however, whether the "leap" which they call for is possible for the vast majority of people who have been brought up in the sceptical tradition. Is it possible even for those sceptics who long for a "new transcendental faith"? Do the theologies of return really speak to their condition? Do they speak to Julien Delattre?

At this point it is well to remind ourselves of what Delattre actually did say when confronted with Father Millet's "faith" as a possible answer to his "longing" (presumably he would have returned the same answer to the Protestant orthodoxies described above). His language could scarcely be stronger. "I won't have any of your patent medicine," Koestler makes him say to the priest; "what you ask of me is the unconditional surrender of my critical faculties" (see p. 190). His rejoinder recalls the categorical refusal of various characters in Camus' novels to take the leap of faith, and Camus' equation, in *The Myth of Sisyphus,* of the "leap" with "philosophical suicide." In a later work, as we have also seen, Koestler further refers to the churches as "venerable anachronisms," and to their type of religion as "archaic." "Archaic" and "obsolete" are indeed adjectives which one encounters frequently in this sort of sceptical critique of orthodoxy. Jung, for example, in his famous analysis of "the spiritual problem of modern man" spoke of the latter's "psychic energy which can no longer be invested in obsolete forms of religion." "Our age," he wrote, "wishes to have actual experiences in psychic life. [But] it wants to experience for itself, and not to make assumptions based on the experience of other ages." [37] And more recently Toynbee, in language strikingly similar to Koestler's, has observed that

Archaistic religious movements are intellectually indefensible because the antecedent Rationalism that has driven a traditional religious faith off the field does not in reality just come and go like the fog. . . . Souls that have once had the experience of intellectual enlightenment can never thereafter find spiritual salvation by committing intellectual suicide; and, though the quest of recapturing their lost faith is in itself both intellectually and morally legitimate, agnostics who embark on this quest will not find themselves able to worship God again in spirit and in truth if they seek to open for themselves a homeward spiritual path by deliberately closing their mind's critical eye.[38]

Specifically, the archaistic label means that the sceptic, even a sceptic favorably inclined to religion, like those mentioned above, has trouble with the words and concepts of the theologies. Their language, he would say, is in large part an archaic language which is not only troublesome but frequently unintelligible to a twentieth-century man. Words like "revelation," "incarnation," and "atonement"

[37] Jung, *Modern Man in Search of a Soul,* pp. 239-40.
[38] Arnold Toynbee, *A Study of History,* Vol. IX, p. 631.

simply do not strike the same responsive chord in him as
they did in a Luther or a John Wesley. Furthermore, they
make assumptions about the nature of the universe—assumptions about supernature, about God and his ways with
men, about revelation in the Bible and Christ—which raise
more questions for him than they answer. How can he
make such assumptions without a prior leap of faith such
as only a man living in the age of Abraham or an utterly
anguished soul like Søren Kierkegaard finds it possible to
make? In short, there is in these theologies, even in those
which claim to repudiate natural theology altogether, a certain presumption of metaphysical knowledge, a definiteness
of metaphysical conception which leaves the sceptic gasp-
ing (and which, incidentally, even Tillich has warned
against). And there is in them, too, a certain presumption
of Christian superiority, of the finality of revelation in
Christ, at which even a person so close to the Roman
Catholic faith as Simone Weil ultimately boggled.

If, then, "return" presents serious if not insuperable difficulties to most sceptics, what sort of religious conviction
is possible for them? Of course, it is impossible to say what,
precisely, is possible in any individual case. To the Camus
who wrote *The Myth of Sisyphus* no sort of religion is
possible, though he may wish that it were. At the other end
of the pole is Professor Joad who, having persuaded himself that "the religious hypothesis" covered "more of the
facts of experience than any other," found it possible to join
the Church of England. In between are people like Simone
Weil and Delattre. Simone Weil stopped just short of
baptism, meanwhile attending mass and discovering new
riches in Christian symbolism. Delattre, on the other hand,
prefers simply "to wait" without committing himself to any
religious notions in particular: "Religions are not invented";
all we can do is to "wait" for them "to materialise." Con-

ceding these and other individual varieties, it seems possible nevertheless to detect the materializing of a more general conviction, a sort of "Layman's Religion" which has been growing up, almost imperceptibly, alongside the new theologies. This "Layman's Religion," if such it can be called, is not easy to describe, for it is quite inchoate and tentative. It is not set down, at least not in all its fullness, in any one place or by any one person. It patently does not command the allegiance of all sceptics, and even those who can be said to adhere to it in general are not always or fully conscious of its existence. Since, however, traces of it are to be found in so many places, and since parts of it *are* quite fully explicated, one can scarcely doubt its existence. To the extent that it does exist, it is the work, largely though not exclusively, of lay intellectuals who have obviously been trying to find a religious *modus vivendi* which does not do violence to the "critical faculties." Thus, it might be said to be a sort of *via media* which embraces the search for religious meaning without, however, abandoning the questioning attitude inculcated by the sceptical tradition.[39]

The term "Layman's Religion" is not contemporary, or at least I have found no reference to it in contemporary literature. It is borrowed from the *De Religione Laici* of Lord Herbert of Cherbury who, it will be recalled, disgusted with the religious and theological warfare of the early seventeenth century, tried to find some common ground upon which laymen if not clergymen could agree (see pp. 97-8). However, Herbert's "common notions" imply a much more positive conception than this "Layman's Religion" of the twentieth century would warrant. The latter is more like the vague "religion of the layman" which

[39] A preliminary sketch of this *via media* notion will be found in my address "Religion and the Sceptical Tradition," in *Henry Wells Lawrence Memorial Lectures,* New London, 1959, Vol. IV, pp. 23-6.

Walter Pater described as "something more than what is called 'natural,' yet less than ecclesiastical, or 'professional' religion." [40] Unlike the clergyman's religion, it does not consist of definite articles of faith such as might be embodied in a credo and expounded in a theology. Though it is not necessarily anticlerical or antichurch, it is antitheological. It consists more of attitudes which have not yet crystallized into articles of faith, or even such broad "notions" as Herbert described. Yet it is like Herbert's "Religion" in its comprehensiveness and its groping for a minimal standard of agreement. As might be expected of a "sceptical" religion it contains strong negative as well as positive constituents. For the purpose of analysis we shall designate these constituents as (1) Polymorphism; (2) The Vanity of Dogmatizing; and (3) Religious Experience as expressed in Myth and Symbol. It should be noted that these constituents are not set down in any particular order, since to do so would be to give them more logical consistency than they exhibit in actual writings.

Polymorphism, a word frequently used by Ernst Troeltsch in his later days, signifies that religious truth, however it be understood, is not confined to any particular "revelation" or church, nor to any particular culture. On the contrary, religion clearly assumes not one but many valid forms (polymorphism) in both time and space, and no sect which does not recognize this fact can hope to appeal widely to the educated and thoughtful community. The sects, if they are to hold their ground and grow, must renounce "naive claims to absolute validity" and affirm their willingness, as Toynbee says, "to tolerate, respect, and revere one another's religious heritages." It is important to note that what polymorphism usually calls for is not a new religion representing a bizarre mishmash of ideas east and

[40] Pater, *Works*, Vol. V, p. 136.

west, nor a renunciation of the religious symbols of one's own culture, but simply a broadening of horizons to include the religious insights of other cultures and to recognize in them parallel attempts to reach the same ineffable end. This antiparochialism is obviously a reflection in the sphere of religion of what Oswald Spengler called the "Copernican viewpoint" in history, i.e., the view that in the writing of history the West can no longer be conceded a unique or privileged position vis-à-vis the other great cultures of the world. The "Copernican viewpoint" in religion, as we may call it, has been growing ever since the Crusades and the great voyages of discovery of the sixteenth and seventeenth centuries. It was strongly represented in the deisms and theisms of the eighteenth-century Enlightenment, as we have seen, and it has gained ever wider expression today in a world brought close together by rapid communications and in which, furthermore, the West has begun to lose its conviction of superiority.

Ernst Troeltsch stated the "Copernican viewpoint" admirably in a lecture entitled "The Place of Christianity among the World-Religions" which he prepared for delivery at Oxford in 1923. Troeltsch, it will be recalled, had been wrestling for years with the problem of historicism and the threat which it posed to religious beliefs. An early work affirmed the "absolute validity" of the religion in which he had been reared and whose theology he had professed at Heidelberg and Berlin. But gradually, as he became better acquainted with the other religions of the world, and because he could not rid himself of his conviction of "individuality" in history (i.e., the relativity and diversity of all things, including religious beliefs), he came round to a concepton of "polymorphous truth." "A study of the non-Christian religions," he said, "convinced me more and more that their naïve claims to absolute validity are also genuinely such. I found Buddhism and Brahminism especially to be really humane and spiritual religions." Thus, Troeltsch had come to think of Christianity, not as "absolutely valid," but as one manifestation of religious truth among many; as evidence, certainly, of a profound inner experience, but not as the only valid one.

This experience is undoubtedly the criterion of its validity, but, be it noted, only of its validity *for us*. It is God's countenance as revealed to us; it is the way in which, being what we are, we receive, and react to, the revelation of God. . . . But this does not preclude the possibility that other racial groups, living under entirely different cultural conditions, may experience their contact with the Divine Life in quite a different way, and may themselves also possess a religion which has grown up with them, and from which they cannot sever themselves so long as they remain what they are.[41]

And since God alone could determine which was relatively best, Troeltsch stressed the common ground of all the religions, urging mutual understanding between them and the renunciation of self-will and the spirit of violent domination. "In our earthly experience," he concluded, "the Divine Life is not One, but Many. But to apprehend the One in the Many constitutes the special character of love."

Echoes of this viewpoint can be heard in a thousand places—in the increasingly wide currency of phrases like "polymorphous truth," the "relativity of the gods" (Jung), the "perennial philosophy" (Aldous Huxley), "multiple revelation" (Simone Weil); in Toynbee's Gifford Lectures of 1952 and 1953; in Jung and his school, and in what Jung calls the *Drang nach Osten*, the drive, which has been gaining momentum since the publication of books like Edward Carpenter's *Pagan and Christian Creeds* (1920), to appre-

[41] Troeltsch, *Christian Thought. Its History and Application*, p. 26.

ciate and assimilate the spiritual wisdom of the East; and in life histories like those of Simone Weil and Hugh l'Anson Fausset. Simone Weil found herself drawn to Roman Catholicism after passing through a free-thinking phase. However, she persisted in refusing Christian baptism, and one of the reasons she gave was her conviction that the Roman Church, great as it was, had no monopoly on truth. "I felt that I could not honestly give up my opinions concerning the non-Christian religions and concerning Israel," she wrote to Father Perrin in 1942, "—and as a matter of fact time and meditation have only served to strengthen them—and I thought that this constituted an absolute obstacle." [42] She preferred to remain therefore at the point where she had been ever since her birth, "at the intersection of Christianity and everything that is not Christianity." The English poet and literary critic Hugh l'Anson Fausset was brought up as a Christian but soon found that he could not accept "the claim of any race or religious fraternity to be the elect of God." He was confirmed in this view chiefly by his discovery of Indian philosophy. Christian missionaries, he observes, would once have smiled at the suggestion that a man might be saved by following the teachings of Vedanta. "To-day the smile would, perhaps, be less assured. For during the last fifty years our knowledge of the comparative qualities and defects of different religions has grown considerably." [43]

Toynbee might almost seem to be picking up the thread of Troeltsch's argument when in his Gifford Lectures he urged "the sacrifice of self-centredness" among the higher religions of the world, all of which are carriers of religious

[42] Simone Weil, Letter to Father Perrin, May 15, 1942, in *Waiting for God*, p. 70.

[43] Hugh l'Anson Fausset, *The Flame and the Light* (New York: Abelard-Schuman, 1958), pp. 11-13.

truth. He quotes the Roman, Quintus Symmachus, who in a controversy with St. Ambrose about "Absolute Reality" declared that "the heart of so great a mystery cannot ever be reached by following one road only." Symmachus' argument, Toynbee feels, "has never been answered by his Christian opponents. . . . For, though Symmachus' ancestral religion is long since extinct, Hinduism lives to speak for Symmachus today."

In the world in which we now find ourselves, the adherents of the different living religions ought to be the readier to tolerate, respect, and revere one another's religious heritages because, in our generation, there is not anyone alive who is effectively in a position to judge between his own religion and his neighbour's. An effective judgement is impossible when one is comparing a religion which has been familiar to one in one's home since one's childhood with a religion which one has learnt to know from outside in later years. . . . The missions of the higher religions are not competitive; they are complementary. We can believe in our own religion without having to feel that it is the sole repository of truth. We can love it without having to feel that it is the sole means of salvation.[44]

Where Toynbee likes to quote Symmachus a follower of Jung quotes the Vedas: "Truth is one, the sages speak of it by many names." [45] This is essentially Jung's position. Jung postulates certain "religion-creating archetypes" in the human psyche, certain original "types" or "categories" as it were, which are refracted in a great many different and yet similar images "according to time, place, and milieu." "In the West," he says in an essay on "The Religious and Psychological Problems of Alchemy," "the archetype is

[44] Arnold Toynbee, *An Historian's Approach to Religion* (Oxford, 1956), pp. 297-99.
[45] Joseph Campbell, *The Hero with a Thousand Faces* (New York: Pantheon Books, 1949).

charged with the dogmatic figure of Christ; in the East, with Purusha, the Atman, Hiranya-garbha, Buddha, and so on." In later years Jung has preferred to call this archetype the "self" which, he says, "refers neither to Christ nor to Buddha but to the totality of the figures that are its equivalent, and each of these figures is a symbol of the self." This seems to be what he means by "the relativity of the idea of God" which he expounded at some length in *Psychological Types*. The archetype or the "self" remains the same, but man's consciousness of it, the images or symbols into which he tries to project it, vary from one epoch or culture to another. "People," he concludes, "have dwelt far too long on the fundamentally sterile question of whether the assertions of [a particular] faith are true or not." [46] The important thing is the assertion itself which necessarily and also as a matter of historical fact speaks a different language in different cultures.

The second and third constituents of the "Layman's Religion"—the "Vanity of Dogmatizing" and Experience as expressed in Myth and Symbol—are complementary to each other and need therefore to be considered together. They are, so to speak, the negative and positive sides of the same coin. The "Vanity of Dogmatizing" (the title of a book written by Joseph Glanvill at the height of the religious and philosophical warfare of the seventeenth century) is the negative side. It signifies (as it signified to Glanvill) a profound conceptual and semantical scepticism; a scepticism that concepts and words—what is sometimes called discursive language, the language which dogma and theology necessarily use to a large extent—can ever convey the religious realities. On this view dogma is "vain," not only because it is parochial, but also because it is prone to literal pronouncements about realities which are essentially

[46] Carl Jung, in *Psychology and Alchemy*, pp. 17-18.

unknowable and unspeakable—at any rate, by ordinary discursive language. "Experience," on the other hand, signifies that what is essentially unspeakable can perhaps be reached in some sort of inner awareness, and expressed in forms which are not primarily discursive in nature, e.g., by myth, symbol, and perhaps "negative theology." Unquestionably, these twin notions are present to some degree in every age, even among theologians, but they would seem to be especially pronounced in the sceptical lay thought of today.

Students of comparative religion and culture have often remarked on the tendency in Western culture to define everything, to reduce even its most profound religious insights to "the logical formulae of normal verbal thought." "The West demands clearness. . . . There is an anxiety for definition and form in the Western religions," says one such student, and he traces this "anxiety," which he says begets "definite creeds and absolutist dogmatism," back to the Roman emphasis on organization and to Greek intellectualism with its straining for systems tested by logical consistency.[47] What has not been sufficiently remarked, at least not in this context, is the increasing resistance to this tendency ever since the great battle between "words" and "things" in the seventeenth century. The history of this resistance to the literal word, this scepticism of discursive language as a vehicle for religious truth, still remains to be written, and all that can be done here is to cite a few examples of it in the contemporary era. It was already much in evidence in the late nineteenth century in, for example, the writings of Matthew Arnold and Herbert Spencer, both of whom were concerned to end the warfare between science and religion, but who were left aghast at the verbalisms and conceptualisms of the theologians. In *Literature and Dogma* Arnold castigated "our mechanical and materialising theol-

[47] S. Radhakrishnan, *East and West in Religion* (London, 1933), p. 49.

ogy, with its insane licence of affirmation about God, its insane licence of affirmation about a future state." Theologians, he said, "know a great deal, far too much" about God; the trouble with dogma is "that it assumes [and tries to put into words] what cannot be *verified*." Hence, he called for a religion in which verbal affirmation would be held to a minimum, a religion concentrating on ethics and therefore very different from what he repeatedly called the "licence" of the creeds. Spencer's criticism, embodied in the first volume of his *System of Synthetic Philosophy*, was even more pointed. The trouble with religious people, he said—and herein lies the "impiety of the pious"—is that they have professed "to know in the minutest detail" what is essentially a mystery. Their error consists in mistaking symbolic conceptions, "definite assertions," for real ones.

Very likely [he concluded] there will ever remain a need to give shape to that indefinite sense of an Ultimate Existence, which forms the basis of our intelligence. We shall always be under the necessity of contemplating it as *some* mode of being; that is—of representing it to ourselves in *some* form of thought, however vague. And we shall not err in doing this so long as we treat every notion we thus frame as merely a symbol, utterly without resemblance to that for which it stands.[48]

This semantical scepticism is writ large in the twentieth century, as can be readily seen from the spate of books on language and its relation to meaning.[49] It is conspicuous among the neo-positivists and psychoanalysts who are, by and large, no friends to religion, but it is also to be found among thinkers who are—lay philosophers like Alfred

[48] Arnold, *Literature and Dogma,* pp. xiv, 308, and *passim;* Herbert Spencer, *First Principles* (London, 1870), p. 113.

[49] See Susanne K. Langer, *Philosophy in a New Key* (Cambridge: Harvard University Press, 1942), chap. 1, for a list of some of these books.

North Whitehead, Ernst Cassirer, and Unamuno, for example, and even some theologians, particularly those who follow an existentialist line of thought. The neo-positivists literally cut the ground out from under dogma by their severe limitation upon what can be expressed in words. According to Ludwig Wittgenstein and Rudolf Carnap, most words are utterly misleading, and facts are radically transformed when they are rendered as verbal propositions; hence, most philosophical and, by inference, theological propositions are not only false but senseless. Likewise, for the psychoanalyst words are pitifully inadequate for expressing man's deepest experience, for, as Otto Rank says in *Beyond Psychology*, they constitute "a rational phenomenon meant to communicate thoughts and to explain actions in rational terms"; hence, they can give but a "mere impression of the irrational." Whitehead, a philosopher who was profoundly concerned about religion, had much the same attitude toward words—and hence toward dogma. He was not, of course, opposed to theology as such; indeed, he propounded a natural theology of his own which has had considerable influence in theological circles. Nevertheless, he severely criticized orthodox theology, first of all, because of its insistence upon encasing its principles in verbal forms of statement better "suited to the emotional reactions of bygone times" than the present; but more profoundly, I think, because of its penchant for saying too much about what ultimately "eludes apprehension." In his "dialogues," Whitehead was always alluding to "the imprecision of language," "monstrous inexactitude in the use of words," "the fallacy of dogmatic finality."

I am impressed [he said on one occasion] by the inadequacy of language to express our conscious thought, and by the inadequacy of our conscious thought to express our subconscious. The curse of philosophy has been the supposition that language is an exact medium. Philosophers verbalize and then suppose the idea is stated for all time.[50]

Whitehead noted this same tendency in Christian theology and for him it signified a "disaster," no less; a disaster because, among other things, it attempted to freeze in words and formulae what is in reality utterly beyond the limits of rationality. "All we can do, in venturing on such subjects," he once said apropos of an analogous subject, namely the metaphysical ideas discussed in his *Process and Reality*, "is to offer suggestions." It may be remarked parenthetically that this conviction of the "Vanity of Dogmatizing"—or *Odium anti-theologicum*, as Unamuno somewhat extremely calls it—undoubtedly accounts for much of the contemporary attraction of the Eastern religions, particularly Buddhism. Whitehead himself did not feel this attraction (he described Buddhism as a "religion of escapism"), but others do, because they see in Buddhism the prototype of a genuinely nondogmatic religion. "Questions which have given rise to violent arguments and persecutions in the West," says Erich Fromm, "have been treated by Hinduism and Buddhism with fine humor and irony." "Such notions" [for example, refusal to discuss the gods, the future of the soul], Karl Pearson had said a long time before, "render Buddhism perhaps the most valuable study among concrete religious systems to the modern freethinker." [51]

Having defined the limits of theology, Whitehead, however, then goes on to suggest (he does so, for example, in the chapter on God in *Science and the Modern World*) that "what further can be known about God must be sought in the region of particular experiences, and there-

[50] *Dialogues of Alfred North Whitehead*, ed. Lucien Price (Boston: Little, Brown, 1954), p. 368.

[51] Fromm, *Psychoanalysis and Religion*, pp. 104-105; Pearson, *The Ethic of Freethought*, pp. 20-21.

fore rests on an empirical basis." "Experience," then, constitutes the positive counterpart to the negative *antitheologicum*, the third and last constituent of the new "Layman's Religion"; and with this notion is often coupled, though not conspicuously in Whitehead, the notion of myth and symbol as the language which best expresses "particular experiences" in religion.

It is remarkable, and certainly significant, how often the word "experience" or some variant of it crops up in contemporary lay thought about religion. William James might almost be said to have set a fashion when he chose to entitle his Gifford Lectures of 1902 "The Varieties of Religious Experience." Following James, Carl Jung, for example, speaks of an "original experience" of the Self, Otto Rank of "vital experience" which takes man "beyond psychology," Aldous Huxley of an "immediate experience" or "direct apprehension of spiritual Fact," Basil Willey of "self-knowledge," Koestler of the "inner voice of conscience" exhibited by the Yogi. Nor is this experiential emphasis lacking among clergymen, as can be readily seen in Germany's two influential Rudolfs, Rudolf Otto and Rudolf Bultmann. Rudolf Otto's *The Idea of the Holy* (1917), unquestionably one of the most important and influential books on religion in the twentieth century, emphasizes that "profounder religion" which, says its author, is based on experience of the "numinous," i.e., the *"mysterium tremendum"* of God which comes "not by demonstration, but by pure contemplation," "from first-hand personal divination." More recently Rudolf Bultmann, anathema to orthodox theologians because of his program of "demythologization" (to which we shall return), has urged the reinterpretation of the Christian message of salvation, not as faith in a historical event, but as the experiencing of man's relation to God here and now.

Just what does "experience" signify as it is used by these and similar writers? Insofar as there is any consensus, it means "personal religion," as William James called it, as differentiated from dogmatic and theological religion; further, the "intuition" or "divination," by individuals, of a wider self or a metaphysical reality (the terms vary) which, as Otto says, citing Goethe, "goes beyond all 'conceiving,' surpasses 'understanding' and 'reason,' and consequently is 'inapprehensible' and cannot properly be put into a statement." [52] It does not necessarily mean *odium* of theology, but it does mean that theology and dogma are at best only "second-hand" and even fumbling renditions of a primordial state of mind or feeling which eludes rational and historical explanations. As Aldous Huxley says in *The Perennial Philosophy*, "the verbal statements of theology's more or less adequate rationalizations of experience have been taken too seriously and treated with the reverence that is due only to the Fact they are intended to describe."

Theological speculation [he adds] is valuable insofar as it enables those who have had immediate experience of various aspects of God to form intelligible ideas about the nature of the divine Ground, and of their own experience of the Ground in relation to other experiences. . . . In no circumstances, however, can the study of theology or the mind's assent to theological propositions take the place of what [William] Law calls "the birth of God within." For theory is not practice, and words are not the things for which they stand.[53]

There is, of course, nothing strictly new in this predilection for "experience," nor, as Otto is careful to point out, has it been wholly lacking in Christian theology. The new

[52] Otto, *The Idea of the Holy*, pp. 154-55, and *passim*.
[53] Aldous Huxley, *The Perennial Philosophy* (New York: Harper and Brothers, 1945), p. 131.

thing is the emphasis put upon it by laymen in an age which for a variety of historical reasons has lost faith in traditional dogma and traditional religious symbols. In such an age the emphasis is understandably upon what comes *before* theology, upon the search for fresh or "first-hand" experience by the individual, and without commitment meanwhile to any more verbal and conceptual definition than is absolutely necessary to the search. This notion of experience is perhaps doubly appealing at the present time because of the approval it might seem to have from the natural sciences and the new science of psychology. "In religion as in natural science," says Huxley, "experience is determined only by experience. It is fatal to prejudge it, to compel it to fit the mould imposed by a theory which either does not correspond to the facts at all, or corresponds to only some of the facts." [54] Huxley might have added that the Jungian school of psychology has similarly made the religious experience rest on supposedly indubitable "psychical facts" which are discoverable in the "unconscious" mind.

Carl Jung explains the new experiential emphasis by reference to "Protestantism." The modern world, he argues, is full of "Protestants"—meaning by "Protestants," not Protestants in the technical sense, but people for whom the old religious symbols no longer work, to whom the old dogmatic formulations make little or no appeal, yet people who are straining for religious illumination. For such people, the only way out of their dilemma is a new interiorizing of religion, a new experiment in "self-experience" from which faith can come again. Jung describes himself as a member of the extreme left wing in the parliament of Protestantism, and that is indeed precisely what he is. As

[54] *Ibid.*, p. 132.

Hans Schaer says of him, he "sets the individual in the very centre of religion as no Church has ever done." [55] He throws man back on the primordial "Self" in which all the "archetypes" of religion have their source, and which he thinks might well become the religious symbol of the new age of the West. Though he differs somewhat from Jung, another psychologist, Erich Fromm, likewise defines "religious experience" as the individual's wonder and "ultimate concern" with the problem of the meaning of life, his attitude of oneness, not only with his fellow men but also "beyond that, with the universe," his "getting in touch with the unconscious." Conspicuous in his conception, as in Jung's, is a reaction against the norms laid down by "authoritarian systems."

Central to Jung's thought, and to the "Layman's Religion" generally, is also, and finally, the notion that myth and symbol constitute the language best suited to express the findings of "experience." Presumably there comes a time when experience must speak, and if it does not find it possible—at any rate, just yet—to speak in the discursive language of dogma and theology, what then? Perhaps the semantical dilemma explains, at least in part, why the re-emphasis on experience has been accompanied by a rehabilitation of myth and symbol. "We must needs mythologize," says Unamuno in a fairly typical statement in his chapter on "The Mythology of the Beyond" in *The Tragic Sense of Life*. For whenever we try to give a form which is "concrete, conceivable, or in other words, rational" to our religious longings, we inevitably become involved in "contradictions and inconsistencies." "But has not the mythological dream its content of truth? Are not dream and myth per-

---

[55] Hans Schaer, *Religion and the Cure of Souls in Jung's Psychology* (New York: Pantheon Books, 1950), p. 211.

haps revelations of an inexpressible truth, of an irrational truth, of a truth that cannot be proven?" [56]

Myth, in the sense that Unamuno uses it, is obviously something quite different from the interpretation put upon it by an older generation of anthropologists. It no longer connotes a world of illusion, a naïve explanation by primitive peoples of physical processes they did not understand, which would afterwards give way to a scientific explanation. For the German philosopher Ernst Cassirer, who devoted a lifetime to its study, myth is no mere fanciful story, but a genuine way of seeing and expressing "primary experience" of reality. The human mentality, says Jung, "does not invent myths, it experiences them." "Myths are original revelations of the pre-conscious psyche, involuntary statements about unconscious psychic happenings, and anything but allegories of physical processes." [57] Stated in other words, myths are projections of the religion-creating archetypes in the soul, akin to dreams yet more than dreams in that they mirror not only the experience of the individual but also the collective experience, the "big dreams" of the race. As we have seen, Toynbee, in his "Acknowledgments and Thanks" appended to the last volume of his *Study of History*, praises Plato—and Jung too—for being neither too proud nor timid "to take to a myth for the sake of reconnoitering regions of the Spiritual Universe beyond the Reason's range." Rudolf Bultmann might seem to represent a reverse tendency with his program for the "demythologization" of Christianity. But Bultmann is clearly

[56] Miguel de Unamuno, *The Tragic Sense of Life in Men and Peoples* (London, 1926), p. 257.

[57] Carl Jung and C. Kerényi, *Essays on a Science of Mythology* (New York: Pantheon Books, 1949), p. 101. For two similar statements by Jungians, see Joseph Campbell, *The Hero with a Thousand Faces*, Prologue, and Laurens Van der Post, *The Dark Eye in Africa*, pp. 182-84.

using myth in another sense, as the expression of a pre-scientific picture of nature. Christianity must be shorn of this sort of outmoded myth, he says, if it is to survive in the modern world. But this only means that it should not be made to rest on views of nature which modern man can no longer accept. I doubt very much that Bultmann would object to Unamuno's usage, though he obviously prefers existential to mythological language when, for example, he explains the meaning of the Easter faith.

What has been said of myth can also be said of symbol, for the two are almost interchangeable in contemporary usage.

Religion in its teachings as well as in its rituals [says Erich Fromm] speaks in a language different from the one we use in daily life, that is, in symbolic language. . . . Symbolic language is the only universal language the human race has known. It is the language used in myths five thousand years old and in the dreams of our contemporaries.[58]

Thus, ideas of God, indeed all religious beliefs and images, are to be regarded as symbols which seek to mediate a "spiritual reality" which cannot be described or defined. They are not descriptions or explanations of anything. They do not give literal truth or exact knowledge in the scientific sense. They are, as John Herman Randall, Jr., puts it, "nonrepresentative and noncognitive." The important thing about them is what they do, not what they describe. They provoke emotional responses in men, and stimulate them to certain types of activity. But principally, they give men "insight" or "vision," they enable men to descry a wider, religious dimension of the world. Thus, they belong to the

[58] Fromm, *Psychoanalysis and Religion*, p. 111.

order of "wisdom" rather than "science," *sapientia* rather than *scientia*.[59]

The advantages which myth and symbol are presumed to have over dogma and theology must now be clear. Myth, says Toynbee in *An Historian's Approach to Religion*, involves the "poetic" rather than the "scientific" usage of words and is by that token the better notation for reconnoitering the "mysterious hinterland" which is beyond the grasp of the human intellect. The assumption behind this statement is that there is a certain kind of experience, viz., the religious experience, which cannot properly be expressed save mythically or figuratively, and that to try to transpose it into scientific or discursive language is to destroy its meaning and efficacy. As Fromm says, trouble arises only when the contents of symbolic language are mistaken for "real events in the realm of things instead of for symbolic expression of the soul's experience." Heinrich Zimmer, the great scholar of the myths and symbols of India, expresses this view, which is evidently also his own, in a statement on Indian philosophy.

To express and communicate knowledge gained in moments of grammar-transcending insight metaphors must be used, similes and allegories. These are then not mere embellishments, dispensable accessories, but the very vehicles of the meaning, which could not be rendered, and could never have been attained, through the logical formulae of normal verbal thought. Significant images can comprehend and make manifest with clarity and pictorial consistency the paradoxical character of the reality known to the sage: a translogical reality, which,

[59] See the account of religious symbols in John Herman Randall, Jr., *The Role of Knowledge in Western Religion* (Boston: Starr King, 1958), chap. 4; also Erwin Goodenough, *Toward a Mature Faith* (New York: Prentice-Hall, 1955), chap. 3.

expressed in the abstract language of normal thought, would seem inconsistent, self-contradictory, or even absolutely meaningless. Indian philosophy, therefore, frankly avails itself of the symbols and images of myth.[60]

From the standpoint of the "Layman's Religion," mythological and symbolic language has the additional advantage of being less parochial than dogmatic and theological language, of availing itself of the religious experience of more than one culture, of uniting rather than separating men in the religious adventure, therefore of fitting in with the polymorphic attitude.

These three constituents of a "Layman's Religion" have been slowly developing for a long time, side by side with the clergyman's religion, sometimes interwining, but more often at loggerheads with it. They have not yet jelled into anything conclusive or even very concrete, and possibly they may never do so. However, they are undoubtedly widely held attitudes at the present time among sceptics who are looking for a religious home. They are the way to a home, not the home itself. For some, the way may lead back into the churches, though only after considerable reinterpretation and decoding of traditional beliefs. For others, the way will continue to lead away from the churches.

Religiously speaking, the present age would seem to be a great age of experimentation. It is, of course, a profoundly sceptical and secular age. Yet there does seem to have been something like a break-through in recent years among an appreciable number of erstwhile sceptics—not toward solid belief, to be sure, but toward an awareness of the importance of religion both for the individual soul and for

[60] Heinrich Zimmer, *Philosophies of India* (New York: Pantheon Books, 1951), p. 25.

civilization. One gets the impression of hundreds of experiments by individuals: Whitehead's speculations about "organism," Jung's "Self," Huxley's "divine Ground," John Cowper Powys' "divine Aether," Hermann Hesse's "journey to the East," Nikos Kazantzakis' "Great Combatant." Unless I misread the signs completely this is not and cannot be a great theological age, and this is said with full knowledge of the present vigor of Christian theology. For theology is built upon a solid rock of faith, and faith is precisely what the modern "layman," reared in the sceptical tradition, does not have. Hence, his innumerable experiments with new myths which will satisfy his "longing." "Layman's Religion" is only a generic label for this species of experiment.

Significantly, the direction of these experiments is mostly (though by no means solely) inward rather than outward. This is not an age in which most men can take comfort from the outer spectacle of either nature or history, especially history. Hence, their instinct is to take "the road inside," as Hesse calls it, hoping thereby to find in some sort of inner experience what the world of appearances does not reveal to the intellect. Doubtless, "the road inside" is a dangerous road which can lead to madness as well as meaning. But it is a sign at least of a new religious vitality which aims to find meaning where it was once widely believed that there was none.

And much would seem to depend on the success of this experimentation. This is indeed one of the insights of the past two generations of visionary sceptics, namely that religious creativity is a *sine qua non* of a truly creative civilization. In a recent work, Sir Maurice Bowra attributes the greatness of Greek civilization partly to the consciousness of the Greeks of "dimensions outside the human sphere."

This "desire for another dimension," he says, was denied by Protagoras' doctrine that "man is the measure of all things."

[But] before Protagoras undermined the ancient confidence, it was commonly accepted that man, so far from being the centre of the universe and being encompassed by an infinite Unknowable, was in fact part of a larger, more embracing scheme. In this belief the Greeks found both comfort and inspiration, comfort because they felt that they were not lost and alone in an impenetrable darkness, and inspiration because, in their desire to grasp this 'beyond,' they released unsuspected forces in themselves. The natural and first place to find it was in the gods.[61]

This is a judgment with which an ever increasing number of European sceptics would agree, even though they see only vaguely how to apply it in their own age of experimentation.

[61] C. M. Bowra, *The Greek Experience* (Cleveland and New York: World Publishing Co., 1957), pp. 193-94.

INDEX

Absolutes, 15, 157, 236, 257;
   Frazer on, 151-52; scepticism
   about, 64
Age of Anxiety, The (Auden),
   216, 217
Age of Longing, The (Ko-
   estler), chap. IV, *passim*, 19,
   24, 186, 188 *ff.*, 206, 213, 223
Age of Reason, The (Paine),
   48, 50, 53
Agnosticism, 7, 62, 65, 93, 202,
   212, 223, 242; "biological,"
   251; Gladstone on, 135-36;
   in the nineteenth century,
   144-46; origin of the word,
   133; "tragic," 207-09, 211;
   Voltaire's, 54
Agnostics, 7, 32, 175
Agnostic's Apology, An
   (Stephen), 145
Albertus Magnus, 99
Alembert, D', 67, 68, 76
Alexander, Samuel, 262
"Altruism," 164
*Analysis of the Influence of
   Natural Religion on the
   Temporal Happiness of Man-
   kind* (Bentham), 142

Annan, Noel, 201, 202
Annet, Peter, 50
Anticlericalism, 5, 6, 23, 41, 100,
   142
Antiquity, 125
Anxiety: and scepticism, 13-14;
   of modern man, 204 *ff.*
"Apology for Raimond Sebond"
   (Montaigne), 32, 105
Apology (Pomponazzi), 114-15
Aquinas, St. Thomas, 53, 68,
   80, 99, 105, 165, 240
Archetypes, religious, 277, 286,
   287
Aristotle, 81, 91, 100, 105, 115,
   124, 203, 240, 251
Aristotelianism, heterodox, 97,
   98, 99 *ff.*; *see also* Averroism
Aristotelians, 78
Arnold, Matthew, 132, 162,
   182, 279-80
Art-for-art's sake, 183
Ash-Wednesday (T. S. Eliot),
   213, 220
Astrology, 100; *see also* Religion
Atheism, 41, 64, 66, 96, 108, 111,
   135; Bayle on, 104; deists
   and, 54; Voltaire on, 47

BF 1083

CATHOLIC THEOLOGICAL UNION
BL2747.8.B35   C001
RELIGION AND THE RISE OF SCEPTICISM [1S

3 0311 00008 1385